SOCIAL ARCHAEOLOGIES OF TRADE AND EXCHANGE

SOCIAL ARCHAEOLOGIES OF TRADE AND EXCHANGE

Exploring Relationships among People, Places, and Things

Alexander A. Bauer
Anna S. Agbe-Davies
Editors

Walnut Creek, California

LEFT COAST PRESS, INC.
1630 North Main Street, #400
Walnut Creek, California 94596
http://www.LCoastPress.com

Copyright © 2010 by Left Coast Press, Inc. First paperback edition 2011.

All rights reserved. No part of this publication may be reproduced, stored in a retrieval system, or transmitted in any form or by any means, electronic, mechanical, photocopying, recording, or otherwise, without the prior permission of the publisher.

Hardback ISBN 978-1-59874-029-5
Paperback ISBN 978-1-59874-030-1
eISBN 978-1-59874-711-9

Library of Congress Cataloging-in-Publication Data

Social archaeologies of trade and exchange : exploring relationships among people, places, and things / edited by Alexander A. Bauer and Anna S. Agbe-Davies.
    p. cm.
Includes bibliographical references and index.
    ISBN 978-1-59874-029-5 (hardcover : alk. paper)—ISBN 978-1-59874-030-1 (paperback : alk. paper)—ISBN 978-1-59874-711-9 (e-ISBN)
1. Social archaeology. 2. Commerce—Social aspects. 3. Exchange—Social aspects 4. Material culture—Social aspects. I. Bauer, Alexander A. II. Agbe-Davies, Anna.
CC72.4.S628 2010
930.1—dc22
                    2010006395

Printed in the United States of America

∞™ The paper used in this publication meets the minimum requirements of American National Standard for Information Sciences—Permanence of Paper for Printed Library Materials, ANSI/NISO Z39.48—1992.

Cover design by Jane Burton

Cover photo: The Mısır Çarşısı, or Egyptian Bazaar, in Istanbul, August 2009. Photo by Alexander A. Bauer.

Contents

Foreword by Robert W. Preucel		7
Preface		9
1.	Rethinking Trade as a Social Activity: An Introduction *Anna S. Agbe-Davies and Alexander A. Bauer*	13
2.	Trade and Interaction in Archaeology *Alexander A. Bauer and Anna S. Agbe-Davies*	29
3.	Landscapes of Circulation in Northwest Argentina: The Workings of Obsidian and Ceramics during the First Millennium AD *Marisa Lazzari*	49
4.	Social Aspects of the Tobacco Pipe Trade in Early Colonial Virginia *Anna S. Agbe-Davies*	69
5.	Arenas of Action: Trade as Power, Trade as Identity *Kenneth G. Kelly*	99
6.	Greeks and Phoenicians: Perceptions of Trade and Traders in the Early First Millennium BC *Susan Sherratt*	119
7.	Those Who Were Traded: African-Bahamian Archaeology and the Slave Trade *Laurie A. Wilkie and Paul Farnsworth*	143
8.	Broads, Studs, and Broken Down Daddies: The Materiality of "Playing" in the Modern Penitentiary *Eleanor Conlin Casella*	165
9.	Buying a Table in Erfelek: Socialities of Contact and Community in the Black Sea Region *Owen P. Doonan and Alexander A. Bauer*	183
10.	Objects, Social Relations, and Cultural Motion *Greg Urban*	207
About the Authors		227
Index		231

Foreword

It might seem that trade and exchange are among the most enduring concepts in archaeological theory. After all, they were central to both the cultural-historical archaeology of the 1940s and 1950s and the processual archaeology of the 1960s and 1970s. Yet, as Alexander Bauer and Anna Agbe-Davies point out, studies of trade and exchange have fallen on hard times in recent years. With some notable exceptions, they have not been central to the agendas of most postprocessual archaeologies. This neglect may be due in part to the early postprocessual critiques of the extreme formalism of the spatial models then in vogue. But methodological difficulties should not obscure the central role of trade in theories of culture change. Indeed, there is every reason to believe that trade can contribute to and expand postprocessual concerns.

This volume marks an important advance in trade and exchange studies. It draws inspiration from its processual antecedents and at the same time engages with new postprocessual theories of agency, identity, meaning, and materiality. Collectively, the chapters point towards a theory of trade with the following three components. First, trade is contextual. The objects of trade can only be understood from within their cultural, ideological, and historical contexts. Second, trade is a communicative activity. It is about not only the movement of things but also what those things signify in terms of persons, places, and meanings. Trade studies must thus look "beyond the material" in order to explore the social constitution of society. Third, trade cannot be divorced from questions of production and consumption. The former refers to the process of the creation of trade objects, while the latter is the process by which the circulation of objects is temporarily slowed. The biography of the object reveals important information about society, particularly labor relations, power differentials, and ideological understandings.

Trade and exchange thus lie at the heart what has come to be called "social archaeology." Social archaeology can be described as the study of the ways in which we express ourselves through the things we make and use, collect and discard, value or take for granted, and seek to be remembered by. It is linked to how we conceptualize the relationships between ourselves and others and between society and history in both past and present contexts. It involves an appreciation of the multiple entailments of our very being-in-the-world.

Trade and exchange encompass the physical and cognitive processes and the social and political practices that link together people, places, and things. These new studies of trade are about the relationships that are created more than they are about the things that circulate. These relationships, the objects traded, and the ideas they convey underpin the very motion of culture.

In the end, the essays in this volume cause us to consider culture in a new way. Rather than thinking about culture as a discrete entity associated with a distinct people occupying a specific geographical locality at a particular time, these studies acknowledge the fluidity of culture, its ever-shifting and always negotiated boundaries. More specifically, they draw attention to what Benjamin Lee and Edward LiPuma (2002) call "cultures of circulation," the cultural practices that underwrite and propel the process of circulation itself. These essays emphasize how material and immaterial cultural forms traverse social space and in the process build particular interpretive communities with their own internal logics and dynamics. Trade and exchange are back on the agenda!

Robert W. Preucel
University of Pennsylvania

Preface

Like the objects of trade discussed in the chapters here, this volume is in many ways a product of social interaction, both predictable and unpredictable, institutional and informal. While we both did our doctoral work at the University of Pennsylvania in the waning years of the processual-postprocessual debates, which clearly influenced our thinking, our engagements with the subject of trade took distinctive trajectories, and it was not until encountering each other's work some time later that we realized that we had been grappling with parallel issues, if in very different contexts—Alex in the Bronze Age Black Sea, Anna in colonial Virginia.

As if to illustrate the ideas about agency, perspective, and meaning in the past that are explored in this volume, we have very different recollections of how our ideas developed and how we came to work together on this project. Alex remembers this conversation taking place at the 2002 Society for American Archaeology (SAA) meeting, where he had just delivered a paper he had co-authored with Owen Doonan that raised the question of where trade studies in archaeology had gone (Owen and Alex's chapter in this volume is a descendant of that paper). Having then stopped to hear a paper that Anna was giving on her research into the pipe trade in Virginia, Alex remembers finding Anna at that meeting and talking over a takeout lunch about the intersections between the papers and the possibility of developing a larger project to reinvigorate theorizing about trade. Anna remembers that she was imposing on the hospitality of Alex and his family on one of many trips to Philadelphia to consult with her advisor about her dissertation research. In the course of discussing the winding paths of our respective projects, we realized our common concerns, especially finding a suitable body of theory for thinking about how the meanings of objects shift from one cultural context to the next and coping with the problem of imports versus locally made copies and the various meanings each might hold for the people who rendered, traded, and used them.

It is clear to us now that there are significant holes in each of our stories. But whichever version most closely approximates what "really" took place in the past (a dilemma that speaks to the challenge of archaeology itself), it is certainly true that our prior connection created the pathways that allowed for the exchange of ideas behind this book. We both came to believe that trade was a central issue in archaeology and yet had been ignored in recent years for no good reason, and that there was a need for a dynamic re-engagement with the subject. In fact, we were confident that a renewed focus on trade would provide new tools for engaging with questions about identity and meaning.

Like many of the participants in the trade activities discussed here, we want to think critically and reflexively about the contexts within which human interaction takes place. While we see ourselves as active agents in the realization of our research goals, "structuring structures" (pace Bourdieu) and larger historical and social contexts have clearly had an influence on the pathways of our thinking and, more broadly, our development as anthropologists. At Penn, we were immersed in a social network in which our peers thought seriously and creatively across anthropology's subfields about signs and the cultural work that they do. Our mentors encouraged innovation and critical thinking but at the same time ensured that our work was grounded in an understanding of what had been done before and the ways in which each generation's contribution might complement and not simply undermine its predecessor's. From such a setting, it is not surprising that we emerged skeptical of theoretical or topical agendas that proposed to toss out babies as well as bathwater. Rather, we were determined to unite the data-driven approach that we admired in earlier scholarship with the close attention to context and the *humanity* of those we studied that made newer approaches so important.

For the new examination of trade presented in this book, we set out deliberately to recruit a group of scholars who work all over the world in many different time periods, in order to highlight the comparative and generalizable qualities of the problems we were wrestling with. It was particularly important to us to include the perspective of sociocultural anthropologists, in recognition of the historic links between our subfields and in the spirit of mutual endeavor.

Our social and professional networks are made material in the final configuration of this work. And true to the themes discussed in the book, the session "Rethinking Trade as a Social Activity" that we organized for an SAA meeting, and the subsequent exchanges related to the editing process—the object making—have in turn shaped those relationships. The trivialities that attend requests for revisions, permissions, and queries about deadlines have indeed bound us more tightly together. Not all of the people initially involved in the conversation appear in the final product, but each of them has been instrumental to the process that led to this volume and we thank all of them for their valuable input. First, we are grateful to the participants in the SAA session. Lisa Beyer, Michael Frachetti, Teddi Setzer, John Edward Terrell, and Robert H. Tykot were a part of the initial group and brought stimulating arguments and novel datasets to the discussion of what a social archaeology of trade might look like.

The contributors who elected to become part of this book were models of patience and promptness as the volume took shape. We are pleased and proud to include their studies in this collection. Mitch Allen with Left Coast Press shepherded us through the process of bringing this book to completion with considerable finesse and good humor. We especially benefited from the comments of three anonymous reviewers who both encouraged and challenged us to articulate more forcefully the volume's contribution. Several of the chapters developed as a direct result of their interventions, and the format of the book as a whole also changed for the better. Finally, we wish to thank two of our mentors, Greg Urban and Bob Preucel, for their participation in this volume, as their work exemplifies the intellectual values of "both…and" that have shaped our thinking.

Finally, we would like to note that Anna's work on this volume was undertaken in part while she was a recipient of a Ford Foundation Postdoctoral Fellowship and on a leave sponsored by the University Research Council of DePaul University, buttressed by a course release from the University of North Carolina, Chapel Hill. The patient support and artistic talent of Eric Deetz was no less instrumental. For his part, Alex would like to thank his wife, Colleen McCarthy, MD, for putting up with his preoccupation with his laptop, which unfortunately will not likely end soon.

Alexander A. Bauer and Anna S. Agbe-Davies

 CHAPTER 1

Rethinking Trade as a Social Activity: An Introduction

Anna S. Agbe-Davies and Alexander A. Bauer

Trade acts as an important mechanism for establishing and maintaining the social bonds that hold societies together, regardless of whether kin (Lévi-Strauss 1969 [1947]), gifts (Mauss 1990 [1950]), or commodities (Appadurai 1986) are being exchanged. As such, trade has long been an important topic in archaeological and anthropological inquiry. Archaeological interest in trade and exchange, however, has declined somewhat in recent decades, perhaps in connection with the postmodern turn toward the social and ideological realms and away from what Lewis Binford (1962) termed the *technomic*—so closely associated with questions of economy and subsistence. Yet, even with increased attention to the social and ideological in archaeology (Meskell and Preucel 2004), the study of trade may still be central to archaeology's intellectual project.

With this volume, we argue for a concept of trade as a fundamentally *social* activity, a concept that focuses not just on the movement of goods but also on the social context and consequences of the exchange. We aim to contribute to the literature on both trade and social life in the past by examining some of the many social aspects of trade overlooked in archaeology: how trade operates as a communicative act, the ways in which exchange transforms the relationship between people and things, the significance of agency and power in contexts of trade, and how archaeologists use sites of consumption and discard to address issues of exchange and social interaction. The chapters discuss trade at a range of scales and in a wide variety of settings but are linked by their attention to its social dimensions.

Here, the contrast between the goods owned by particular actors at the commencement and completion of an exchange is not the full or sole meaning of that exchange. Rather, the contributors to this volume acknowledge the fact that when goods are in motion, they are moving through social spaces and that there is meaning in the event itself, not merely in the accomplished fact of an exchange. We address not only the ends but the means (and the consequences and the implications) of trade.

Refocusing on Trade

The declining interest of archaeologists in the subject of trade is clear. While significant treatments of the subject were published more than two decades ago (Adams 1974; Brumfiel and Earle 1987; Ericson and Earle 1982; Sabloff and Lamberg-Karlovsky 1975), and though world-systems theory (Wallerstein 1974) influenced a series of important edited volumes and syntheses in the 1980s and early 1990s (Algaze 1993; Blanton and Feinman 1984; Champion 1989; Rowlands et al. 1987; Schortman and Urban 1987), few new perspectives have developed since then. As one of us (AAB) observed in a paper that grew to become Bauer and Doonan's contribution to this volume,

> of the 625 articles that appear in the *Anthropological Literature* database when doing a keyword search of "archaeology" and "trade," only 127 were published in the 1990s, compared with numbers almost double that in both the 1970s and 1980s.... Moreover, of those 127, only 43 have appeared in the five years from 1996 to 2000. [Bauer and Doonan 2002:4]

Noting that this decline coincided with the growing influence of postprocessual approaches to archaeology, the authors suggested a link and proposed that the revitalization of trade studies in archaeology might come about through an integration of the *themes* of the postprocessual turn with the *evidence* traditionally deployed in materialist studies concerned with the movement of goods. Such an approach would allow archaeologists to "bring to the forefront the more subtle aspects of social interaction which have often been obscured by universalizing models" (Bauer and Doonan 2002:5).

One reason for the decline in interest among those practitioners who take a postprocessual or interpretative approach to the past may be that trade's close association with positivist forms—artifact distribution curves, economic modeling, and the like—has tended to turn archaeologists oriented more toward the social off the subject. Given the importance of trade and interaction in social life, however, trade should not be the exclusive domain of positivist approaches but can and should be dealt with in a range of ways, including more contemporary approaches that focus on meaning, communication, and the experience of those engaged in the exchange.

In his distinguished lecture to the American Anthropological Association, Gil Stein (2002) likewise remarked on the problems facing traditional approaches to trade and interregional interaction. He then went on to describe the development of a new paradigm built on both processual and postprocessual approaches. He promoted an approach that goes beyond a top-down emphasis on structural and systemic aspects of intersocietal exchange to take into account the impact of such factors as social identity and ideology (Stein 2002:907). While clearly we agree with the sentiment, we wonder whether the new synthesis actually is at hand. The chapters presented here may be considered a step in the right direction, however, as they illustrate that the processual models and techniques so thoroughly developed in the 1970s and 1980s and more current postprocessual concepts such as agency are not so much contradictory as complementary. In a phrase, we are aiming for a synthesis: "both…and" as opposed to "either…or" (for further discussion, see Bauer and Agbe-Davies, chapter 2, this volume).

Coming to Terms with Trade and Exchange

As Kohl (1975) remarked over thirty years ago, when archaeologists use the terms *trade* and *exchange*, they often do so interchangeably, without adequately addressing the ways in which trade differs from other forms of exchange. In Renfrew's (1975) classic study of trade models, for example, he states explicitly that the terms are synonymous, and perhaps for his purpose (differentiating the intensity of contact for different artifact distribution patterns), they were. In this volume, we take *exchange* to refer to the transfer of goods from one party to another through a wide range of mechanisms, from ritualized gift exchange to the negotiated transactions of barter and markets and the one-way exchange of coercion and piracy. *Trade* is a more specific category of activity in which the exchange is more formalized and market based, both in the individual interaction and on a systemic scale. Trade is thus one type of exchange relationship in which each interaction is usually "closed," or completed in a single moment of exchange of x for y, and which often occurs across otherwise powerful social and geographic boundaries. This formulation differs from that put forth by Rahul Oka and Chapurukha Kusimba (2008:340), in which they distinguish "the material-economic component" (trade) from a more encompassing category of "interaction among humans" (exchange).

For the most part, archaeological studies of trade and exchange have tended to emphasize a limited set of problems. But as John Edward Terrell has observed as a result of his work on coastal New Guinea, trading activities are more diverse and multifaceted than archaeologists have typically recognized, and an act of exchange is not just economic but "is often also social, emotional, traditional and sometimes sexual" (Terrell 2001:69). He thus suggests that the networks that these activities promote are personal, creating "social fields" that crosscut and extend beyond other assumed cultural boundaries, such as language, territory, or ethnicity.

Within a more traditional paradigm, excavators may identify finds as exotic in material or design and therefore indicative of exchange. For example, archaeologists are very familiar with the broad range of resources—whether marine shell from the Gulf of Mexico or copper from the Great Lakes—that residents of the middle Mississippi Valley regularly obtained from Archaic through Mississippian times. Likewise, finished objects in the Cahokian style found their way across a broad swath of North America (Pauketat 2004:35–36, 120–124). Similarly, discussions of the nature and scale of Late Bronze Age trade in the Mediterranean are often built on listlike inventories of the "foreign" materials found in each of the regions assumed to be involved in the trade (e.g., Lambrou-Phillipson 1990; Cline 1994). In other cases, such as Knapp and Cherry's (1994) volume on Mediterranean trade based on their study of artifact provenience, researchers have inferred exchange from the existence of specialized production within particular sites or regions. Each of these lines of evidence has been used to discover exchange networks or relationships. Yet the actors comprising the networks often remain ciphers. In this volume, the contributing authors propose to find meanings largely unacknowledged in previous treatments of trade and exchange by emphasizing the "social, symbolic, and ideational roles of exchange over the economic" (Kirch 1991:158) for a change. The chapters come together along several themes that have helped us organize our thoughts about the social aspects of exchange and the manifestation of these themes in the archaeological record. They are context, communication, and consumption.

Context

Sensitivity to the contexts of social action in the past and the construction of meaning in both the past and the present have been central elements of the postprocessual critique (Barrett 1987), a stance no less cogent for the study of trade. Here, we draw explicitly on several meanings of "context," as the environmental or behavioral setting within which action takes place and as an interest in "particular data rather than general theory" (Hodder 1987:2). From this perspective, objects of trade should be considered in light of their cultural, ideological, and historical contexts (Hodder 1982:207). An item has a caloric value or a use value, to be sure, but we can also speak in terms of its social value. In this respect, we also begin to address the issues suggested in Pierre Bourdieu's (1986) work on transformations among economic, social, and cultural capital.

Investigations along such lines might focus on the social context within which trade activities were performed and trade networks established. For example, when considering the mutual effects between context and exchange relationships, we might well ask, why are some attempts to develop connections successful and others not? What aspects of the larger social context foster or discourage acts of trade? "The human relationships that constitute trade are fickle—people do not act within a system but within a matrix of community and individual goals," remark Owen Doonan and Alexander Bauer (chapter 9, this volume:190). Connections among participants may develop for a host of reasons, from carrying out formal, top-down agendas to more informal and personal reasons, and even by chance.

Attention to social context could also lead one to consider the extent to which trade connections exploit or enhance existing relationships or even forge new ones, as in the classic case of the *kula* described by Bronislaw Malinowski (1922). We might ask, what obligations link trading partners and how does the very act of exchange deepen those ties? For example, archaeology has revealed the importance of exchanges in creating networks of support among enslaved and free washerwomen in Cape Town as they negotiated their lives in colonial South Africa (Jordan 2005:223–224). Exchange can also communicate or reinforce values, as is the case in the "exchange" of bridewealth for women, reminding them and their families of the roles of wives and daughters (Evans-Pritchard 1946). In her contribution to this volume (chapter 8), Eleanor Casella considers the ways that material and sexual exchanges shape life in modern prisons and how social relationships may be converted into goods and back again. Like the other investigations in this volume, hers focuses on the social context within which trade activities are performed and trade networks established.

Considerations of context must also recognize the physical dimensions of these interactions: in what kinds of social and spatial settings do trade interactions take place? Marketplaces, certainly, are the spatial manifestation of ritualized, if not institutionalized, trade practices, but family gatherings, parties, pilgrimages, and even seasonal migrations all provide physical contexts where repeated and predictable (and therefore patterned and archaeologically analyzable) connections may be made among willing participants in a trade network. In this volume, Doonan and Bauer (chapter 9) describe just such an example in the contemporary Black Sea region of Turkey, and they use that experience to inform a larger understanding of how space may have both facilitated trade relationships and been exploited by them since the Bronze Age. Conversely, the physical context of trade is also constructed or reconceptualized by the things being exchanged. Exotic goods or the traders themselves might simultaneously make distant places seem nearer and further away. For example, in her chapter on how trading activities helped the ethnic concept of *Phoenician* take shape in the Iron Age Greek psyche, Susan Sherratt (chapter 6, this volume) illustrates the power of long distances to influence not only ideas about trade items but also ideas about the places they came from and, most importantly, those who brought them.

Clearly, concepts of place are important in trade studies, for as Bender (2001) has noted, landscape is not merely a backdrop to human experience but part of a complex web of relationships among people, places, and things, two of which are continually "on the move," in a circulating and shifting relationship with one another. In chapter 5 (this volume), Kenneth Kelly explains how African traders participating in the transatlantic exchange of human beings used specific landscape features as well as what archaeologists often gloss as "trade goods" to maintain their position of power vis-à-vis both European partners and African rivals. Marisa Lazzari looks at the circulation of obsidian and ceramics in prehispanic Northwest Argentina to illustrate how trade items may index both specific places in the landscape and the lived experience of moving within and across it. As she remarked in her paper, "'Landscape' redefines regional space as a lived, active dimension of social life" (2004). Landscape is clearly a context that shapes and is shaped by the circulation of people and items within it. Together, they create a web of experience in which the meanings of all three—people, places, and things—continually transform and comment on each other.

Communication

Trade studies in archaeology have tended to emphasize the circulation of things rather than the movement of more intangible aspects of culture, such as traditions, ideas, and values. This emphasis may be expected, given archaeology's reliance on a material dataset. Until recently, it meant that archaeologists often fell into the habit of focusing on Kent Flannery's "artifact" and "system" at the expense of the "Indian" he also mentions (Flannery

1967:120). But our necessary connection to the material does not mean that we should ignore nonmaterial factors. In fact, it is becoming increasingly recognized in archaeology that the divide between things and how we talk about and analyze them can be misleading (Joyce 2002). This division is arguably nowhere more extreme than in archaeological studies of trade, which have been dominated by statistical models and distribution curves and have frequently ignored the fact that trade is at heart a social activity, depending on interactions among people. Certainly, material objects play a role in shaping these engagements, but they do not in themselves comprise the whole substance of trade. Rather, material exchange also needs to be recognized as being part of a broader process—or perhaps set of strategies—for establishing and maintaining social relations that looks "beyond the material," as Renfrew (1993:5) suggested over a decade ago. With this approach, archaeologists consider exchange as a communicative act, one that facilitates the exchange of nonmaterial things, such as information, ideas, and values (Wobst 1977). Such exchange also metadiscursively creates or reinforces notions of connectivity between participants (Urban 1996, chapter 10, this volume). As Urban asks (1996:162), "Is it exchange, or the idea of exchange, that binds? Must commerce take place, or is it sufficient to believe in the idea of commerce?" That discourse about trade and traders can determine social roles and even bring about ethnic consciousness is illustrated in Sherratt's work (chapter 6, this volume) on the Phoenicians. Likewise, Bauer (2008) has raised the possibility that imported or imitative materials may be more significant for what they represent—indices of connection between regions and people—than as tangible items of exchange. For if culture can be located within contexts of social interaction and discourse, then trade as a communicative practice may not be merely a feature to be measured in a given society but a key process in the creation and circulation of culture itself.

Indeed, the question of what is communicated and to whom might also be applied to the artifacts themselves, in both their systemic and archaeological contexts (Schiffer 1972). Linguists and others influenced by the writings of Charles Sanders Peirce (e.g., 1965) find utility in the distinction between signs acting as symbols and signs acting as indices. For archaeologists, this distinction often means considering the style of an artifact as part of its meaning. However, many studies normatively link objects with certain groups (pots = people), which undertheorizes style as being *only* symbolic, that is to say, conventional. But as several authors in this volume suggest (Lazzari, chapter 3, and Agbe-Davies, chapter 4, most explicitly), artifact style is much more than symbolic; in fact, it may more often act indexically, pointing to a particular referent by virtue of a direct spatiotemporal link—in the case of trade and exchange, links with the person(s) who made, transported, offered, accepted, used, and discarded what is now, in our archaeological context, an artifact (Keane 2003; Parmentier 1997, Preucel and Bauer 2001). What has been neglected in archaeology, then, is a full understanding of the indexical meanings of artifacts, what they signify (communicate) *to us* when divorced from their systemic contexts. These indexical meanings are crucial to an understanding of social relations yet are relatively neglected in archaeological studies of cultural meaning.

While recent analyses of material culture may be grounded in postprocessual and active concepts of things, the underlying method often calls to mind the work of archaeologists operating in the cultural-historical framework that made such tight links between the style of artifacts and the identity of their makers. Likewise, explanations that cast the primary significance of goods in purely economic terms capture only part of their meaning. In this volume, we have set up an opposition between processual attention to and postprocessual neglect of trade. Although it may be premature to declare ourselves to be in a "post-postprocessual" moment, we still might envision an early twenty-first-century synthesis between the thesis of the New Archaeology and the antithesis of the new-new Archaeology, applying the toolkit of the former to the problems, issues, and themes of the latter (on the synthesis of processual and postprocessual paradigms, see the discussion of Stein 2002 above).

Consumption

Although we are emphasizing the human element in instances of exchange, we must not neglect the goods entirely. Another concept that brings these two factors—people and things—together is consumption. While we appreciate Daniel Miller's definition of consumption as "an increasing reliance on commodities produced by others," we are more inspired by his insight that consumption may be a medium through which social relations are constructed and maintained, a process that is perhaps accelerating in the modern world (Miller 1995:143, 154).

In their contribution to this volume (chapter 7), Laurie Wilkie and Paul Farnsworth confront consumption on two levels. First, they consider the men, women, and children who were themselves converted into commodities and, in a manner of speaking, *consumed* through the process of enslavement. (For commoditization as it applies to people, see Kopytoff [1986].) Wilkie and Farnsworth also reflect on the choices made by these people as *consumers* and active agents in the marketplace, particularly as revealed by their selection of ceramic tableware. This and other essays in this volume begin to address James Carrier and Josiah Heyman's (1997) critique of anthropological analyses of consumption by paying attention to the agency of households, rather than individuals. The contributions furthermore resituate consumption in a matrix in which decisions are structured by social position and consequences as much as taste and price.

But even here we can move "beyond the material" by extending the work of those who have recently revitalized the discussion of production "as a social activity" (see, for example, contributions to Brumfiel and Earle 1987; Costin and Wright 1998; Wailes 1996; or reviews by Clark 1995; Costin 1991). Innovations such as articulating the distinction between independent and attached specialists and otherwise considering the social context of production have given archaeologists the tools to repopulate the production process. Chapter 4, by Anna Agbe-Davies, links the aforementioned focus on relations of production to the relations of consumption. In it, she compares the distribution of clay tobacco pipes at eleven sites linked by known kin and affective networks to discover the influence of those prior social connections on the trade in these locally produced goods. In turn, these findings have implications for our interpretations of the mode(s) of production employed in the manufacture of these goods. Here, again, contributions to this volume engage with an emerging critique of consumption studies that such research, in monopolizing the space formerly taken by production studies, often privileges cultural and semiological over social and structural explanations for agents' actions, and furthermore erases the effect of work and class in shaping individuals and groups (Wurst and McGuire 1999). Much of the work on consumption seems to rest on the assumption that consumer acts are generated in a free, ideal space constrained only by tradition or a desire to communicate meanings, especially to communicate (high) social or economic status. We wish to combine this emphasis on the meanings of material culture with the strengths of production studies, which are good at getting us to think about structured interaction among social actors (if sometimes rendered "faceless"), and which acknowledge that agents often act because they want to accomplish some particular end in the world or because social structures constrain or channel their choices.

We should note, finally, that each of the papers collected here could have been used to illustrate any of the three principles: context, communication, or consumption. For example, Sherratt turns prosaic ideas about foreign imports on their head to highlight instead how the consumption of goods can create and solidify the ethnic identities of the consumer versus producer or merchant (as supplier). Kelly indirectly deals with consumption as well, in that the consumer's desire to obtain is part of why traders and goods are powerful. In fact, no small part of our task in introducing this volume and outlining its themes has been deciding which chapter to use to illustrate which of our larger points. We view the overlap among the chapters as further evidence of the cohesiveness and utility of this social approach to trade.

Conclusion

In his discussion of prehistoric exchange in Melanesia, Patrick Kirch (1991:157) observes that "one goal of archaeological studies of prehistoric exchange is to explain the origins and particular configurations of these networks" but that, as Timothy Earle has written, "no coherent body of theory exists to explain exchange and its linkage to broader sociocultural forms" (Earle 1982:3). The contributors to this volume work in far-flung corners of the world and study periods in some cases separated by millennia, but they are united by a common vision of trade as a social process grounded in interactions among people—people who moved through particular landscapes, engaged in relationships with others, and used the things that these relationships brought their way.

The volume begins with a review of the history of trade studies in archaeology and their connection with other classic themes, such as diffusion and migration. In chapter 2, Bauer and Agbe-Davies outline the waxing and waning fortunes of trade as a research focus and explanatory model. With roots in early efforts to explain the movement of objects and ideas (a theme taken up in the final chapter by Urban) as well as cultural change, trade studies held little appeal for archaeologists with an evolutionist orientation. The expansion of economic anthropology and the introduction of new analytical techniques revived interest in the field, and the authors further suggest that archaeology's turn toward the social may herald yet another renewal of trade studies.

The substantive chapters that follow indicate what such a resurgence might look like. Lazzari (chapter 3) explores how a social concept of landscape—one created through the circulation of entities instead of being defined by geography or topography—contributes to new understandings of trade during the Formative period in the Andes. Specifically, her chapter concerns what are commonly termed exotic materials in contexts of daily use and how those artifacts may have created an enduring sense of place. The chapter by Agbe-Davies (chapter 4) considers the extent to which existing social relations shaped the distribution networks that brought tobacco smoking pipes to plantations and towns in Tidewater Virginia during the seventeenth century. The analytical techniques she employs owe a great debt to the developments of a more processual approach to the archaeological record, but the analysis is also informed by previous studies of the pipes that emphasize their symbolic content and their role in reflecting and framing power relationships in the intensely hierarchical world of the plantation.

Power is a central motif in chapter 5 by Kelly, in which he argues that, while power can derive from or be signaled by the possession of certain goods, the exchange process itself is an arena in which individuals and groups can exercise and augment their power. His analysis of the arrangement of landscapes, structures, and artifacts in the town of Savi informs a discussion of how Hueda elites used trade relationships with European outsiders during the era of the transatlantic slave trade. Kelly's secondary idea, that trading roles and relationships formed an important part of group identity, is echoed in Sherratt's contribution (chapter 6), in which she considers how recipients of goods in Early Iron Age Greece regarded both the material items and the traders who brought them. Particularly striking are the ways in which Greek notions of their own identity were bound up in their perceptions of "Phoenician" traders and the items they carried.

Identity also plays a role in the chapter by Wilkie and Farnsworth (chapter 7), in which they point out its significance to slave traders and planters in their selection and disposition of Africans as commodities. Furthermore, the authors demonstrate how the inhabitants of a Bahamian plantation, after being enslaved, used mass-produced consumer goods—namely ceramics—to maintain identities that were meaningful and productive within their inter- and intraplantation communities. In chapter 8, on Anglo-American and Anglo-Australian prisons, Casella emphasizes the role of goods in establishing and maintaining interpersonal relationships. Prisoners need goods, to be sure, but they also need each other to survive the hazards posed by the institution itself and their fellow inmates. As she observes, "To cope, one must trade."

The final case study, chapter 9 by Doonan and Bauer, returns us to the problems that motivated this volume and illustrates how refocusing on the social dimensions of trade may deepen our interpretations of how and why things move, and reshape the methodologies employed in archaeological analyses. Inspired by a personal experience during fieldwork, the authors seek to re-envision their project as one that "identifies the multiple ways in which culture moves among individuals, communities, and regions, and the ways in which those players both actively shape and are shaped by the circulation of cultural elements" (188). Whether or not *trade* is the appropriate term to use as the focus of such an approach is worth asking, however, as John

Terrell did in his remarks on the session from which this volume developed. Offering instead the term "community of culture" to acknowledge both the indeterminacy and the connective power of such a formation, Terrell suggested that archaeology might be better served by discarding *trade* altogether for the kinds of relations explored in the essays here.

The volume concludes with a commentary by linguistic anthropologist Greg Urban, who relates his notions of how materialized culture moves through the world to the problem of trade and particularly the social consequences of the exchange of goods (e.g., Urban 2001:61). For Urban, the circulation of material exemplifies the circulation of culture itself, as each object may be seen as a momentary materialization of culture, able to be passed around and capable of both establishing and maintaining social relationships. His treatment of trade, production, and material culture in *Metaculture* (2001) convinces us that he takes the archaeologist's interest in material culture seriously and that subfields of anthropology still have some common ground, given our shared emphasis on the circulation of ideas, whether they are embedded in objects or in instances of social interaction and social learning.

References

Adams, Robert McC.
1974 Anthropological Perspectives on Ancient Trade. *Current Anthropology* 15:239–258.

Algaze, Guillermo
1993 *The Uruk World System: The Dynamics of Expansion of Early Mesopotamian Civilization*. University of Chicago Press, Chicago.

Appadurai, Arjun (editor)
1986 *The Social Life of Things: Commodities in Cultural Perspective*. Cambridge University Press, Cambridge.

Barrett, John C.
1987 Contextual Archaeology. *Antiquity* 61:468–73.

Bauer, Alexander A.
2008 Import, Imitation, and Communication: Pottery Style, Technology, and Coastal Contact in the Early Bronze Age Black Sea. In *"Import" and "Imitation": Methodological and Practical Problems with an Archaeological Key Concept*, edited by P. Biehl and Y. Rassamakin, pp. 89–104. Schriften des Zentrums für Archäologie und Kulturgeschichte des Schwarzmeerraumes Band 11. Beier & Beran, Langenweiβbach, Germany.

Bauer, Alexander A., and Owen P. Doonan
2002 Buying a Table in Erfelek: A New Look at the Social Nature of Trade. Paper presented at the 67th Annual Meeting of the Society for American Archaeology, Denver.

Bender, Barbara
2001 Landscapes On-the-Move. *Journal of Social Archaeology* 1:75–89.

Binford, Lewis R.
1962 Archaeology as Anthropology. *American Antiquity* 28(2):217–225.

Blanton, Richard, and Gary L. Feinman
1984 The Mesoamerican World System. *American Anthropologist* 86:673–82.

Bourdieu, Pierre
1986 The Forms of Capital. In *Handbook of Theory and Research for the Sociology of Education*, edited by J. G. Richardson, pp. 241–258. Greenwood Press, New York.

Brumfiel, Elizabeth M., and Timothy Earle
1987 *Specialization, Exchange and Complex Societies*. Cambridge University Press, Cambridge.

Carrier, James G., and Josiah McC. Heyman
1997 Consumption and Political Economy. *The Journal of the Royal Anthropological Institute* 3(2):355–373.

Champion, T. (editor)
1989 *Centre and Periphery: Comparative Studies in Archaeology*. Unwin Hyman, London.

Clark, John E.
1995 Craft Specialization as an Archaeological Category. *Research in Economic History* 16:267–274.

Cline, Eric H.
1994 *Sailing the Wine-Dark Sea: International Trade and the Late Bronze Aegean*. BAR International Series 591. British Archaeological Reports, Oxford.

Costin, Cathy Lynne
1991 Craft Specialization: Issues in Defining, Documenting, and Explaining the Organization of Production. *Archaeological Method and Theory* 3:1–56.

Costin, Cathy Lynne, and Rita P. Wright (editors)
1998 *Craft and Social Identity*. Archaeological Papers of the American Anthropological Association Vol. 8. American Anthropological Association, Arlington, Virginia.

Earle, Timothy K.
1982 Prehistoric Economies and the Archaeology of Exchange. In *Contexts for Prehistoric Exchange*, edited by J. E. Ericson and T. K. Earle, pp. 1–12. Academic Press, New York.

Ericson, J. E., and Timothy K. Earle (editors)
1982 *Contexts for Prehistoric Exchange*. Academic Press, New York.

Evans-Pritchard, E. E.
1946 Nuer Bridewealth. *Africa: Journal of the International African Institute* 16(4):247–257.

Flannery, Kent V.
1967 Culture History v. Cultural Process: A Debate in American Archaeology. *Scientific American* 217(2):119–22.

Hodder, Ian
1982 Toward a Contextual Approach to Prehistoric Exchange. In *Contexts for Prehistoric Exchange*, edited by J. E. Ericson and T. K. Earle, pp. 199–211. Academic Press, New York.

Hodder, Ian (editor)
1987 *The Archaeology of Contextual Meanings*. Cambridge University Press, Cambridge.

Jordan, Elizabeth Grzymala
2005 "Unrelenting Toil": Expanding Archaeological Interpretations of the Female Slave Experience. *Slavery and Abolition* 26(2):217–232.

Joyce, Rosemary A.
2002 *The Languages of Archaeology: Dialogue, Narrative, and Writing*. Blackwell, Oxford.

Keane, Webb
2003 Semiotics and the Social Analysis of Material Things. *Language & Communication* 23:409–425.

Kirch, Patrick V.
1991 Prehistoric Exchange in Western Melanesia. *Annual Review of Anthropology* 10:141–165.

Knapp, A. Bernard, and John F. Cherry
1994 Provenience Studies and Bronze Age Cyprus: Production, Exchange and Politco-Economic Change. Monographs in World Archaeology 21. Prehistory Press, Madison, Wisconsin.

Kohl, Philip L.
1975 The Archaeology of Trade. *Dialectical Anthropology* 1:43–50.

Kopytoff, Igor
1986 The Cultural Biography of Things: Commoditization as Process. *In* The Social Life of Things: Commodities in Cultural Perspective, edited by Arjun Appadurai, pp. 64–91. Cambridge University Press, Cambridge.

Lambrou-Phillipson, C.
1990 *Hellenorientalia: The Near Eastern Presence in the Bronze Age Aegean, ca. 3000–1100 b.c.* Mediterranean Archaeology 95. Paul Åströms Forlag, Göteborg, Sweden.

Lazzari, Marisa
2004 Circulation of Things, Production of Social Spaces: The Roads of Ceramics and Obsidian in Northwest Argentina (1st Millennium AD). Paper presented at the 69th Annual Meeting of the Society for American Archaeology, Montreal.

Lévi-Strauss, Claude
1969 [1947] *The Elementary Structures of Kinship*. Translated by James Harle Bell, John Richard von Sturmer, and Rodney Needham, editor. Beacon Press, Boston.

Malinowski, Bronislaw
1922 *Argonauts of the Western Pacific*. E. P. Dutton & Co., Inc., New York.

Mauss, Marcel
1990 [1950] The Gift. Translated by W. D. Halls,. W. W. Norton, New York.

Meskell, Lynn M., and Robert W. Preucel (editors)
2004 *A Companion to Social Archaeology*. Routledge, London.

Miller, Daniel
1995 Consumption and Commodities. *Annual Review of Anthropology* 24:141–161.

Oka, Rahul, and Chapurukha Kusimba
2008 The Archaeology of Trading Systems, Part 1: Towards a New Trade Synthesis. *Journal of Archaeological Research* 16:339–395.

Parmentier, Richard J.
1997 The Pragmatic Semiotics of Cultures. *Semiotica* 116:1–115.

Pauketat, Timothy R.
2004 *Ancient Cahokia and the Mississippians*. Cambridge University Press, Cambridge.

Peirce, Charles Sanders
1965 Division of Signs. In *Collected Papers of Charles Sanders Peirce*, edited by Charles Hartshorne and Paul Weiss, pp. 134–155. The Belknap Press, Cambridge, Massachusetts.

Preucel, Robert W., and Alexander A. Bauer
2001 Archaeological Pragmatics. *Norwegian Archaeological Review* 34:85–96.

Renfrew, A. Colin
1975 Trade as Action at a Distance: Questions of Integration and Communication. In *Ancient Civilization and Trade*, edited by Jeremy A. Sabloff and C. C. Lamberg-Karlovsky, pp. 3–60. University of New Mexico Press, Albuquerque.
1993 Trade Beyond the Material. In *Trade and Exchange in Prehistoric Europe*, edited by C. Scarre and F. Healy, pp. 5–16. Oxbow Monographs, Vol. 33. Oxbow, Oxford.

Rowlands, M., M. T. Larsen, and K. Kristiansen (editors)
1987 *Centre and Periphery in the Ancient World*. Cambridge University Press, Cambridge.

Sabloff, Jeremy A., and C. C. Lamberg-Karlovsky (editors)
1975 *Ancient Civilization and Trade*. University of New Mexico Press, Albuquerque.

Schiffer, Michael B.
1972 Archaeological Context and Systemic Context. *American Antiquity* 37(2):156–165.

Schortman, Elizabeth M., and Patricia A. Urban
1987 Modeling Interregional Interaction in Prehistory. In *Advances in Archaeological Method and Theory*, vol. 11, edited by M. B. Schiffer, pp. 11–35. Academic Press, New York.

Stein, Gil J.
2002 From Passive Periphery to Active Agents: Emerging Perspectives in the Archaeology of Interregional Interaction. *American Anthropologist* 104:903–916.

Terrell, John Edward
2001 Archaeology, Material Culture, and the Complementary Forms of Social Life. In *Fleeting Identities: Perishable Material Culture in Archaeological Research*, edited by P. B. Drooker, pp. 58–75. Southern Illinois University Press, Carbondale.

Urban, Greg
1996 *Metaphysical Community*. University of Texas Press, Austin.
2001 *Metaculture: How Culture Moves through the World*. University of Minnesota Press, Minneapolis.

Wailes, Bernard (editor)
1996 *Craft Specialization and Social Evolution: In Memory of V. Gordon Childe*. University Museum, Philadelphia.

Wallerstein, Immanuel
1974 *The Modern World System*. Academic Press, New York.

Wobst, H. Martin
1977 Stylistic Behavior and Information Exchange. In *Papers for the Director*, edited by C. Cleland, pp. 317–342. Museum of Anthropology, Anthropological Papers 61. University of Michigan Press, Ann Arbor.

Wurst, LouAnn, and McGuire, Randall H.
1999 Immaculate Consumption: A Critique of the "Shop till You Drop" School of Human Behavior. *The International Journal of Historical Archaeology* 3(3):191–199.

 CHAPTER 2

Trade and Interaction in Archaeology
Alexander A. Bauer and Anna S. Agbe-Davies

Archaeologists have long considered the sharing and exchange of material objects within and among communities to be a fundamental indicator of social relations and social cohesion. In effect, shared material culture indicates shared culture (a view originally formulated by Kossina (1911) and later developed by Childe [1929, 1956]). At its most extreme, this view has resulted in the ascription of culture to the objects themselves, most clearly illustrated by the definition of groups such as the "Bell Beaker Culture" (see discussion in Clarke 1968:230ff.). While a direct and normative association between material culture and specific ethnic or cultural groups has been seriously called into question and can no longer be simply assumed (Kramer 1977), archaeologists still look to the sharing of material culture as an indicator of shared practices or identity, largely because in most cases, material culture is all we have to work with (see discussion in Shennan 1989).

When it comes to the study of interaction, archaeologists may interpret similarities between distant areas as an indicator of trade relations or, in the absence of direct imports, local imitation or the arrival of new people in a region. Whether an object was made locally and by whom are questions that lie at the heart of such differentiations and that allow archaeologists to label the material an import, an imitation, or an object made locally but in a foreign style, presumably by a foreigner. These three cases are thought to correspond to and be an index of the larger social processes of trade, diffusion, and migration. In this way, trade in archaeology has been both theoretically and methodologically linked with these other forms of cultural interaction (Bauer 2008).

But in spite of the fact that trade has been included among these and other core cultural processes—and perhaps because of it, the subject has suffered repeated abandonment by the field of archaeology as its paradigms have shifted. For the early culture historians, concerned with identifying and describing past cultures, trade was a primary vehicle for explaining the spread of objects and ideas among cultures, and Childe (1950) included the existence of trade among the primary features of urban societies. But as the descriptive approach was abandoned in favor of process-centered models of human behavior and social evolution, trade was cast aside as a concept with little predictive or explanatory power. Yet, when archaeologists developed improved methods of quantification and materials sourcing, trade re-emerged as a central subject for inquiry and soon achieved prominence in archaeological studies as a possible prime mover for the development of complex societies (e.g., Flannery 1968; Rathje 1971; Renfrew 1969; Wright 1972). Its prominence within the processual studies of the 1970s, however, sowed the seeds of its own demise. With the emergence of the postprocessual critique of the hypothetico-deductive approach, of which trade had since become exemplary, the subject was once again cast aside as passé or, worse, lacking in salience for understanding the past. The recent attention to social relations and communication on a range of scales, from networks to individual action, suggests once again that trade may be central to our understandings of the past. The aim of this chapter is to review the main phases of the archaeological study of trade and show how, in spite of their repeated abandonment, trade and exchange persist as core concerns for archaeology in the twenty-first century.

Cultural Interaction and Diffusion

Beginning with theories of diffusion first articulated at the turn of the twentieth century by the *Kulturkreise* school (Montelius 1899), trade and external relations have been thought to play an important role in cultural development and change (Schortman and Urban 1987). Based on a conception of culture as a complex of multiple, isolable traits, diffusion represented the mechanism through which individual traits or clusters thereof were thought to spread from one culture to the next (Childe 1925, 1929; Dixon 1928). Cultural differences and culture change in this view were thus seen to result from historical processes of cultural borrowing that were unique to each region and culture, as opposed to resulting from a generalized evolutionary trajectory shared by and internal to each culture (Boas 1924; Kroeber 1940; Lowie 1929). On a practical level, the idea that cultures were comprised of a set of traits allowed archaeologists to then define culture areas by mapping the distribution of those individual traits spatially. Archaeologists also began to identify the relationships between these areas by tracking the appearance of specific traits through time and space.

This approach is exemplified by the work of V. Gordon Childe, who presented a synthesis of European prehistory over the course of a prolific career. His early work was particularly focused on defining and mapping the relationships among culture groups in Neolithic and Bronze Age Europe to show how innovations such as farming and metallurgy—and the artifact types related to them—spread across the region. By mapping cultures in time and space (fig. 2.1) and then plotting the points at which specific innovations or traits appeared in different groups, he was able to show the direction and spread of features among them, allowing him to argue that the most significant innovations had their origins in the Middle East and then spread westward through Europe (Childe 1928, 1929). This *ex oriente lux* perspective was partly undermined only with the revision to chronology brought by radiocarbon dating (Renfrew 1973), and the endurance of the model is illustrated by the fact, for example, that it is still customary to date the Bronze Age later the farther west one goes.

Though the idea of diffusion brought attention to the importance of considering intersocietal contact in studies of cultural variability and change, growing criticism that the concept was undertheorized subsequently led to attempts to refine it. Specifically, the mechanisms of diffusion were thought to be insufficiently explained or just assumed (Rands and Riley 1958), particularly with respect to the similarly sweeping process of migration, which had also featured prominently in early syntheses of prehistory (Hawkes 1954). For example, some anthropologists used the concept of acculturation to specify which processes would allow or impel members of a society to borrow traits from its neighbors (Redfield, Linton, and Herskovits 1936), and to determine the parameters under which such borrowing might occur (Willey 1953; Willey and Lathrap 1956).

At the same time that this critique of diffusionist analyses was growing, evolutionary explanations of culture change were making a resurgence in anthropology and archaeology (Binford 1962; Steward 1955; White 1949, 1959). In evolutionary models, culture was seen as humans' "extrasomatic means of adaptation" (White 1959:8). Cultures changed primarily in relation to environmental factors and for the most part on an implicitly unilinear continuum from simple to complex (Sahlins and Service 1960). In such a scheme, diffusion and intercultural contact were secondary issues, when considered at all (White 1945, 1957). Julian Steward (1955:182) famously

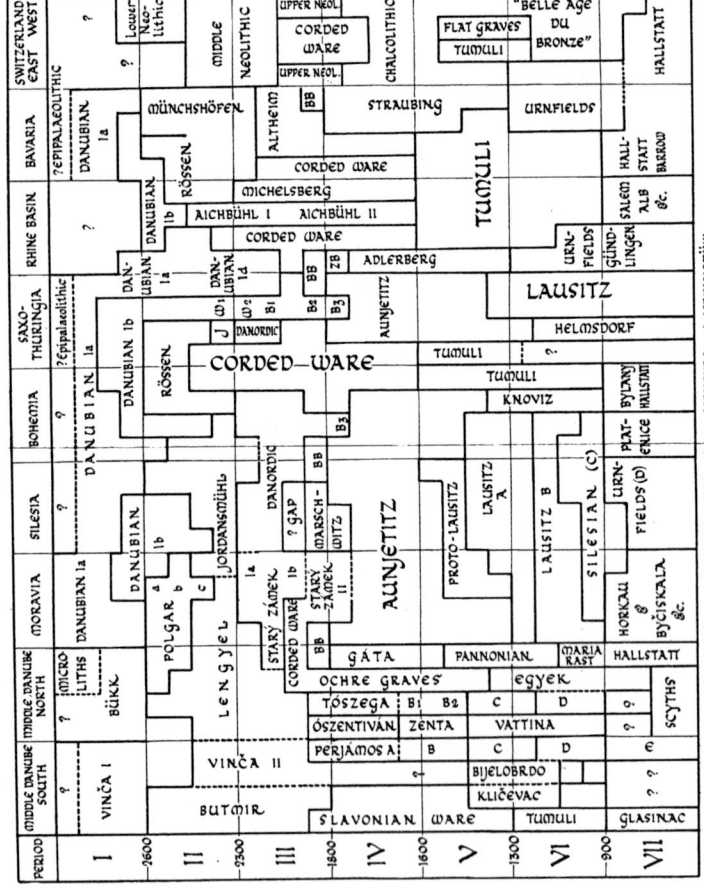

Figure 2.1 Childe's (1929) spatial and chronological chart of central European cultures in the Neolithic and Bronze Ages from *The Danube in Prehistory*.

dismissed diffusion as "mechanical and unintelligible," a way "to avoid coming to grips with problems of cause and effect" that "explains nothing." As Schortman and Urban (1987:48) point out, diffusion and evolution, having developed as responses to each other, were perceived as incompatible, opposing approaches to culture change, despite several attempts to reconcile the two views.

One such attempt was Willey's study of settlement patterns in Peru's Virú Valley, in which he used spatial data to examine how patterns of activities—not simply artifacts—were linked to the choices that groups made to organize their society in a given region (Willey 1953; Willey and Lathrap 1956). By focusing on activity areas and clusters of artifacts rather than the presence or absence of individual objects, he was able to improve on older and more simplistic diffusionist models to identify the spread of practices and cultural actions across sites and regions. Willey's attention to social organization and both the external and internal factors producing change may thus be understood as merging earlier diffusionary studies with the growing interest in ecology and adaptation at that time.

Among the efforts to reconcile diffusionist and ecological/evolutionary approaches, Caldwell's (1964) "interaction sphere" model is also worthy of note, not simply for its attempt to integrate interaction and culture change in a single model but also because it anticipated many of the concerns of the world-systems approaches that emerged in subsequent years. In Caldwell's formulation, interaction among disparate communities, expressed through sets of behavior patterns and material culture, allowed the development of more complex societies, either in a subset of the regions taking part in the interaction or in the interaction area as a whole. Although focused superficially on the mechanisms of interaction and the flow of cultural ideas, this model also considered their evolutionary implications with respect to emerging state societies, effectively bridging the two dominant views at the time and highlighting the importance of interaction for understanding culture change.

Trade and Exchange

Although diffusion's vague conceptualizations of interaction may have faded with the emergence of evolutionary models in archaeology, concerns with intersocietal contact found a new and even more comfortable home in the study of trade and the development of economic anthropology in the 1960s (Dalton 1969; Polanyi et al. 1957; Sahlins 1965). A specific focus on trade offered a way to approach interregional relationships in tangible and measurable ways absent in diffusionist approaches. It provided a way to theorize interaction more rigorously by focusing on the system of reciprocal exchanges that facilitates the spread of objects and ideas constituting diffusion (Adams 1974:240–41). Moreover, such trade studies could fit with evolutionary or adaptationalist models because trade could be understood as one of many strategies employed by a social group to adapt to its environment and exploit the resources afforded it (e.g., Adams 1966; Sanders 1956). Thus trade, with its easy fit with both methodologies of quantification and adaptationalist theory, replaced diffusion as the primary way archaeologists came to study interaction in the past.

Archaeological approaches to the trade and exchange of objects developed in large part out of economic anthropology and studies of both gift exchange and early market systems. Building on observations by Malinowski (1922) and others about the system of long-distance reciprocal exchange in the Trobriand Islands known as the "kula ring," in which objects were circulated among participants in order to maintain social relations with each other, Mauss stated explicitly that the exchange of goods is often more significant socially than economically. Thus in noncapitalist societies, it could be more appropriate to consider these goods as "gifts" (1990 [1950]). Exchange is a social act embedded within and acting to reinforce a system of social relationships between individuals, between an individual and his or her group, and between a group and its neighbors. For archaeologists, without access to living people for information about these relationships, measuring the scale (through distribution) and intensity (through quantification) of exchange was thought to be a way to identify what kinds of relationships existed, even if their individual meanings remained elusive (Renfrew 1972, 1975). The growth of scientific applications in archaeology and studies of provenience (artifact sourcing) went a long way toward addressing the earlier criticisms of diffusionary approaches for their inability to establish firmly the existence and extent of contacts among societies by, for example, distinguishing imports from imitations (Brothwell and Higgs 1963; Renfrew, Cann, and Dixon 1965; Renfrew et al. 1966).

While the addition of sourcing techniques represented a significant development in the field of archaeology and the study of trade, their easy incorporation into statistical models had the effect of promoting a study of trade that was more formally economic and not so concerned with the social meanings stressed by Mauss and others. The primary concerns of such formalist approaches to trade and exchange in archaeology included identifying and isolating the rational decisions driving trade, as well as developing predictive models and spatial distribution curves to analyze and measure its extent (Earle and Christenson 1980; Renfrew 1972, 1975; Tourtellot and Sabloff 1972; Wright 1972). In Renfrew's (1975) classic analysis, for example, he suggested that the scale and intensity of trading relationships could be measured though quantification of imports in assemblages. Comparisons of the percentage of imports at various sites in a region could be matched with the types of distribution curves that corresponded to different kinds of trading systems: down-the-line, directional, freelance, or prestige-chain (fig. 2.2a–d).While these studies provided a productive avenue for research into ancient interaction systems, they were criticized not only for their inattention to noneconomic dimensions of trade but also for not dealing adequately with the problem of equifinality in explaining artifact distribution patterns (Hodder 1978), and for not recognizing the potential for multiple kinds of trade systems to operate simultaneously or in a nested fashion (Knapp and Cherry 1994).

A more fundamental criticism of such formalist approaches has its foundations in the work of Karl Polanyi (1975; Polanyi et al. 1957), who, influenced by Malinowski and other social anthropologists, argued that rational economics could not adequately explain how premodern and noncapitalist economies worked. He argued for what he called "substantive" understandings (or a kind of locally embedded equivalence) of terms such as *market*, *trade*, and *money*, recognizing that these terms suggest qualitatively and quantitatively different things in non-industrial contexts. Moreover, Polanyi (1957) distinguished between "administered" and "market" trade, asserting that the latter, characterized by entrepreneurial mercantile activity, standard currency, and market behavior, has only been a feature of modern societies. Trade in premodern and non-industrial contexts, on the other hand, is "administered" in that it is largely under institutionalized control and occurs under conditions decided by that institution, whether a local chief, the temple economy, or socially-embedded systems of redistribution such as the potlatch, the kula, or dowries (Polanyi 1975:150–51). In the years since, Adams (1974:239) and others have pointed out that the distinction between administered and market exchange is not so clear, as there is increasing evidence that entrepreneurial, market-sensitive activities existed in premodern contexts, the Phoenicians of the early Iron Age Mediterranean being a prime example (see Sherratt, chapter 6, this volume). Moreover, it is equally clear that nonmarket systems, socially and institutionally embedded, also exist in industrial, market-based societies (see, e.g., Casella, chapter 8, this volume), suggesting that both market and nonmarket systems may operate simultaneously and at different scales in a wide range of contexts (see also Knapp and Cherry 1994).

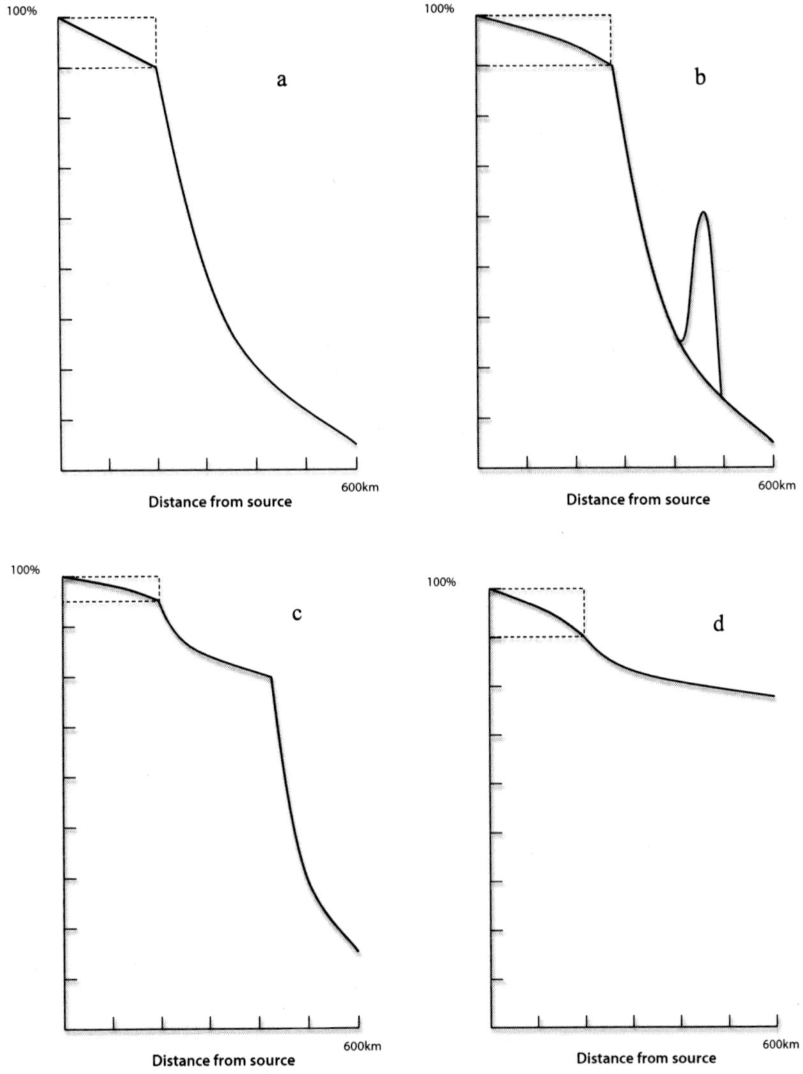

Figure 2.2 Renfrew's distribution curves illustrating falloff in abundance of a traded commodity with distance from source, representing (a) down-the-line trade, (b) directional trade, (c) freelance trade, and (d) prestige-chain trade (after Renfrew 1975).

Symbols and Systems

Recognizing the shortcomings of the formalist and substantivist approaches when used in isolation, archaeologists made several attempts in the 1970s and 1980s to bridge them and, as Earle (1982:3) says, "to explain exchange and its linkage to broader sociocultural forms." Jane Schneider (1974), for instance, looked at social interactions and pointed out that social relations of all kinds involve the exchange of both material and nonmaterial items and that such exchanges act economically and symbolically to solidify social hierarchies and structures. This kind of approach, what Hodder (1982b) calls "social exchange" theory, involves both formalist conceptualizations of trade systems along with a discussion of social strategies common in substantivist approaches. Similarly, Adams (1974) argued that a false dichotomy between the two perspectives prompted archaeologists to choose between them (with formalism seeming to win out), when in fact both the economic and the more historically contingent social dimensions of trade and exchange needed to be explored archaeologically. While not offering a specific way forward, Adams' warning in many ways anticipated the problems facing current studies of trade that this volume seeks to address.

In confirmation of Adams' suspicion regarding where the field was headed, in 1982 Hodder observed that few if any studies of trade considered its symbolic and ideological aspects, central issues in his "contextual" approach to archaeological interpretation (Hodder 1982a, 1987). As he (1982b:207) says, the "artifacts exchanged are not arbitrary." Rather, objects are imbued with and convey meanings for those creating, using, and exchanging them. These meanings are variable (they shift), multiple (they act simultaneously), and contextually embedded in an "interlinked network of exchange relations, social strategies, and symbolism." The objection to Hodder's view, however, was that it went too far in the other direction: it seemed to leave little room for cross-cultural theorizing about and systematic analysis of cultural interaction. As Earle (1982:3) points out, while an emphasis on meaning may be seen to follow from the substantivist approach because it recognizes that exchange is embedded in social relations and structures, contextual approaches also share with substantivism the problem of how to discover these relationships and structures *archaeologically*. One way forward, suggested by several of the cases in this volume, is to bring classic archaeological concepts and tools, common and thus comparable across contexts and approaches, to bear on relatively newer concerns about social action and meaning.

Schneider (1974, 1977), another scholar who emphasized social interactions, was also among the first to introduce the concept of world-systems into archaeology. This approach to interregional interaction has had lasting effects on the discipline and in many ways represents the most recent major theoretical development in the study of trade in archaeology. The world-systems perspective initially developed as a critique of prevailing theories in development economics that regarded the modern world as divided between independent and dependent nation-states. Within development economics, the latter were thought to lack some quality or qualities that would enable them to become fully "developed," and thus they were unable to enter into trade as equal partners with the former. Influenced by the French Annales approach to history of Fernand Braudel (1972 [1949]) and others, as well as emerging critiques of unilinear views of the evolution of societies, Immanuel Wallerstein (1974, 1980, 1989) acknowledged that states supplied labor and goods to each other in an unequal exchange, but he argued that their inequality was fundamental to the *system* within which all states operated, rather than a manifestation of dependent states' inability to catch up. He proposed a model in which unequal exchange has a spatial dimension and the division of labor is not contained within individual societies but crosses societal boundaries, with peripheries supplying labor and commodities and cores accumulating the surplus. In his original formulation, semi-peripheries also played a role in the system, being "peripheral" to dominant cores and a core of sorts to their own peripheries (Wallerstein 1976). All of the elements were interdependent, with cores just as dependent on the system as peripheries. This view foregrounded the importance of interaction and dependence among societies of different scales and suggested that the appropriate unit of analysis was the system as a whole, not the individual society (which, in the modern era that Wallerstein was considering, was the state).

World-systems theory has been used most often as a way of explaining the unique dynamics of the capitalist world-economy since the sixteenth century, but Jane Schneider (1977), Janet Abu-Lughod (1989), and Andre Gunder Frank (e.g., Frank and Gills 1993), among others, have argued that versions of world-systems operated in earlier periods. Most notably, Schneider (1977) argued that in precapitalist times, asymmetrical world-systems configurations developed around trade in luxury goods, which were then exchanged for raw materials from the periphery. Her application of world-systems analysis to the trade in both commodities *and* prestige items subsequently influenced several archaeological treatments applying world-systems theory to cases ranging from Central Asia and the Indus (Kohl 1979, 1987) to early Mesoamerica (Blanton and Feinman 1984) and the southwestern United States (Upham 1982). Offering an alternative to social evolution by stressing the importance of interaction in the development of societies, world-systems analysis found favor among archaeologists interested in understanding how interaction effects culture change and became a productive line of inquiry for the field (e.g., Champion 1989; Ekholm and Friedman 1979; Friedman and Rowlands 1977; Rowlands et al. 1987; Schortman and Urban 1987; Sherratt

1993a). In this way, the study of trade in archaeology became embedded in a broader phenomenon, "interaction," wherein researchers considered not only the movement of traded items but also the intersocietal relations of production that allowed for their movement.

Some alternatives to world-systems theory developed out of dissatisfactions with its emphasis on commodities rather than the symbolic value often embedded within traded objects (Appadurai 1986; Fotiadis 1999; Sherratt and Sherratt 1991). In fact, most archaeological analyses inspired by world-systems theory reject Wallerstein's exclusive consideration of commodities and use his model to analyze the trade in preciosities as well as nonmaterial factors such as information and symbolic content (Schneider 1977; Upham 1982). Renfrew and Cherry (1986), for example, developed the peer-polity interaction model, in which changes in social structure develop as a result of the interaction among neighboring, similarly structured social units. Their model represents an important step in the study of the role of trade in culture change because of its broad understanding of interaction, including social competition and emulation as well as symbolism and the exchange of information (see also Marcus 1990; Sherratt 1993b). A broader perspective is also developed in the models of Schortman and Urban (Schortman 1989; Schortman and Urban 1987) and Kohl (1987), which, although heavily influenced by world-systems perspectives, also focus on the exchange of information and technology.

Two modified world-systems models are notable for their attempt to deal with aspects of exchange beyond the economic. First, Schortman and Urban (1987:68) have developed a model of "interregional interaction" in which people exchange not just objects but also information in "energy, materials, social institutions and ideas" (see also Wobst 1977). Drawing on world-systems theory as well as the earlier concept of an "interaction sphere" developed by Caldwell (1964), they reinforce Wallerstein's original point that the position of the periphery is as important as that of the core and that "all developments of social complexity [are] inseparably linked with intersocietal interaction" (Schortman and Urban 1987:80). Like other systems approaches, theirs attempts to address the multiple processes involved in intersocietal relationships. However, their assumption that only the responses of the "dominant group of identity holders will have developmental significance for the rest of society" (70) reproduces a normative view of culture that more current analyses seek to avoid.

Second and more recently, Gil Stein (2002) has sought to bring a world-systems approach into accommodation with many of the perspectives espoused by postprocessual archaeologies, particularly concepts of agency and practice theory. He rightly notes that most archaeological models of trade and exchange have tended to emphasize intersocietal over intrasocietal dynamics. He also notes a tendency towards a "misplaced directionality" in analyses of interregional relationships, insofar as archaeologists label cores and peripheries before we even begin, and then proceed to emphasize the influence of the former on the latter, seldom considering the impact of peripheries on their cores (Stein 2002:903–4). For example, he points out that traditional anthropological and archaeological terms such as *acculturation* imply that the dynamic of cultural change is unidirectional. Stein does not explicitly develop a way around this problem but suggests that the recent focus on agency, practice, and social identity (e.g., Dobres and Robb 2000, 2005; Lightfoot et al. 1998) provides archaeologists with better conceptual tools with which to approach these questions.

Stein (2002:905ff.) suggests that a new paradigm is developing for the study of interregional interaction in archaeology, fusing the economically focused comparative approach of processual archaeology with the postprocessual emphasis on agency, practice, and ideology, as well as the latter's recognition of material culture's role in mediating identities. Other features of the new synthesis he describes include a rejection of unilinear models and the recognition that interaction is both multiscalar and variable, that the societies involved in such interactions are heterogeneous, and that both internal dynamics and human agency are important factors to consider. To illustrate this new model, he replaces the well-worn world-systems approach to the Uruk expansion, which he rightly says has lost its heuristic value because archaeologists have diluted and overused it,[1] with a trade diaspora model that he says "allow[s] for a much broader range of interactional forms than the traditional models" (Stein 2002:913; see also Curtin 1984).

Conclusion: Whither Trade?

Trade has endured as a core concern of archaeology despite shifts in methodologies and theoretical approaches. The emphases of each generation of scholars affect how the study of trade is pursued (or not pursued) by the succeeding one, so that the subject seems to go through periodic lulls as a topic of interest. Early attention to trade as a vehicle for comparing and linking culture groups led to its initial rejection by positivists who sought to develop testable models of human behavior. With the discovery that statistical and spatial analysis could be easily applied to trade, it became so clearly associated with processual approaches that it has been almost entirely ignored by postprocessual archaeologists.

From time to time, archaeologists have developed models that work to reconcile seemingly divergent approaches: formalist and substantavist, diffusionist and evolutionary, processual and postprocessual. Recent articulations of a possible third way in archaeological studies of trade emphasize the importance of balancing understandings of systems and structures with the agency of past actors (Stein 2002) and considering, for example, the possibility that elite hegemony and regulation may share the stage with free markets and actors (Oka and Kusimba 2008:365–366).

Whether such new, integrated approaches to trade are in fact emerging is not yet clear, but one aim of this volume is to explore some aspects of trade that have been relatively neglected. This exploration is not so much a rejection of world-systems and other approaches that have dominated trade studies over the past thirty years but rather an effort to highlight a greater diversity of perspectives into the social dimensions of trade that engage with ethnographic, ethnohistorical, and historical research, as Adams (1974) envisioned. As Wylie (2000) has suggested with regard to archaeological theorizing in general, a multiplicity of approaches may be not only what we are stuck with but also in fact best for the field's continued intellectual development. Trade studies, too, may best be understood in the plural, illustrating that the macro-scale models so thoroughly developed in the 1970s and 1980s and newer concepts such as agency are not so much contradictory as complementary.

The reason why trade has remained an important topic for archaeologists of all perspectives is that, as Malinowski and Mauss pointed out in their early anthropological studies, trade is a fundamental vehicle for establishing and maintaining social relations among individuals and groups, whether accomplished through the exchange of gifts, commodities, or kin through marriage. And as Urban (1996:162) observes, the actual exchange of items is in many cases secondary and may only need to happen occasionally to maintain the idea that social relations exist. Trade is thus clearly a social act. Even in late capitalist times, we may argue that the use of trade embargoes or the signing of free trade agreements among nation-states have important social aims and effects. And so as archaeology moves into the twenty-first century, exploring those social dimensions of trade will maintain the theme among the field's core concerns.

Note

1. Stein's (2002:904) comment that "calling virtually every multigroup interaction network a 'World-System' diminishes the term" is a great understatement.

References

Abu-Lughod, Janet L.
1989 *Before European Hegemony: The World System ad 1250–1350*. Oxford University Press, Oxford.

Adams, Robert McC.
1966 *The Evolution of Urban Society*. Aldine, Chicago.1974 Anthropological Perspectives on Ancient Trade. *Current Anthropology* 15:239–258.

Appadurai, Arjun (editor)
1986 *The Social Life of Things: Commodities in Cultural Perspective*. Cambridge University Press, Cambridge.

Bauer, Alexander A.
2008 Import, Imitation, or Communication?: Pottery Style, Technology, and Coastal Contact in the Early Bronze Age Black Sea. In *"Import" and "Imitation": Methodical and Practical Problems with an Archaeological Key Concept*, edited by P. Biehl and Y. Rassamakin, pp. 89–104. Schriften des Zentrums für Archäologie und Kulturgeschichte des Schwarzmeerraumes Band 11. Beier & Beran, Langenweiβbach.

Binford, Lewis R.
1962 Archaeology as Anthropology. *American Antiquity* 28:217–225.

Blanton, Richard, and Gary L. Feinman
1984 The Mesoamerican World System. *American Anthropologist* 86:673–682.

Boas, Franz
1924 Evolution or Diffusion? *American Anthropologist* 26:340–344.

Braudel, Fernand
1972 [1949] *The Mediterranean and the Mediterranean World in the Age of Phillip II*. Translated by S. Reynolds. 2 vols. Collins, London.

Brothwell, D., and E. Higgs (editors)
1963 *Science in Archaeology*. Basic Books, New York.

Caldwell, Joseph R.
1964 Interaction Spheres in Prehistory. In *Hopewellian Studies*, edited by J. R. Caldwell and R. Hall, pp. 134–143. Illinois State Museum Scientific Papers, Vol. 12. Illinois State Museum, Springfield.

Champion, T. (editor)
1989 *Centre and Periphery: Comparative Studies in Archaeology*. Unwin Hyman, London.

Childe, V. Gordon
1925 *The Dawn of European Civilisation*. Kegan Paul, Trench, Trubner & Co., London.
1928 *The Most Ancient East: The Oriental Prelude to European Prehistory*. Kegan Paul, Trench, Trubner & Co., London.
1929 *The Danube in Prehistory*. Clarendon Press, Oxford.
1950 The Urban Revolution. *Town Planning Review* 21:3–17.
1956 *Piecing Together the Past: The Interpretation of Archaeological Data*. Routledge and Kegan Paul, London.

Clarke, David L.
1968 *Analytical Archaeology*. Methuen and Co., London.

Curtin, Philip D.
1984 *Cross-Cultural Trade in World History*. Cambridge University Press, Cambridge.

Dalton, George
1969 Theoretical Issues in Economic Anthropology. *Current Anthropology* 10:63–102.

Dixon, Roland B.
1928 *The Building of Cultures*. Charles Scribner's Sons, New York.

Dobres, Marcia-Anne, and John Robb
2000 Agency in Archaeology: Paradigm or Platitude? In *Agency in Archaeology*, edited by J. Robb, pp. 3–17. Routledge, London.
2005 "Doing Agency": Introductory Remarks on Methodology. *Journal of Archaeological Method and Theory* 12:159–166.

Earle, Timothy K.
1982 Prehistoric Economics and the Archaeology of Exchange. In *Contexts for Prehistoric Exchange*, edited by J. E. Ericson and T. K. Earle, pp. 1–12. Academic Press, New York.

Earle, Timothy K., and Andrew L. Christenson
1980 *Modeling Change in Prehistoric Subsistence Economies*. Academic Press, New York.

Ekholm, K., and J. Friedman
1979 "Capital" Imperialism and Exploitation in Ancient World Systems. In *Power and Propaganda: A Symposium on Early Empires*, edited by M. T. Larsen, pp. 41–58. Akademisk Forlag, Copenhagen.

Flannery, Kent V.
1968 The Olmec and the Valley of Oaxaca: A Model of Interregional Interaction in Formative Times. In *Dumbarton Oaks Conference on the Olmec*, edited by E. P. Benton, pp. 79–110. Dumbarton Oaks, Washington, DC.

Fotiadis, Michael
1999 Comparability, Equivalency, and Contestation. In *Material Symbols: Culture and Economy in Prehistory*, edited by J. E. Robb, pp. 385–398. Southern Illinois University, Carbondale Occasional Papers, Vol. 26. Center for Archaeological Investigations, Carbondale, IL.

Frank, Andre Gunder, and Barry K. Gills (editors)
1993 *The World System: Five Hundred Years or Five Thousand?* Routledge, London.

Friedman, J., and Michael Rowlands (editors)
1977 *The Evolution of Social Systems*. Duckworth, London.

Hawkes, Christopher F. C.
1954 Archaeological Theory and Method: Some Suggestions from the Old World. *American Anthropologist* 56:155–168.

Hodder, Ian
1978 *The Spatial Organization of Culture*. Duckworth, London.
1982a Theoretical Archaeology: A Reactionary View. In *Symbolic and Structural Archaeology*, edited by I. Hodder, pp. 1–16. Cambridge University Press, Cambridge.
1982b Toward a Contextual Approach to Prehistoric Exchange. In *Contexts for Prehistoric Exchange*, edited by J. E. Ericson and T. K. Earle, pp. 199–211. Academic Press, New York.

Hodder, Ian
1987 *The Archaeology of Contextual Meanings*. Cambridge University Press, Cambridge.

Knapp, A. Bernard, and John F. Cherry
1994 *Provenience Studies and Bronze Age Cyprus*. Prehistory Press, Madison, WI.

Kohl, Philip L.
1979 The "World Economy" in West Asia in the Third Millennium BC. In *South Asian Archaeology 1977*, edited by M. Taddei, pp. 55–85. Instituto Universitario Orientale, Naples.
1987 The Ancient Economy, Transferable Technologies and the Bronze Age World System: A View from the Northeastern Frontier of the Ancient Near East. In *Centre and Periphery in the Ancient World*, edited by M. Rowlands, M. T. Larsen, and K. Kristiansen, pp. 13–24. Cambridge University Press, Cambridge.

Kossina, Gustav
1911 *Die Herkunft der Germanen: zur methode der Siedlungsarchäologie*. C. Kabitzsch: Würzburg.

Kramer, Carol
1977 Pots and People. In *Mountains and Lowlands: Essays in the Archaeology of Greater Mesopotamia*, edited by T. C. Young, Jr., pp. 99–112. Bibliotheca Mesopotamica, Vol. 7. Undena, Malibu, CA.

Kroeber, Alfred L.
1940 Stimulus Diffusion. *American Anthropologist* 32:1–20.

Lightfoot, Kent, Antoinette Martinez, and Ann Schiff
1998 Daily Practice and Material Culture in Pluralistic Social Settings: An Archaeological Study of Culture Change and Persistence from Fort Ross, California. *American Antiquity* 63:199–222.

Lowie, Robert H.
1929 *Culture and Ethnology*. Peter Smith, New York.

Malinowski, Bronislaw
1922 *Argonauts of the Western Pacific*. Routledge, London.

Marcus, Michelle I.
1990 Center, *Province* and Periphery: A New Paradigm from Iron Age Iran. *Art History* 13:129–150.

Mauss, Marcel
1990 [1950] *The Gift*. Translated by W. D. Halls. W. W. Norton, New York.

Montelius, Gustaf Oscar Augustus
1899 *Der Orient und Europa: Einfluss der Orientalischen Cultur auf Europa*. Königl Hofboktryckeriet, Stockholm.

Oka, Rahul, and Chapurukha M. Kusimba
2008 The Archaeology of Trading Systems, Part 1: Towards a New Trade Synthesis. *Journal of Archaeological Research* 16(4):339–395.

Polanyi, Karl
1957 Marketless Trading in Hammurabi's Time. In *Trade and Market in the Early Empires*, edited by H. W. Pearson, pp. 12–26. The Free Press, New York.

Polanyi, Karl
1975 Traders and Trade. In *Ancient Civilization and Trade*, edited by Jeremy A. Sabloff and C. C. Lamberg-Karlovsky, pp. 133–154. University of New Mexico Press, Albuquerque.

Polanyi, Karl, C. H. Arensberg, and H. W. Pearson (editors)
1957 *Trade and Market in the Early Empires*. The Free Press, New York.

Rands, R. L., and C. L. Riley
1958 Diffusion and Discontinuous Distribution. *American Anthropologist* 60:274–297.

Rathje, William L.
1971 The Origin and Development of Lowland Classic Maya Civilization. *American Antiquity* 36:275–285.

Redfield, Robert, Ralph Linton, and Melville J. Herskovits
1936 Memorandum on the Study of Acculturation. *American Anthropologist* 38:149–152.

Renfrew, A. Colin
1969 Trade and Culture Process in European Prehistory. *Current Anthropology* 10:151–169.
1972 *The Emergence of Civilisation: The Cyclades and the Aegean in the Third Millennium bc*. Methuen, London.
1973 *Before Civilization: The Radiocarbon Revolution and European Prehistory*. Cambridge University Press, Cambridge.
1975 Trade as Action at a Distance: Questions of Integration and Communication. In *Ancient Civilization and Trade*, edited by Jeremy A. Sabloff and C. C. Lamberg-Karlovsky, pp. 3–59. University of New Mexico Press, Albuquerque.

Renfrew, A. Colin, J. R. Cann, and J. E. Dixon
1965 Obsidian in the Aegean. *Annual of the British School at Athens* 60:225–247.

Renfrew, A. Colin, and John F. Cherry
1986 *Peer Polity Interaction and Socio-Political Change*. Cambridge University Press, Cambridge.

Renfrew, A. Colin, J. E. Dixon, and J. R. Cann
1966 Obsidian and Early Culture Contact in the Near East. *Proceedings of the Prehistoric Society* 32:30–72.

Rowlands, M., M. T. Larsen, and K. Kristiansen (editors)
1987 *Centre and Periphery in the Ancient World*. Cambridge University Press, Cambridge.

Sahlins, Marshall
1965 On the Sociology of Primitive Exchange. In *The Relevance of Models for Social Anthropology*, edited by M. Banton, pp. 139–227. ASA Monograph, Vol. 1. Tavistock Publications, London.

Sahlins, Marshall D., and Elman R. Service (editors)
1960 *Evolution and Culture*. University of Michigan Press, Ann Arbor.

Sanders, William T.
1956 The Central Mexican Symbiotic Region: A Study in Prehistoric Settlement Patterns. In *Prehistoric Settlement Patterns in the New World*, edited by G. R. Willey, pp. 115–127. Viking Fund Publications in Anthropology, Vol. 23. Wenner-Gren Foundation for Anthropological Research, New York.

Schneider, Jane
1974 *Economic Man*. Free Press, New York.
1977 Was There a Pre-Capitalist World-System? *Peasant Studies* 6:20–29.

Schortman, Edward M.
1989 Interregional Interaction in Prehistory: The Need for a New Perspective. *American Antiquity* 54:52–65.

Schortman, Edward M., and Patricia A. Urban
1987 Modeling Interregional Interaction in Prehistory. In *Advances in Archaeological Method and Theory* Vol. 11, edited by M. B. Schiffer, pp. 11–35. Academic Press, New York.

Shennan, Stephen (editor)
1989 *Archaeological Approaches to Cultural Identity*. Unwin Hyman, London.

Sherratt, Andrew
1993a What Would a Bronze Age World System Look Like? *Journal of European Archaeology* 1(2):1–57.
1993b Who Are You Calling Peripheral? Dependence and Independence in European Prehistory. In *Trade and Exchange in Prehistoric Europe*, edited by F. Healey, pp. 245–255. Oxbow, Oxford.

Sherratt, Andrew, and Susan Sherratt
1991 From Luxuries to Commodities: The Nature of Bronze Age Trading Systems. In *Bronze Age Trade in the Mediterranean*, edited by N. H. Gale, pp. 351–384. Studies in Mediterranean Archaeology Vol. 90. Paul Åströms Förlag, Göteborg, Sweden.

Stein, Gil J.
2002 From Passive Periphery to Active Agents: Emerging Perspectives in the Archaeology of Interregional Interaction. *American Anthropologist* 104:903–916.

Steward, Julian H.
1955 *Theory of Culture Change*. University of Illinois Press, Urbana.

Tourtellot, Gair, and Jeremy A. Sabloff
1972 An Analysis of the Hopewell Interaction Sphere. In *Social Exchange and Interaction*, edited by E. N. Wilmsen, pp. 126–135. Museum of Anthropology, Anthropological Papers, Vol. 37. University of Michigan Press, Ann Arbor.

Upham, Steadman
1982 *Polities and Power: An Economic and Political History of the Western Pueblo*. Academic Press, New York.

Urban, Greg
1996 *Metaphysical Community*. University of Texas Press, Austin.

Wallerstein, Immanuel
1974 *The Modern World-System: Capitalist Agriculture and the Origins of the European World-Economy in the Sixteenth Century*. Academic Press, New York.
1976 Semi-Peripheral Countries and the Contemporary World Crisis. *Theory and Society* 3(4):461–483.
1980 *Mercantilism and the Consolidation of the European World-Economy, 1600–1750*. Academic Press, New York.
1989 *The Second Era of Great Expansion of the Capitalist World-Economy, 1730–1840s*. Academic Press, New York.

White, Leslie A.
1945 "Diffusion vs. Evolution": An Anti-Evolutionist Fallacy. *American Anthropologist* 47:339–356.
1949 *The Science of Culture*. Grove Press, New York.
1957 Evolution and Diffusion. *Antiquity* 31:214–218.
1959 *The Evolution of Culture*. McGraw-Hill, New York.

Willey, Gordon R.
1953 A Pattern of Diffusion-Acculturation. *Southwestern Journal of Anthropology* 9:369–384.

Willey, Gordon R., and Donald W. Lathrap
1956 An Archaeological Classification of Culture Contact Situations. In *Seminars in Archaeology: 1955*, edited by R. Wauchope, pp. 3–30. Society for American Archaeology, Salt Lake City.

Wobst, H. Martin
1977 Stylistic Behavior and Information Exchange. In *Papers for the Director*, edited by C. Cleland, pp. 317–342. Museum of Anthropology, Anthropological Papers, Vol. 61. University of Michigan Press, Ann Arbor.

Wright, Henry T.
1972 A Consideration of Interregional Exchange in Greater Mesopotamia: 4000–3000 B.C. In *Social Exchange and Interaction*, edited by E. N. Wilmsen, pp. 95–105. Museum of Anthropology, Anthropological Papers, Vol. 37. University of Michigan Press, Ann Arbor.

Wylie, Alison
2000 Questions of Evidence, Legitimacy, and the (dis)Union of Science. *American Antiquity* 65:227–237.

CHAPTER 3

Landscapes of Circulation in Northwest Argentina: The Workings of Obsidian and Ceramics during the First Millennium AD

Marisa Lazzari

Andean studies scholars have long explored the exchange of goods and services at various levels, from kin groups to state societies. There is a substantial record of the circulation of all kinds of materials across very long distances since ancient times, and ongoing archaeological, ethnohistorical, and ethnographic research keep further unveiling the complexity of these networks. In this context, scholars have debated whether transactions were mainly conducted within kinship and ethnic groups or whether exchange was also conducted outside the boundaries of ethnic units (compare Murra 1975, 1985, 1987; Rostworowski 1977; Salomon 1985, 1986). To what extent the latter might have involved specialization or the existence of trade in the sense of a market economy in which some people specialized as merchants (Polanyi 1977) in precolonial times has been a particularly contentious point of the debate.

Although the social aspects of different forms of exchange have long been a central concern in this tradition of research, most scholars have based their interpretations on the structuring role of reciprocity. Reciprocity has often been seen as an overarching cultural rule that defines an Andean lifestyle, also known as *lo andino*. In this view, the circulation of things and services between kinfolk is a key mechanism that balances the unequal distribution of resources in the highly diverse Andean environment, what is usually referred as Andean "ecological complementarity" (Alberti and Mayer 1974; Murra 1975).

Such a rule-bound vision of social and economic exchanges resonates with Lévi-Strauss' (1969 [1948]) objectivist interpretation of the reciprocity norm. Originally defined by Malinowski (1961 [1926]:40; see also 1984 [1922]:139) as "a chain of reciprocal gifts and countergifts, which in the long run balance, benefiting both sides equally," reciprocal transactions were seen by Mauss (1967 [1925]:10–18, 44, 70) as social integration devices put in motion by the compelling powers of those objects given as gifts. Mauss observed that such objects were considered extensions of the giver's self in a social field that combined normative rules with strategic cunning, a field in which a plethora of transactional forms could occur simultaneously. Although Mauss (1967 [1925]:25, 45) agreed that non-Western reciprocal exchanges ultimately achieved the balancing of self-interest, he aptly observed that neat typologies were unhelpful when studying circulatory practices and sociality as constituted through giving.

When interviewed by Myers and Kirshenblatt-Gimblett (2001:287–288), anthropologist Annette Weiner fittingly commented that though the principle of reciprocity helped to explain social interaction and exchange throughout the world, too often it had been misused as a perfect opposite to a market economy. In this role, it serves as an all-explaining, ready-made, and almost automatic principle that guarantees social integration and exists prior to the people involved in its practice.

The interpretation of reciprocity as a rule has been thoroughly criticized by Bourdieu (1977:8–9) and various other scholars (e.g., Humphrey and Hugh-Jones 1992; Miller 2001; Strathern 1992; Weiner 1992, 1994), who emphasized the inadequacy of conceiving reciprocity as a fixed cultural principle or rule to be decoded. Such a view can hardly account for the overwhelming empirical evidence showing that reciprocity is an arena of constant struggle and negotiation. Its meaning changes in response to the unforeseeable consequences of the actual implementation of seemingly unchangeable rules. Even Mauss (1969 [1925]: 46, 70), who believed in the essential difference between Western and non-Western modes of exchange (i.e., the former was motivated by self-interest, the latter by social integration), was a keen observer of the strategic nature of the actual operation of reciprocity.

Andean scholars have certainly discussed the limits of the conceptualization of reciprocity as a rule and have acknowledged the romantic underpinnings of the idea of *lo andino* (Mayer 2002:71, 135–138; Salman and Zoomers 2003; Salomon 1991; Starn 1994; Van Buren 1996). Yet these assumptions still underwrite most studies in the region, particularly archaeological investigations conducted in the south-central Andes. In opposition to these assumptions, I argue that archaeological research in the region would benefit from focusing on the general category of circulation as a domain of social practices that both result from and generate social meanings. This move aligns archaeology with more recent works in the social sciences that reposition circulation as a constitutive domain of social life (Gaonkar and Povinelli 2003:385; Lazzari 2006; Lee and Li Puma 2002:193). It is also my contention that, while the formative role of ecological complementarity in Andean life cannot be overlooked, our understanding of it needs to be expanded. In addition to being an efficient way of managing land and resources, complementarity is organized through a series of social practices and discourses (with cosmological and political implications; see Lecoq 1987), while being also a deeply lived bodily experience. As has been argued for other areas of the world (Roepstorff and Bubandt 2004:15), ecological complementarity can be categorized as a "practice of nature," that is, a way of engaging with the physical world that is inseparably imaginary and pragmatic.

To better address such inseparability, I argue that the concept of landscape—understood as indivisibly natural and cultural (Ingold 2000:190–193)—challenges the traditional notion of the archaeological region that has often been favored in the study of ancient circulation. The space that emerges from circulatory practices is not a passive domain traversed by people and objects. Rather, this space has enormous potential to shape human consciousness and social formations in unique ways. The circulation of human and nonhuman bodies (whether artifacts, animals, plants, or any other material or immaterial cultural category of being; see Lazzari 2005) weaves lived landscapes. That is, the engagement of such bodies with particular topographies over the long term produces large-scale social spaces. This kind of landscape can be seen as a deep-time version of what anthropologist Nancy Munn (1990:2) has defined as *regionality*: the experience of the world beyond the local through people's involvement in ceremonies, exchanges, and the spread of information through complex networks of alliances and rivalries. Artifacts and materials used and displayed in such events and exchanges, particularly those objects that have circulated through long distances and participated in several transactions prior to their arrival to the context of use under study, may enable the experience of the landscape as a large-scale social space.

The evocative powers of material culture (Rowlands 1993) can be intensively perceived in those nonlocal artifacts and materials used in everyday activities, as these link the user to distant people and places both metaphorically and concretely. Using such objects in concrete tasks provides a tangible lesson to the user about the artifacts' social life: the previous transactions, users, and routes through which the objects circulated become a concrete reality that shapes local practical knowledge. Although most anthropological studies of exchange have identified such properties in highly formalized artifacts or ceremonial spaces (e.g., Weiner 1994), archaeology reveals that the humblest of objects used in quotidian spaces can also link distant people and places and expand the horizon of meaning of everyday life.

In this way, non-utilitarian approaches to the production of social space and the role of material culture in social and economic transactions (Lazzari 2005) can better guide us to explore how unique "cultures of circulation" (Lee and LiPuma 2002:192) were created in the past. These cultures of circulation were produced as material and immaterial cultural forms that traversed social spaces, building around them communities with their own forms of interpretation and evaluation. This complex entanglement of practices and social significances cannot be adequately tackled by homogenizing conceptions of spheres of interaction or regional space. Trying to explore the multilayered social space during part of the Formative period in Northwest Argentina (first millennium AD) as a field of contesting meanings and competing practices, this article discusses lithic and ceramic materials from early sedentary settlements on the western side of the Aconquija Mountains (Catamarca province).

Nature, Culture, and Circulation: A Closer Look at the Andean Debate

Andean communities are often conceived as self-sufficient, as they typically participate in a system of land tenure that grants access rights to land and dwellings in microenvironments located at different altitudes to all members of one ethnic group. This system, known as the "vertical archipelago" (also referred as "verticality"), is thought to provide ethnic group members with fluid access to multiple resources through interfamily exchanges of goods and services. Murra (1975, 1985) and others (e.g., Alberti and Mayer 1974) argued that this kind of self-sufficiency was a widespread organizing principle(one often discussed as an ideal that communities aim to achieve; see Shimada 1985a:xi) and considered nonqualitative exchange with strangers to be logically incompatible with the Andean lifestyle because community members could seemingly satisfy their subsistence needs by means of qualitative exchanges conducted under the rule of reciprocity. Yet numerous forms barter and non-ceremonial exchange have been identified throughout the Andes, and researchers continue to debate the extent to which these forms were part of local precolonial developments (Espinoza Soriano 1987; Mayer 2002; Murra 1985; Rostworowski 1989; Shimada 1985a, 1985b).

The conceptualization of community exchange as incompatible with less personal exchanges with outsiders is largely based on substantivist economic anthropology and its otherwise commendable goal of understanding noncapitalist economies in their own terms. In works in this school of thought, barter has usually been demonized as the historical precedent of market economies (Humphrey and Hugh-Jones 1992:3). However, it is worth remembering that Polanyi himself was ambiguous about whether quantitative forms of exchange such as barter could be conflated with market transactions, and he did not argue that the former necessarily preceded the latter (Halperin 1993:291). At any rate, anthropologists have often shown (e.g., Gell 1992; Humphrey 1992) that barter is as embedded in social relations as gift exchange, and the practice of barter does not imply the existence of a separate economic sphere of quantitative exchanges comparable to present-day market economies.

Given the proliferation of dichotomous approaches to exchange, the point made by anthropologists working on similar issues in other areas of the world is indeed relevant for Andean studies. Significantly, the area offers ample evidence of a wide variety of intercommunity exchanges since the earliest settlement. As Lecoq (1987) and Nielsen (2001b) have shown for contemporary llama caravan traders, one cannot assume that mundane exchanges are detached from multiple orders of signification. There is also considerable evidence of the coexistence of multiple modalities of transactions and circulation in both early colonial and precolumbian times in different areas of the Andes (e.g., Assadourian 1995; Salomon 1985, 1986; Van Buren 1996). Although some archaeologists have sought to demonstrate the long duration of the constitutive elements of Murra's (1972) archipelago model (Aldenderfer 1993; Stanish 1992), the diversity of empirical data challenges the idea that Andean circulation was regulated by similar cultural principles with minor variations across regions. Many scholars have feared that speaking of multiple forms of exchange and fluid interactions across communities undermines our understanding of Andean cultural specificity and perpetuates the Western ideological separation of economy from social life. Yet the available evidence of creativity and diversity in forms of transactions can be embraced without discarding the idea that economy is embedded in social practice. As argued before, forms of circulation that may transcend the limits of intragroup transactions are also constitutive of meaningful social domains, albeit at different spatial and temporal scales.

It is my contention that Andean scholars' traditional distrust of archaeological models that emphasize fluid and multiple forms of circulation and interaction is rooted in the entrenched belief that nature determines the social division of labor in the Andes and thus functions as the fundamental regulator of basic human needs. In this sense, Andean ecological complementarity is considered the foundation for transactions. The capacity of the landscape to affect human action is conceived of as physical causality only; that is, a topography that both limits and enables particular behaviors. The landscape is seen as a passive backdrop, a stage of sorts that makes possible the unfolding of particular human histories.

In this framework, the value of things is only determined by what is considered "objective need," while distance is a major limiting factor defining desirability. In archaeology, distance has been usually combined with estimations of the amount of labor invested in the manufacture or acquisition of materials to establish what is deemed their objective value, understood as directly linked to the existence of an objective need. This approach often disregards broader, more cultural aspects of the value of things, thus flattening out the diversity of social strategies in the past.

Beyond the necessary consideration of their particularities, trade, barter, and gift exchanges are all social forms of circulation (Lazzari 1999, 2006; see also Agbe-Davies and Bauer, chapter 1, this volume), a sphere of social practice that has been taken for granted and undertheorized in the study of past social life. Inseparably economic, political, and cultural, circulation is always in "infinite reciprocity" with other spheres of social practice (Simmel 1990: 56). The value of things is neither intrinsic nor solely determined by the investment of labor in their manufacture or acquisition, although the value is always related to the substantive transformation of matter to produce social life, be it through labor, childbirth, or even storytelling (Turner 1979, 1989). Largely a cultural phenomenon, the value of things emerges from a field of strategies and negotiations in which the capacity of people and things to influence each other is of key importance (Munn 1986:7).

It is in this sense that it is crucial to acknowledge that landscapes are more than mere backdrops for human development. A landscape is a collective (in the sense of Latour 1993), an assemblage of human and nonhuman factors and agents that configures the concrete and imagined spaces making up social worlds. This configuration is not carried out through physical causality only. A landscape is a fully lived and imagined entity that is simultaneously shared and contested by the communities that inhabit it. The shapes of a lived landscape are understood through practices of exchange, in ceremonies that use exchanged objects, and in daily tasks that employed materials from faraway places; they can be also learned by exclusion, through the absence of those materials that one does not have access to but others do. Understanding the landscape in these intimate, bodily terms enables us to move beyond the need to prove the existence of particular modalities of circulation in the past, toward an understanding of the constitutive role of circulating material culture in the configuration of social worlds.

The Landscape and Culture of Circulation in the First Millennium AD

The Aconquija chain is a mountain fringe that spreads north to south, separating the provinces of Tucumán and Catamarca in northwestern Argentina (fig. 3.1). As a consequence of its high altitude (5,600 m above sea level [asl]), this chain creates a stark contrast between the eastern areas and the dry western lands. The settlements on the western side are constituted by households dispersed among agricultural fields and corrals dating to the first millennium AD and located on the fertile zone between 2,500 and 3,100 m asl.[1]

Unlike other areas in the Andes, in Northwest Argentina Formative period societies were small-scale sedentary or semi-sedentary communities with loosely structured internal hierarchies.[2] Despite their size, they acquired objects and resources from several areas, including the subtropical forest and eastern lowlands. Raw materials, minerals, shells, drugs, feathers, wood, and foodstuffs, as well as artifacts with and without representational traits, circulated across long distances, materializing relationships with myriad people and places. In the south-central Andes, lithics have been largely overlooked in the study of social interaction (but see Browman 1998; Escola 2004; Giesso 2003), while fine ceramics have been largely privileged as indicators of the direction and intensity of the flow of information, objects, and resources. However, ongoing sourcing analysis of obsidian and ceramics reveals that both classes of material culture circulated in socially significantly ways (Lazzari 2005, 2006; Scattolin and Lazzari 1998).

In this sector of the Andes, it is generally believed that highland llama caravans connected diverse microenvironments, bringing goods to settled valley communities in exchange for their products (Albeck 1994; Dillehay and Núñez 1988). Although it is unlikely that only one modality can account for the circulation of things throughout the whole prehistory of Northwest Argentina (Lazzari 2001) and the evidence of systematic caravan circulation in the Formative period is scarce (Haber 2001; but see Korstanje 1998), caravans have left a substantial material record constituted by paths, roads, temporary settlements, and rock art (e.g., Aschero 2000b; Nielsen 2001a).

Most of the Aconquija sites are located on ancient trails connecting both sides of the mountain chain. Several classes of evidence indicate artifactual

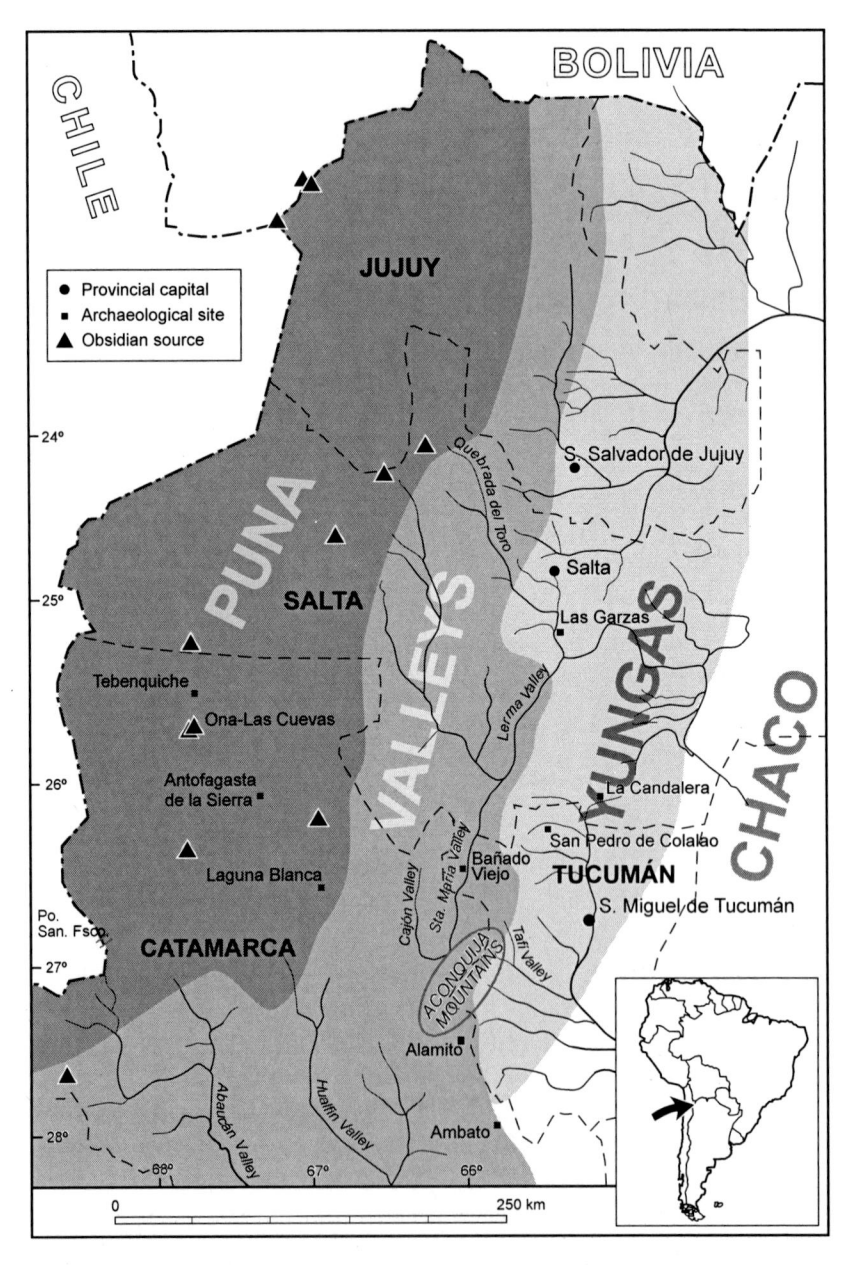

Figure 3.1 Map of Northwest Argentina, indicating archaeological localities, valleys, and areas mentioned in the text.

and architectural similarities with settlements in nearby valleys, such as Santa María, Tafí, Cajón, Campo del Pucará, and Hualfín, as well as with more distant areas, such as Laguna Blanca or Tebenquiche in the *puna*, a high-altitude desert shared by Argentina, Chile, and Bolivia. Given the distances between the archaeological sites in the Aconquija Mountains and many of the places mentioned above, and the lack of evidence of political centralization, it is safe to assume that Aconquija dwellers did not gain access to the resources and material culture of these various locations through directly controlled colonies.[3] However, the generally sedentary nature of the settlements in the area does not preclude the possibility of periodic trips to other regions to obtain resources whenever there was a relative reduction in local crop-related activities. Most likely, several modalities coexisted according to the rhythms and circuits of tasks, both in the Aconquija and beyond (Lazzari 2006).[4] This network of objects, traits, raw materials, and places hints at the existence of a shared regional world of social experience during the period. A closer look at the ceramics and lithics may illustrate the benefits of a more holistic approach to archaeological materials traditionally studied separately, as if belonging to mutually exclusive domains of past life (Lazzari 2006).

Ceramics and Lithics in the Aconquija: Contrasting Relations

Obsidian sources in Northwest Argentina are located in the *puna*. Obsidian from one of the main sources, Ona-Las Cuevas (see fig. 3.1), appears at sites in different microenvironments and with very different material assemblages (Yacobaccio et al. 2002, 2004). Published information regarding obsidian in eastern lowland sites indicates very low frequencies, suggesting less access in these areas (Ortíz 2003).

Obsidian occurs in very low frequencies in lithic assemblages (3–9 percent) at western Aconquija sites. The obsidian that reached these sites had a much higher knapping quality than locally available raw materials, yet the tools manufactured with it were rather informal. While most of the tools manufactured with this material were projectile points, the assemblages are mainly characterized by unretouched or minimally retouched flakes and scarcely shaped flake tools with a minimum investment in their sharpening (Andrefsky 1998; Koldehoff 1987; Tomka 2001). This lack of investment contradicts the usual expectations for technologies applied to high-quality raw materials at sites that are far from the original sources (Andrefsky 1994). The informality of the lithic assemblage could imply that in the Aconquija, obsidian was not seen as a scarce resource because of access through frequent long-distance treks, exchanges with neighbors who had frequent access, or visits from travelers bringing the material with them. Regarding the first possibility, the main subsistence tasks conducted in the Aconquija were agricultural; therefore, long-distance treks may have not been easy to practice on a frequent basis. Yet several lines of evidence indicate the existence of a complex web of short- to medium-distance connections between the villages of the time. At any rate, the combined low technological investment and low frequency of obsidian in the assemblages suggest that there was not much interest in acquiring, accumulating, or preserving this raw material.

It is difficult, if not impossible, to assess the "objective" exchange value or equivalence of the obsidian found in these sites, that is, what this material was exchanged for. Yet it is certainly possible that obsidian reached the area as the by-product of transactions involving the exchange of local produce for other things, such as salt, shells, beads, clay, and fine ceramics, with neighbors or visiting travelers who obtained the items through the previous transactions along the road. The copper ores common in the southern end of the chain were probably a main attraction to the area, given the importance of this metal in early metallurgy in Northwest Argentina (González 1999). It is possible that, as well-documented ethnographic cases indicate (Göbel 1998; Lecoq 1987; Mayer 2002), obsidian played in the past a role comparable to that of the small gifts often used to initiate present-day barter transactions. This ethnographic example may hint at one of the possible ways in which this raw material was incorporated by Aconquija dwellers into their daily artifactual assemblages.

The question one should ask at this point is whether the seeming lack of special treatment (technological and contextual) of this high-quality material means that obsidian was a less *socially* significant material than others, such as ceramics. Performance-oriented phenomenological studies of materiality indicate that it would be advisable to avoid following established interpretations of this fact (Lazzari 2005). The corporeal presence of obsidian artifacts, even the humblest debris, intervened in daily life and added another level to people's perception of their surroundings. Obsidian's concrete presence indicated their connection with highland places, a connection experienced in action and performed through use, rather than represented or expressed.

Besides obsidian, Aconquija household assemblages included tools of and debris from local (quartz, schist, coarse-grained andesite) and medium range (dacite and fine-grained andesite) lithic raw materials, as well as faunal remains, metalwork and copper minerals, and ordinary and fine ceramic wares. While fine ceramics were mostly locally produced, many of them were manufactured with clays obtained from deposits a short to medium distance away

(10–50 km, Lazzari 2006). These fine ceramics usually display a repertoire of Formative period motifs and manufacturing techniques widely available in the southern section of Northwest Argentina. Most fine ceramics show incised geometric designs, but anthropomorphic and zoomorphic motifs are also well represented. The stylistic repertoire of the period shows a consistent interest in the fluidity of form; many of the representational motifs used in pottery, sculpture, and metalwork depict half-human and half-nonhuman beings (Scattolin 2006). Contrary to traditional archaeological taxonomies (e.g., Tartusi and Núñez Regueiro 1993), recent research has demonstrated that these ceramics show highly diverse combinations of motifs and forms traditionally been considered as part of different, mutually exclusive styles (Scattolin and Bugliani 2005). These studies revealed a technical style that emphasized representational and formal *fluidity* in a wide range of vessel shapes. Yet these vessels were not altered or reshaped to adapt to practical purposes (as lithics were). Through ceramics, the cultural quality of fluidity became embodied in a fairly fixed material form.

Obsidian on the contrary, embodied fluidity in a nonrepresentational manner. These poorly defined and constantly reshaped artifacts prompt our imagination to question what might have been exchanged for them (e.g., corn, potatoes, copper, reputation of hospitality, information of trading possibilities in further spots along the road, and so on), things that departed the Aconquija to travel to several other directions and left obsidian and other items behind as testimony to the transactions. Much escapes our understanding of such transactions, yet it is possible to argue that past people's imagination was also shaped and stimulated, albeit in radically different ways compared to the present, as a consequence of the daily use of these artifacts. Far from preventing archaeological analysis, the difficulties posed by obsidian are also the source for our inquiries into a broader sense of cultural value. For more than any of its physical properties (brilliance, sharpness, brittleness, darkness), obsidian has the capacity to materialize the awareness of people and places that are not present. This quality is, however, not comparable to a sign detached from its invisible signified, but an "incarnate significance," an inseparable conjunction of local and nonlocal dimensions of social life in a material form (Keane 2003; Lazzari 2005).

This property of obsidian became relevant in this particular culture of circulation because ceramics, by way of their decoration and morphology, made visually explicit connections with neighboring valleys by using decorative motifs popular in neighboring areas. Some of the areas favored by Aconquija ceramists when "citing" in vessel decoration were the Campo del Pucará, Santa María, Hualfín, Cajón, Lerma, and Tafí valleys, La Candelaria and Colalao in the eastern lowlands or *yungas*, and Laguna Blanca and Tebenquiche in the *puna*. These visual and material references nevertheless contradicted the actual origin of the clay employed. For instance, the Aconquija sites and those in the surrounding valleys shared clay sources with those in the Ambato Valley (150 km south). However, almost none of the characteristic iconographic motifs produced in the Ambato valley (e.g., sacrificial imagery, feline and trophy head motifs) were actually depicted in the ceramics found in the Aconquija area. The Ambato Valley is one of the key archaeological areas concerning the origins and expansion of the renowned La Aguada cultural complex, characterized by a profusion of male and sacrificial iconography, as well as formalized ritual centers (González 1998; Tartusi and Núñez Regueiro 2001). Simultaneously, obsidian from the Ona-Las Cuevas source was used in most of the Formative period sites located in most of the above-mentioned archaeological areas, despite the fact many of them had ceramic assemblages markedly different in terms of iconography and general technical style. For instance, Ona-Las Cuevas obsidian was used in both the Aconquija and the Antofagasta de la Sierra; however, the latter shared iconographic motifs with the Ambato and Abaucán valleys (see fig. 3.1) that are virtually absent in the Aconquija (Lazzari 2005, 2006; Olivera 1997; Scattolin and Lazzari 1998; Yacobaccio et al. 2004). It is possible to say that at a regional scale, obsidian united places otherwise unconnected; it created a silent network of implicit connections indicated and indirectly experienced through the use of this material in everyday tasks.

As a raw material, obsidian was in perpetual transformation and circulation, thus working as a reminder that the world beyond everyday, face-to-face interactions was constructed through a complex set of alliances and obligations. Ceramics also embodied and portrayed these alliances and obligations, but the representational component of these artifacts reveals a careful selectivity, a subtle yet tangible reminder of the political underpinnings of such a complex web. At any rate, the physical properties of both classes of material culture became handy in this cultural context. On the one hand, obsidian was a more fluid medium than fired clay. While it is true that both vessels and pot shards can be recycled, using obsidian tools demanded their constant resharpening and refashioning into different artifacts. Obsidian thus lent itself to an ambiguous cultural role; neither precious nor fully ordinary, this material compressed social time and space by mediating the embodied experience of the wider social world. Interestingly, and unlike ceramics, obsidian sustained an understanding of the world that did not require image-making for its reproduction. At a sociopolitical level, this phenomenological power of obsidian meant that its presence at a site affirmed the existence of those other places "hidden" by iconographic selectivity. While ceramic decoration referred mostly to nearby valleys and some highland settlements (e.g., Laguna Blanca; see fig. 3.1), obsidian brought the wider regionality—both the sites that shared iconographic motifs with the Aconquija and those that did not—into the realm of intimate domestic space. This can be argued precisely because ceramics made explicit, visually figurative and nonfigurative references to other places through the flexible combinations of motifs, yet the ceramics also selectively established the boundaries for the suitable expression of these qualities. This ambivalence of ceramics toward the qualities of flexibility and social fluidity hints at their cultural relevance both at the local level and the wider region. In this context, the indexical nature and the creative powers of obsidian were probably not insignificant to those using it, as it sustained alternative spatial and social relations.

Conclusion

Beyond the significance of exchange in particular periods, circulating things—whether highly coveted or mundane objects—enable the experience of distant places as both real and imagined (Battaglia 1994). People and objects wove a world of represented and nonrepresented experiences in the Formative period, creating a complex landscape of connections, values, and understandings that affected social strategies. Seeing circulation as social practice means considering value as the capacity of both people and things to act and influence each other. The mutuality between people, objects, and space has to be acknowledged, as well as the inseparability of spheres of social practice. This shift situates ecological complementarity as a sociospatial matrix of value-forming practices, without drawing on the rigid models of sociality or the essentializing dichotomies that ossify indigenous experience into *a priori* categories. Such a new perspective reveals an Andean ecologic complementarity and circulatory sociality closer to Mauss' (1967 [1915]:1) "total social phenomena," albeit discarding the dichotomies that undermined his version. Landscapes of circulation are powerful entanglements of human and nonhuman actors as equal partners, in which beliefs, strategies, and imaginations stir social action into unforeseeable paths by the sheer force of the invisible yet deeply lived aspects of culture.

Acknowledgments

Funds for this research were provided by a Dissertation Research Grant awarded by Fundación Antorchas (Argentina), a Summer Research Grant provided by the Tinker Foundation (Institute of Latin American Studies, Columbia University), the Scholarship Foundation (New York), and partially by a CONICET (Consejo Nacional de Investigaciones Científicas y Técnicas, Argentina) research grant, PIP 02084, "Producción y reproducción aldeana al oeste del Aconquija" (Resol. 1234), granted to the overarching research program (PASCAL [Proyecto Arqueológico Sur Calchaquí]), directed by Professor María Cristina Scattolin. I would like to thank Laura Quiroga and Sean Goddard for the map and the PASCAL team for openly sharing resources and information on the various aspects of the project.

Notes

1. Available radiocarbon dates indicate that most settlements were occupied during the first millennium AD with little use in the Late period, or Periodo de Desarrollos Regionales (Scattolin 2007).
2. In Northwest Argentina, the hunter-gatherer way of life experienced changes around 5000 BP that led to the domestication of plants and camelids. Around 3600–2900 BP, the first evidences of ceramic production and a sedentary way of life started to appear in the dry western highlands or *puna* (Aschero 2000a).
3. Scholars agree that combinations of caravans and colonies are more likely to have occurred in the Late period, 1100–1400 AD (see Albeck 1994; Aschero 2000b).
4. See Mayer (2000:143–171) for a rich ethnographic description of these practices.

References

Albeck, María E. (editor)
1994 *Taller "De Costa a Selva": Producción e Intercambio entre los Pueblos Agroalfareros de los Andes Centro Sur.* Instituto Interdisciplinario Tilcara. Universidad de Buenos Aires, Argentina.

Alberti, Giorgio, and Enrique Mayer (editors)
1974 *Reciprocidad e Intercambio en los Andes Peruanos.* Instituto de Estudios Peruanos, Lima.

Aldenderfer, Mark S. (editor)
1993 *Domestic Architecture, Ethnicity, and Complementarity in the South-Central Andes.* University of Iowa Press, Iowa City.

Andrefsky, William, Jr.
1994 Raw Material Availability and the Organization of Technology. *American Antiquity* 59:21–35.
1998 *Lithics: Macroscopic Approaches to Analysis.* Cambridge University Press, Cambridge.

Aschero, Carlos A.
2000a El Poblamiento del Territorio. In *Nueva Historia Argentina*, edited by Miryam N. Tarragó, pp. 7–60. Editorial Sudamericana, Buenos Aires.
2000b Figuras Humanas, Camélidos y Espacios en la Interacción Circumpuneña. In *Arte en las Rocas: Arte Rupestre, Menhires y Piedras de Colores en Argentina*, edited

by Mercedes Podestá and María de Hoyos. Sociedad Argentina de Antropología, Buenos Aires.

Assadourian, Carlos S.

1995 Exchange in the Ethnic Territories between 1530 and 1567: The *Visitas* of Huánuco and Chucuito. In *Ethnicity, Market, and Migration in the Andes: At the Crossroads of History and Anthropology*, edited by Brooke O. Larson and Olivia Harris, pp. 101–134. Duke University Press, Durham, NC.

Battaglia, Deborah

1994 Retaining Reality: Some Practical Problems with Objects as Property. *Man*, n.s., 29:631–644.

Bourdieu, Pierre

1977 *Outline of a Theory of Practice*. Cambridge University Press, Cambridge.

Browman, David L.

1998 Lithic Provenience Analysis and Emerging Material Complexity at Formative Period Chiripa, Bolivia. *Andean Past* 5:301–324.

Dillehay, Thomas, and Lautaro Núñez A.

1988 Camelids, Caravans, and Complex Societies in South-Central Andes. In *Recent Studies in Pre-Columbian Archaeology*, edited by Nicholas Saunders and Olivier de Montmollin, pp. 603–634. BAR International Series 421 (ii). British Archaeological Reports, Oxford.

Escola, Patricia S.

2004 Variabilidad en la Explotación y Distribución de Obsidianas en la Puna Meridional Argentina. *Estudios Atacameños* (Chile) 28:9–24.

Espinoza Soriano, Waldemar

1987 *Artesanos, Transacciones, Monedas y Formas de Pago en el Mundo Andino, Siglos XV y XVI*. Banco Central de Reserva del Perú, Lima.

Gaonkar, Dillip, and Elizabeth Povinelli

2003 Technologies of Public Forms: Circulation, Transfiguration, Recognition. *Public Culture* 15(3):385–398.

Gell, Alfred

1992 Inter-Tribal Commodity Barter and Reproductive Gift-Exchange in Old Melanesia. In *Barter, Exchange and Value: An Anthropological Approach*, edited by Caroline A. Humphrey and Stephen Hugh-Jones, pp. 142–168. Cambridge University Press, Cambridge.

Giesso, Martín

2003 Stone Tool Production in the Tiwanaku Heartland. In *Tiwanaku and Its Hinterland: Archaeological and Paleoecological Investigations in the Lake Titicaca Basin of Bolivia*, Vol. 2, edited by Alan L. Kolata, pp. 363–383. Washington, DC: Smithsonian Institution Press.

Göbel, Barbara

1998 "Salir de Viaje". Producción Pastoril e Intercambio Económico en el Noroeste Argentino. In *50 Años de Estudios Americanistas en la Universidad de Bonn: Nuevas Contribuciones a la Arqueología, Etnohistoria, Etnolingüística y Etnografía de las Américas*, edited by Sabine Dedenbach Salazar-Sáenz, Carmen Arellano Hoffman, Eva König, and Heiko Prümers, pp. 867–891. Bonner Amerikanistische Studien 30. Verlag Anton Saurwein, Markt Schwaben, Germany.

González, Alberto R.
1998 *Arte Precolombino: Cultura La Aguada, Arqueología y Diseños*. Filmediciones Valero, Buenos Aires.

González, Luis R.
1999 Bronce Bajo el Sol. Metal Prehispánico en el Noroeste Argentino. In *Masked Histories. A Re-Examination of the Rodolfo Schreiter Collection from North-Western Argentina*, edited by Per Stenborg and Adriana Muñoz, pp. 97–131. Etnologiska Studier 43. University of Göteborg, Göteborg, Sweden.

Haber, Alejandro
2001 El Oasis en la Articulación del Espacio Circumpuneño. *Actas del XIII Congreso Nacional de Arqueología Argentina* 1:251–267. Córdoba, Argentina.

Halperin, Rhoda
1993 The Concept of Equivalencies. *Research in Economic Anthropology* 14: 255–298.

Humphrey, Caroline A.
1992 Fair Dealing, Just Rewards: The Ethics of Barter in North-East Nepal. In *Barter, Exchange and Value: An Anthropological Approach*, edited by Caroline A. Humphrey and Stephen Hugh-Jones, pp. 107–141. Cambridge University Press, Cambridge.

Humphrey, Caroline A., and Stephen Hugh-Jones (editors)
1992 *Barter, Exchange and Value: An Anthropological Approach*. Cambridge University Press, Cambridge.

Ingold, T.
2000 *The Perception of the Environment: Essays on Livelihood, Dwelling and Skill*. Routledge, London.

Keane, Webb
2003 Semiotics and the Social Analysis of Material Things. *Language and Communication* 23:409–425.

Koldehoff, B.
1987 The Cahokia Flake Tool Industry: Socioeconomic Implications for Late Prehistory in the Central Mississippi Valley. In *The Organization of Core Technology*, edited by John K. Johnson and Carole A. Morrow, pp. 151–185. Westview Press, Boulder, Colorado.

Korstanje, María A.
1998 El Médano, es un Sitio Caravanero? Apuntes Sobre Contextos de Tráfico y Territorialidad para el Formativo. In *Los Desarrollos Locales y sus Territorios*, edited by María B. Cremonte. Facultad de Humanidades y Ciencias Sociales. Universidad de Jujuy, Argentina.

Latour, Bruno
1993 *We Have Never Been Modern*. Harvester Wheatsheaf, New York and London.

Lazzari, Marisa
1999 Nuevos Datos sobre la Procedencia de Obsidianas en el Aconquija y Areas Aledañas. *Cuadernos del Instituto Nacional de Antropología y Pensamiento Latinoamericano* 18: 243-256. Buenos Aires
2001 La Circulación de Obsidiana en el NOA: Reconsiderando la Complementariedad. *Actas del XIII Congreso de Arqueología Argentina*, 1, p. 108. Córdoba, Argentina.

Lazzari, Marisa
2005 The Texture of Things: Objects, People and Landscape in Northwest Argentina (First Millennium AD). In *Archaeologies of Materiality*, edited by Lynn M. Meskell, pp. 121–161. Blackwell, Oxford.
2006 Traveling Things and the Production of Social Spaces: An Archaeological Study of Circulation and Value in NW Argentina. Unpublished PhD Dissertation, Department of Anthropology, Columbia University, New York.

Lecoq, Patrice
1987 Caravanes des Lamas, Sel et Échanges dans une Communauté de Potosí, en Bolivie. *Bulletin de l' Institute Français des Etudes Andines* 16 (3–4):1–38.

Lee, Benjamin, and Edward LiPuma
2002 Cultures of Circulation: The Imaginations of Modernity. *Public Culture* 14 (1):191–213.

Lévi-Strauss, Claude
1969 [1948] *The Elementary Structures of Kinship*. Eyre & Spottiswoode, London.

Malinowski, Bronislaw
1961 [1926] *Crime and Custom in Savage Society*. Routledge and Kegan Paul, London.
1984 [1922] *Argonauts of the Western Pacific*. Waveland Press, Inc., Prospect Heights, Illinois.

Mauss, Marcel
1967 [1925] *The Gift: The Form and Reason for Exchange in Archaic Societies*. Routledge, London.

Mayer, Enrique
2002 *The Articulated Peasant: Household Economies in the Andes*. Westview Press, Boulder, CO.

Miller, Daniel
2001 Alienable Gifts and Inalienable Commodities. In *The Empire of Things: Regimes of Value and Material Culture*, edited by Fred R. Myers, pp. 91–115. School of American Research Press, Santa Fe, New Mexico.

Munn, Nancy
1986 *The Fame of Gawa: A Symbolic Study of Value Transformation in a Massim (Papua New Guinea) Society*. Duke University Press, Durham, North Carolina.
1990 Constructing Regional Worlds in Experience: Kula Exchange, Witchcraft and Gawan Local Events. *Man*, n.s.,25:1–17.

Murra, John V.
1972 El control vertical de un máximo de pisos ecológicos en la economía de las sociedades Andinas. In *Visita de la Provincia de León de Huanaco (1562)*, Vol. 2, edited by Ortíz de Zuniga, pp. 429–476. Universidad Hermillo Valdizan, Huanaco.
1975 *Formaciones Económicas y Políticas del Mundo Andino*. Instituto de Estudios Peruanos, Lima.
1985 The Limits and Limitations of the "Vertical Archipelago." In *Andean Ecology and Civilization: An Interdisciplinary Perspective on Andean Ecological Complementarity*, edited by Shozo Masuda, Izumi Shimada, and Craig Morris, pp. 15–20. Papers from Wenner-Gren Foundation for Anthropological Research Symposium 91.University of Tokyo Press, Tokyo.

Murra, John V.
1987 Existieron el Tributo y los Mercados antes de la Invasión Europea? In *La Participación Indígena en los Mercados Surandinos: Estrategias y Reproducción Social Siglos XVI a XX*, edited by Olivia Harris, Brooke Larson, and Enrique Tandeter, pp. 51–61. Centro de Estudios de la Realidad Económica y Social, La Paz.

Myers, Fred R., and Barbara Kirshenblatt-Gimblett
2001 Art and Material Culture: A Conversation with Annette Weiner. In *The Empire of Things: Regimes of Value and Material Culture*, edited by Fred R. Myers, pp. 269-313. School of American Research Press, Santa Fe, NM.

Nielsen, Axel E.
2001a Evolución Social en Quebrada de Humahuaca (AD 700–1536). In *Historia Argentina Prehispánica*, Vol. 1, edited by Eduardo E. Berberián and Axel E. Nielsen, pp. 171–264. Editorial Brujas, Córdoba, Argentina.
2001b Ethnoarchaeological Perspectives on Caravan Trade in the South-Central Andes. In *Ethnoarchaeology of Andean South America: Contributions to Archaeological Method and Theory*, edited by L.A. Kuznar, pp. 163–201. International Monographs in Prehistory, Ann Arbor, Michigan.

Olivera, Daniel E.
1997 Los Primeros Pastores de la Puna Sur Argentina: Una Aproximación a Través de su Cerámica. *Revista de Arqueología Americana* 13:69–112.

Ortíz, Gabriela
2003 Estado Actual del Conocimiento del Denominado Complejo o Tradición Cultural San Francisco, a 100 Años de su Descubrimiento. In *La Mitad Verde del Mundo Andino: Investigaciones Arqueológicas en la Vertiente Oriental de los Andes y las Tierras Bajas de Bolivia*, edited by Beatriz N. Ventura and Gabriela Ortíz. Universidad Nacional de Jujuy, S.S. de Jujuy, Argentina.

Polanyi, Karl
1977 *The Livelihood of Man*, edited by Harry W. Pearson. Academic Press, New York.

Roepstorff, Andreas, and Nils Bubandt
2004 General Introduction. The Critique of Culture and the Plurality of Nature. In *Imagining Nature: Practices of Cosmology and Identity*, edited by Andreas Roepstorff, Nils Bubandt, and Kalevi Kull, pp. 9–26. Aarhus University Press, Aarhus, Denmark.

Rostworowski, María
1977 *Etnía y Sociedad: Costa Peruana Prehispánica*. Instituto de Estudios Andinos, Lima.
1989 *Organización Económica en los Andes*. Hisbol, La Paz.

Salman, Ton, and Annelies Zoomers (editors)
2003 *Imaging the Andes: Shifting Margins of a Marginal World*. Aksant, Amsterdam.

Salomon, Frank
1985 The Dynamic Potential of the Complementarity Concept. In *Andean Ecology and Civilization: An Interdisciplinary Perspective on Andean Ecological Complementarity*, edited by Shozo Masuda, Izumi Shimada, and Craig Morris, pp. 511–532. Papers from the Wenner-Gren Foundation for Anthropological Research Symposium 91. University of Tokyo Press, Tokyo.
1986 Vertical Polities in the Inka Frontier. In *Anthropological History of Andean Polities*, edited by John V. Murra, Nathan Wachtel, and Jacques Revel, pp. 89–117. Cambridge University Press, Cambridge.

Salomon, Frank
1991 Tres Enfoques Cardinales en los Actuales Estudios Andinos. In *Reproducción y Transformación de las Sociedades Andinas de Siglos XVI–XX*, edited by Segundo Moreno Y., and Frank Salomon. ABYA-YALA, Quito.

Scattolin, María C.
2006 Contornos y Confines del Universo Iconográfico pre-Calchaquí del Valle de Santa María. *Estudios Atacameños: Arqueología y Antropología Surandinas* (Chile) 32:119–139.
2007 Santa María Antes del Año Mil. Fechas y Materiales para una Historia Cultural. In *Sociedades Precolombinas Surandinas: Temporalidad, Interacción y Dinámica cultural del NOA en el ámbito de los Andes Centro-Sur*, edited by V. Williams, B. Ventura, A. Callegari, and H. Yacobaccio, pp. 203–220. Taller Internacional de Arqueología del Noroeste Argentino y Andes Centro-Sur (TANOA). Instituto de Ciencias Antropológicas, Facultad de Filosofía y Letras, Universidad de Buenos Aires.

Scattolin, María C., and María F. Bugliani
2005 Un Repertorio Surtido. Las Vasijas del Oasis de Laguna Blanca, Puna Argentina. *Revista Española de Antropología Americana* 35:51–74.

Scattolin, María C., and Marisa Lazzari
1998 Tramando Redes: Obsidianas al Oeste del Aconquija. *Estudios Atacameños* 14:189–209. Chile.

Shimada, Izumi
1985a Introduction. In *Andean Ecology and Civilization: An Interdisciplinary Perspective on Andean Ecological Complementarity*, edited by Shozo Masuda, Izumi Shimada, and Craig Morris, pp. xi–xxxii. Papers from Wenner-Gren Foundation for Anthropological Research Symposium 91. University of Tokyo Press, Tokyo.
1985b Perception, Procurement, and Management of Resources: Archaeological Perspective. In *Andean Ecology and Civilization: An Interdisciplinary Perspective on Andean Ecological Complementarity*, edited by Shozo Masuda, Izumi Shimada, and Craig Morris, pp. 357–399. Papers from the Wenner-Gren Foundation for Anthropological Research Symposium 91. University of Tokyo Press, Tokyo.

Simmel, Georg
1990 *The Philosophy of Money*, edited by David Frisby. Routledge, London.

Stanish, Charles
1992 *Ancient Andean Political Economy*. University of Texas Press, Austin.

Starn, Orin
1994 Rethinking the Politics of Anthropology: The Case of the Andes. *Current Anthropology* 35(1):13–38.

Strathern, Marilyn
1992 Qualified Value: The Perspective of Gift Exchange. In *Barter, Exchange, and Value*, edited by C. Humphrey and S. Hugh-Jones, pp. 169–191. Cambridge University Press, Cambridge.

Tartusi, Marta, and Víctor Núñez Regueiro
1993 Los Centros Ceremoniales del N.O.A. *Publicaciones del Instituto de Arqueología* (Tucumán, Argentina) 5:1–49.

Tartusi, Marta, and Víctor Núñez Regueiro
2001 Fenómenos Cúlticos Tempranos en la Subregión Valliserrana. In *Nueva Historia Argentina Prehispánica*, edited by Eduardo E. Berberián and Axel E. Nielsen, pp. 127–170. Editorial Brujas, Córdoba, Argentina.

Tomka, Steve A.
2001 The Effect of Processing Requirements on Reduction Strategies and Tool Form: A New Perspective. In *Lithic Debitage: Context, Form, Meaning*, edited by W. Andrefsky Jr., pp. 207–225. University of Utah Press, Salt Lake City.

Turner, Terence
1979 Anthropology and the Politics of Indigenous People's Struggles. *Cambridge Anthropology* 5(1):1–42.
1989 Agnostic Exchange: Homeric Reciprocity and the Heritage of Simmel and Mauss: A Commentary. *Cultural Anthropology* 4(3):260–264.

Van Buren, Mary
1996 Rethinking the Vertical Archipelago: Ethnicity, Exchange, and History in the South Central Andes. *American Anthropologist* 98(2):338–351.

Weiner, Annette
1992 *Inalienable Possessions: The Paradox of Keeping-While-Giving*. University of California Press, Berkeley.
1994 Cultural Difference and the Density of Objects. *American Ethnologist* 21(2):391–403.

Yacobaccio, Hugo D., Patricia S. Escola, Marisa Lazzari, and Fernando X. Pereyra
2002 Long Distance Obsidian Traffic in Northwestern Argentina. In *Geochemical Evidence for Long Distance Exchange*, edited by Michael Glascock, pp. 167–203. Bergin and Garvey, Westport, Connecticut.

Yacobaccio, Hugo D., Patricia S. Escola, Fernando X. Pereyra, Marisa Lazzari, and Michael D. Glascock
2004 Quest for Ancient Routes: Obsidian Research Sourcing in Northwestern Argentina. *Journal of Archaeological Science* 31:193–204.

CHAPTER 4

Social Aspects of the Tobacco Pipe Trade in Early Colonial Virginia

Anna S. Agbe-Davies

Introduction

For decades, archaeologists have dealt with Chesapeake-made smoking pipes of the early colonial era as symbols—as indicators of social identity or as media for social communication. Here, I address equally compelling themes regarding social life in early Virginia through a consideration of these pipes as objects of exchange. The emphasis on the question of exchange leads us to confront such issues as elite power in a provincial economy, the role of social networks in local trade, and the effect of human relationships on modes of local manufacturing and consumption in a commodity-exporting colony.

The present research uses evidence for the exchange of clay tobacco pipes as a vehicle for approaching other aspects of life in the seventeenth-century Chesapeake. Exchange is the analytical bridge that connects sites of consumption with agents of production, actors who—in the case of locally made tobacco pipes—have been a subject of much discussion for over fifty years. Such a bridge is necessary because archaeologists are unable to agree on the meaning of these artifacts, a meaning that is in no small degree conflated with the identities of the pipe makers. Much of the research that has gone before rests on the implicit assumption that the users and makers of these pipes are one and the same—if not the same individual, then members of the "same" social group who shared an understanding of the significance of these artifacts. Consequently, much of the existing scholarship is devoted to discovering the ethnicity[1] of the pipe makers. The answer to this question has been sought in comparisons of decorative elements on the pipes (fig. 4.1) with the known decorative repertoires of the various groups living in the Chesapeake colonies during the seventeenth century, generally glossed as Native Americans, Europeans, and Africans. Perhaps predictably, the debate defies satisfactory resolution because of the many potential analogous forms and the frequent reliance on a "passive" concept of style (Hegmon 1992:518).

One solution to the current impasse in the scholarship would be to clarify the relationship between pipe makers and pipe users and to understand how pipes got from one to the other, if exchange in pipes indeed even existed. Such investigations would certainly tell us something new about pipes in the seventeenth-century Chesapeake, but they would also give us insight into two key areas of social relationships—those having to do with labor (and by extension, power) and those having to do with race (and by extension, identity), the latter having preoccupied the field for so long.

This chapter, then, begins with a discussion of prior research regarding pipes made and used in the colonial Chesapeake. It then turns to the discussion of a new way to address the problem of social identity by using the evidence for exchange to address questions about control within the pipe-making industry and to ascertain whether these artifacts might reasonably

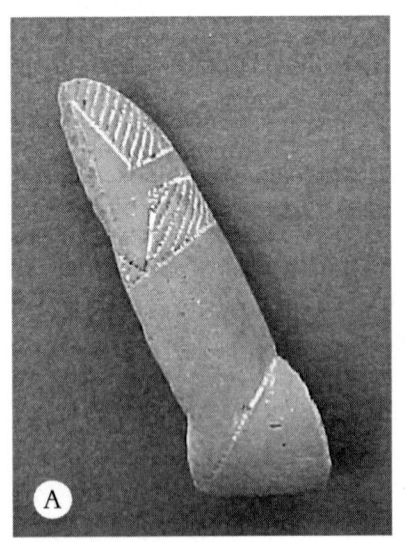

Figure 4.1 The pipe fragment on the left (A) is from Rich Neck and is marked with what Emerson identifies as a kwardata motif (see especially 1999:Figure 4.10). The fragment on the right (B) comes from Jamestown and depicts what Mouer et al. (1999:Figure 5.12) call a "running deer" motif. Photographs by A. S. Agbe-Davies.

be assumed to reflect the desires of the colony's large laboring class. Finally, I discuss new research in which several other scholars have begun to explore the ways in which the exchange of pipes might reveal something about seventeenth-century society in the Chesapeake.

Local pipes in Chesapeake Archaeology

Chesapeake-made pipes are readily distinguished from the contemporaneous clay pipe tradition coming out of western Europe by their clay, the color of which commonly ranges from pale yellow to dark brown, a distinct contrast with the whiter and finer ball clay of pipes made in Europe and exported to the Chesapeake as well as to other locations in the Atlantic world. These latter pipes, sometimes erroneously called "kaolin" pipes, may also be called "imported" in contrast with the "local," "terra-cotta," or "Chesapeake" pipes that were made and used in the colonies bordering the Chesapeake Bay throughout the seventeenth century. The ball clay pipes are a longer-lived and more broadly distributed tradition. They are virtually ubiquitous on sites where residents were members of the European diaspora of the sixteenth through the nineteenth centuries or traded with them. Regardless of where researchers fall on the question of "who" made the local pipes, all agree that the tradition of smoking tobacco in clay pipes (as opposed to taking snuff, smoking cigars, and so on) originated with the Native inhabitants of eastern North America.

The parameters of the "local" in locally made pipes continue to be explored. These artifacts were initially identified at Jamestown in southeastern Virginia (fig. 4.2) (Harrington 1951). Soon, however, archaeologists were reporting these artifacts from sites throughout Virginia and Maryland. In general, the pipes are thought to be limited to sites east of the fall line that marks the limits of navigation on the rivers that feed into the Chesapeake Bay (Emerson 1988). But the tradition appears to extend to the Carolinas. For example, Dane Magoon (1999) has reported pipes from pre- and post-contact sites in northeastern North Carolina that are similar in form and decoration to those found in the Chesapeake colonies. Researchers have also identified small numbers of similar-looking pipes in collections from New England (Capone and Downs 2004), England (Moore 2000:63) and coastal Canada (Luckenbach and Kiser 2006:169). For all of that, however, the principal distribution of these supposedly local pipes remains the coastal reaches of the Mid-Atlantic colonies.

The other striking difference between "imported" and "local" pipes is the degree of decoration. Archaeologists in the Chesapeake have paid particular

72 ❧ Anna S. Agbe-Davies

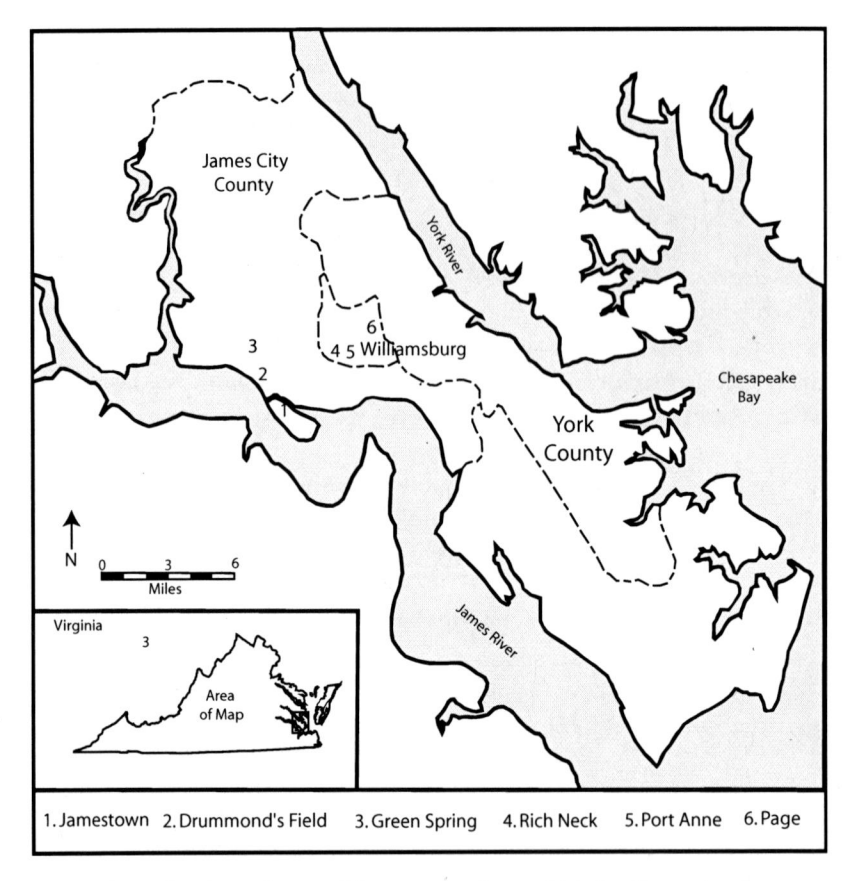

1. Jamestown 2. Drummond's Field 3. Green Spring 4. Rich Neck 5. Port Anne 6. Page

Figure 4.2 Sites in and around Jamestown from which locally made pipes were selected. Illustration by J. E. Deetz. Adapted from Agbe-Davies 2004c:Figure 1.3, original illustration by H. M. Harvey.

attention to the wide range of decorative styles found embellishing the locally made pipes, elements that distinguish this pipe tradition from the more restricted decorative repertoire of the pipes produced in British and Dutch workshops in the metropole. Although the ball clay pipes tend to restrict decoration to a band of indentations at the lip or a stamp impressed on the heel (see fig. 4.3a for a similarly decorated local pipe), many local pipes include elaborate striping, geometric forms, figural elements, and sometimes even letters, particularly on the bowl, on occasion highlighted with a white slip or paint (figs. 4.3b and 4.3c). Researchers have sought to understand the significance of these decorations according to the prevailing methodological and theoretical frameworks of their times. By bringing together the strengths of these various approaches, we can achieve a more synthetic understanding

Social Aspects of the Tobacco Pipe Trade ❧ 73

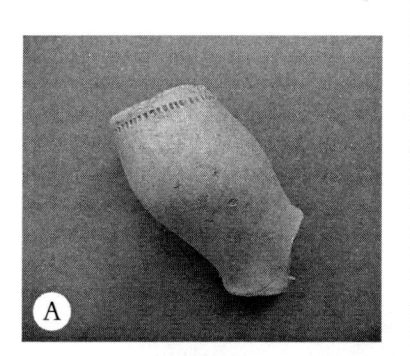

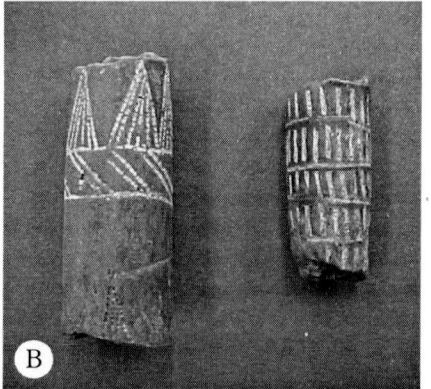

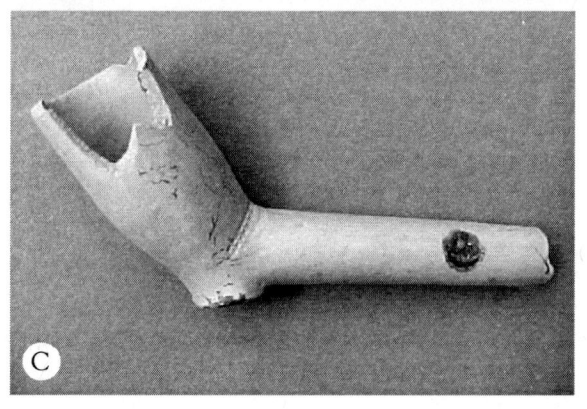

Figure 4.3 Some locally made pipes are direct imitations of imported styles, with very little decoration beyond some rouletting at the lip, as with this pipe (A) from Jamestown. Others are very fancifully decorated, including even the stems. Sometimes these impressed decorations are infilled with white, as in example B from Port Anne. A common decorative technique in the present assemblage was a line or two of rouletting at both the lip and the juncture of the bowl and stem, as seen in example C from Green Spring. Photographs by A. S. Agbe-Davies.

of local pipes and through them of the seventeenth-century colonies of the Chesapeake and the exertion of power.

Archaeologists working in the middle of the twentieth century, operating in what we might now call a cultural-historical framework, saw the attributes of these pipes directly reflecting the traditions of their makers. J. C. Harrington, an early pioneer in the field of historical archaeology, wrote of the locally made pipes he found at Jamestown:

> Many are obviously of Indian manufacture, but some may have been made by the settlers following Indian

> styles and techniques...some of these pipes which are most Indianlike in character, have well-formed English initials incorporated in the bowl decoration. Is this a case of the Indian copying an European idea; was the maker an "educated" Indian; or did a white man make an "Indian" pipe and put his initials on it? [Harrington 1951:n.p.]

Much of the contemporaneous scholarship followed in the same vein, linking these pipes to the precontact traditions of the local Native population and using the discovery of pipes as an indicator of the ongoing presence of Native Americans living within or trading with the colony (e.g., MacCord 1969; Mitchell 1983). Most researchers devoted their energies to the description of the pipes from a particular site (e.g., Heite 1972; Noël Hume 1979). The object descriptions emphasized the decorative attributes over other forms of variation, and the assemblage descriptions tended to focus on the presence or absence of the pipes instead of evaluating the finds quantitatively. Other archaeologists developed Harrington's observation that local pipes of the colonial period shared attributes with both Native and European pipe traditions (e.g., McCrery 1968) in the consideration of how "acculturation" influenced artifact assemblages and the societies they represented. There was little concern, however, for the place that these pipes might have in a system of material culture. Nor did these researchers spend much time discussing what the objects and their decorations might signify to their makers and users.

When the New Archaeology took hold, interest in identifying the ethnic identity of the pipes' producers waned somewhat, and many studies shifted to focus on the possible systemic—rather than traditional or "cultural"—forces that encouraged a Chesapeake-based pipe tradition to flourish even while imported pipes continued to arrive from the metropole. Hypotheses explaining the growth and decline of the tradition over the course of the "long" seventeenth century were related to economic and rationalistic ideas about why the tradition existed in the first place: as a stopgap replacement for inaccessible imported pipes. For example, Susan Henry (1979) suggested that the local pipes were produced during periods of economic depression, as a less expensive alternative to imported pipes. Likewise, Henry Miller's (1991) study of the Pope's Fort assemblage showed that local pipes increased concurrently with Dutch pipes, hinting that both may have been replacements for British pipes when trade with the colonial power was interrupted. Such studies may be thought of as processual insofar as they attempted to explain the local pipe phenomenon by setting up testable hypotheses, developing more systematic classifications for the pipes, and using quantitative data. Certainly, some researchers continued to publish descriptive analyses (e.g., Crass 1988). However, research during this period also tended to emphasize the technomic function of the pipes and economic, rather than social, ideological, or identity-driven explanations for their manufacture and use, although the explanations were still historically particular, given the criteria set out by Lewis Binford (1962).

Since the late 1980s, however, much of the scholarship has been in response to the suggestion that these artifacts were a symbolically charged alternative to European pipes for an increasingly African workforce. Matthew Emerson (1988) introduced the possibility of an African dimension to local pipes. In his regional study of the tradition, he identified several hundred individual decorative characters and argued that the combination of "denticulate lines, patterns, or figures, stamped characters, and decorative fill...is closely paralleled in some West African decorative arts" (Emerson 1988:132). He furthermore identified particular decorative motifs that occur on both local pipes and objects produced by artisans in a range of West African societies (see also Emerson 1999). In a study that examined changes in the local pipe tradition over time, J. Cameron Monroe (2002:34–36) has argued that the style of the pipes represents attempts by Afro-Virginians to negotiate their changing status within the colony, as well as the development of an African American ethnicity out of multiple African ethnicities. Research such as that produced by Emerson and Monroe reflects a turn towards what might be regarded as postprocessual themes: a concern with ethnicity and the investigation of how people use material culture in its assertion, an interest in the symbolic (as opposed to functional) meaning of artifacts, and attention to the particular historical contexts within which people acted (Hodder 1985).

The reaction to such studies has been strong and somewhat heated. Significant numbers of archaeologists continue to assert a greater affinity with local native pipe-making and decorative traditions. The contributors to Mouer et al. (1999), in particular, point to decorative similarities with the motifs identified on the pipes in the material culture of Europe and Native America (see also Magoon 1999). The fact of the matter, though, is that the pipes do appear to bear the imprint of multiple groups. There appears to be little hope of resolving the debate by continuing to compare the pipes' decorations with the decorative repertoires of potential source traditions.

So in recent years, archaeologists have treated these artifacts primarily as *symbols*, signs that are arbitrary, historical, traditional, and cultural (Peirce 1965). Or more accurately, the artifacts are seen as vehicles for symbolic decoration. But the qualities of a symbol that make it a powerful kind of sign—multivalency and the underdetermined relationship between signifier and signified—can also generate ambiguous interpretations and irresolvable debates (Emerson 1999; Mouer et al. 1999). Some interesting new approaches emphasize, even if not explicitly, how the pipes signify in other ways.

Kathryn Sikes (2008) has continued the emphasis on the *iconic* dimensions of pipe decoration, but with different spin on the star motif that has attracted so much attention from those who would use it to identify ethnic affiliations (see above) or individual pipe makers (see below). A star motif on a pipe acts as an icon of a celestial star "in so far as it is like that thing" (Peirce 1965:143). Sikes suggests that, because star motifs are prevalent in multiple decorative traditions and seem to reference natural phenomena accessible to all observers, the common experience of "stars" might explain their prevalence on midcentury pipes. Rather than emphasize what the signs might have communicated to just any viewer, she rightly notes that stars are more prevalent on the back (smoker's) side of the bowl. She therefore considers the significance that the referents of such signs might have had for the pipe user (Sikes 2008).

In their paper "Who Smoked Chesapeake Pipes?," Fraser Neiman and Julie King (1999) treat local pipes as *indices*, signs that mark the presence of bound laborers—in contrast to the owners of labor, indicated by white pipes. On the other hand, C. Jane Cox, Al Luckenbach, and Dave Gadsby (2005) argue that the local pipes are more likely an indicator of earlier occupation or frontier settings. Both Neiman and King and Cox et al. are exploring the indexical qualities of these pipes—how they operate as signs that may be thought of as "a fragment torn away from the Object, the two in their Existence being one whole or part of such whole" (Peirce 1965:137), or more plainly, "causal or proximal linkages" (Keane 2003:413). The research on which the present study draws (Agbe-Davies 2001, 2004c), as well as others dealing with local pipes (Luckenbach and Kiser 2006; Monroe and Mallios 2004) likewise treats the distribution of pipes among sites as an index of some past behaviors, particularly production and circulation. In most of these cases, the interpreter of the sign is not likely to be a participant in the society that produced the pipes but rather the analyst herself.

Why Pipes? Why Archaeology?

Archaeology is our best shot at understanding pipe production in the tobacco colonies. Aside from rare references in court records to the digging of pipe clay (cited in Emerson 1988:44) or the ownership of pipe molds (Fleet 1961), the activity leaves barely a trace in the documentary record. Furthermore, we have very little *direct* archaeological evidence of production, such as kilns or wasters (but see Luckenbach and Cox 2002; Outlaw and Outlaw 2000). Our understanding of production relies on reconstructing the social relationships that moved pipes from places of manufacture to places of use and discard.

Descriptions written in the metropole depict that pipe industry as being dominated by small, relatively impoverished producers working at the household level (Arnold 1977; Walker 1977). But the sites and texts of the early colonial Chesapeake indicate clearly that several other industries, including pottery production and brick and tile manufacture, were sponsored or managed by labor-owning elites. For example, William Berkeley, governor of Virginia for much of the seventeenth century, wished to broaden the economic base of the colony beyond the export of tobacco. His writings record his experimentation with a range of cash crops, including rice, wine, and silkworms (Billings 1996). The excavation of his plantation at Green Spring revealed the presence of a pottery kiln (Smith 1981), the wares of which are readily recognized via stylistic criteria at contemporaneous sites throughout the James-York Peninsula (Straube 1995) and have been successfully characterized in terms of material properties by Thomas E. Davidson's (1995) image analysis of locally produced ceramics. Researchers using xeroradiography determined that John Page's kiln at Middle Plantation produced tiles not only for Page's own house but also for several other structures in the community that was to become Williamsburg, as well as at Jamestown itself (Galucci et al. 1994; Metz et al. 1998). Archaeology indicates, perhaps even more clearly than the written record, the extent to which land- and labor-owners diverted resources from tobacco production to satisfy local demand for manufactures.

So elite planters clearly were managing production activities that supplied more than just the needs of their own households. Why might we think that they would be interested in the pipe trade specifically? Analysis of price lists and merchant records in England have revealed that the high price of pipes relative to their weight made their transport over considerable distances profitable (Oak Rhind 1980). Virginia-made pipes in the earliest phases at James Fort have been identified as the work of one Robert Cotton, who, William Kelso and Beverly Straube (2004) argue, had been dispatched to the colony to assay clays for the Virginia Company. That investors would go to such lengths to obtain raw materials for pipe production hints at the potential for profit that some saw in the industry. The assemblages selected for this study came from sites at the center of the Virginia colony, in and around its capital at Jamestown (see fig. 4.2). Sites with evidence for pipe making (Drummond's Field) or other forms of ceramic production—pottery (Green Spring, Jamestown), brick (Rich Neck, Jamestown, Page), or tile (Page)—were given priority.

Working with the premise that elite planters could have found pipe production to be a worthwhile use of their laborers' time and talents, the task is then to determine whether the distribution of locally made pipes followed elite social networks or other pathways. As noted above, archaeological and documentary evidence clearly indicate that productive and exchange networks operated even within this small area. Transatlantic trade links were not the only important ones for seventeenth-century Virginians, despite the colony's location at England's periphery. In addition to—and often congruent with—these economic networks were deep and densely woven social networks, binding together the elite families whose political and economic dominance shaped the colony's social structure (McCartney 2000; Rutman and Rutman 1984; for the nature [and limits] of domination, see Weber 1978).

The analysis of a network requires a focus on a particular segment of time. This one focuses on the latter half of the seventeenth century, a time during which friendships and animosities were brought into high relief by an armed challenge to the social order. It was also a time during which the wealthiest households in the central part of the colony shifted their investment in human labor from indentured servants to slaves (Morgan 1975). These were the years leading up to and following Bacon's Rebellion, in which the working population challenged elites' stranglehold on the colony's economy and political structure and the planter class responded by encouraging the growing fissure between white and black laborers. But not all rebels were landless workers, and not all loyalists were land- and labor-owning elites. The rebellion highlighted other cleavages in the society. Analyses of existing family and social networks show that these played a considerable role in predicting which side of the conflict one selected (Rutman and Rutman 1984; Sprinkle 1992). It was therefore necessary to determine which sites would likely participate in the same social and commercial networks.

A number of the sites included in this study were owned or occupied by the same individual. For example, Richard Kemp owned Rich Neck plantation, was one of the owners of Structure 100 at Jamestown, and possibly also held title to the land now designated Port Anne. Green Spring and Jamestown's Structure 100 were both owned by William Berkeley, who may also have owned either Structure 112 or Structure 144, depending on one's interpretation of the statehouse records. Berkeley's widow went on to marry Philip Ludwell, who owned part of Jamestown Structure 144 and whose family purchased Rich Neck from Kemp's widow in 1665. William Drummond II owned both Structure 100 and the plantation at Drummond's Field (Agbe-Davies 2004c). It might be that plantation owners organized the distribution of pipes from one of their properties to another.

One of the factors favoring elite dominance prior to Bacon's Rebellion was the density and redundancy of ties that connected the members of the planter class. Below are just a few of the many examples of relationships that bound the owners and occupants of the selected sites into a close-knit, interdependent community. John Page had intimate business dealings with an owner of Structure 19 at Jamestown. He hosted William Berkeley at his home as Berkeley returned to Green Spring, after having executed William Drummond for his role in the rebellion. Multiple commercial and marital ties link the various owners of Structure 100 with the Pages. Thomas and Philip Ludwell were secretaries of the colony and right-hand men of Governor Berkeley, demonstrating multiple and overlapping links between Rich Neck, Green Spring, and Structure 144. Structures 127 and 100 were at various points owned by tenants on the governor's land at Pasbehaye who were therefore neighbors of Drummond. Plantations owned by men and women with such dense personal, professional, and commercial networks might reveal a trade in pipes among themselves more so than plantations for which no such networks could be identified.

We could also turn the question of alliances on its head and ask who would be *unlikely* to engage in trans-plantation trade, even if given the opportunity? Clearly one key relationship that began as tenancy, blossomed into patronage, but eventually went sour was the one between Berkeley and Drummond. The latter rented a place on the governor's land in the 1640s, was appointed governor of Albemarle by Berkeley in the 1660s, but began to criticize Berkeley's administration of the colony and the governor's land in that same span and soon earned his enmity (Agbe-Davies 2004c). Thus, we might expect barriers to trade between Green Spring and Drummond's Field, as well as between Drummond's Field and Rich Neck.

The pipes from the sites above were subjected to a quantitative analysis of a broad range of attributes with an emphasis on *technological* over *decorative* style. Instead of focusing on decorative content and the self-conscious symbols that sometimes decorated the pipes—and that, incidentally, are readily imitated or "decoupled" (Urban 2001) from their original referents, this study emphasizes technological attributes, including marks left by the manufacturing process and the *manner*, not the *content*, of the decoration (Agbe-Davies 2006). These unconscious patterns of production—we might also call them motor habits, or even elevate them to the level of *habitus*—are better indices of a pipe's having come from a particular workshop or "school" of pipe making than decoration alone (for technological style and the relationship between style and producers, see Chilton 1999; Eerkens 2000; Eerkens and Bettinger 2001; Hill and Gunn 1977; Lechtman 1977; Sackett 1990). Patterning in the distribution of technological attributes across sites should provide evidence for arguments about the occupants of particular sites trading in particular pipe production networks.

Patterns and Practice

After characterizing pipes from each of these sites using both nominal and metric traits, I conducted a series of comparisons between the sites in an attempt to discover technical similarities among pipe assemblages. From these we might infer which sites seemed to be drawing on the same sources for pipes. In other words, I sought to identify which sites belonged to the same pipe exchange networks.

Nominal traits selected for comparison included such characteristics as bowl shape (in comparison with standard references such as Atkinson and Oswald [1969], Henry [1979], and Oswald [1975]), surface treatment, bowl forming technique, the presence of mold scars, and firing core variants (as described in Orton et al. 1993). Table 4.1 provides a more comprehensive list of these variables. Such characteristics may be used as indicators of particular technological or "isochrestic" styles of production, to index the handiwork of an individual or workshop of makers (Sackett 1990). Such analytical criteria and techniques are commonly found in classic processual studies of material culture (e.g., Deetz 1965; Hill and Gunn 1977). The decision to record attributes as individual modes, rather than identifying artifacts as exemplars of taxonomic types, is likewise a technique with deep roots in archaeology (Rouse 1939).

One important use of nominal traits was to test the identification of particular attributes with a site or subset of sites. The chi-square statistic revealed, for example, that the presence of mold scars, different surface textures, manner of finishing the pipe lip, manner of finishing the mouthpiece, and the presence or absence of decoration were among the traits significantly associated with certain sites rather than others. For instance, pipe fragments from Jamestown were more likely to be highly burnished than fragments from other sites; both Green Spring and Jamestown had unusually high numbers of mouthpiece fragments with rounded ends (Agbe-Davies 2004c:Appendix VI). When the Jamestown sites were compared with one another, some of the same variables that distinguished sites from one

Table 4.1 Nominal variables recorded for the pipe fragments. (For an explanation of the variables not discussed in this chapter, see Agbe-Davies 2004c.)

bowl shape	multiple bores	motif name
fabric texture	lip formation	motif method
surface texture	mouthpiece	motif tool
inclusions	bowl base	motif location
color	scraped or knife-trimmed	scar treatment
core appearance	painted/slipped	scar location
firing cloud	glazed	text method
striation type	waster	text content
bowl formation	post-manufacturing	
pinched	modification	
	smoked	

another also distinguished the assemblages found in the different structures from one another. Several other variables, such as fabric texture, pinching, multiple bores, round versus square heels, and the appearance of the firing core could discriminate among the Jamestown subassemblages, even though they were not useful when comparing the outlying plantations with each other. (Agbe-Davies 2004c:263).

Metric traits allowed for a more precise comparison of individual pipes (particularly those of similar form), as well as the comparison of fragmentary specimens and statistical analysis of standardization (fig. 4.4). The coefficient of variation (CV) is a statistic that can be used to compare the variability of metric traits (Blackman et al. 1993; Eerkens and Bettinger 2001). Because CV scores (expressed as percentages) are scaled, one can use them to compare the variability of, for example, the thickness of pipe bowls at the lip (in the present assemblage averaging 2.33 mm) and the exterior diameter of pipe bowls at the lip (averaging 20.61 mm), without worrying about the difference in size of the measurements themselves. Replicative and ethnoarchaeological studies have demonstrated that nonspecialists can consistently produce a CV range of 2.5–3 percent for objects of familiar sizes and shapes (Eerkens 2000). It appears that skilled potters are capable of producing wares with CVs ranging from 2 percent to 6 percent and often perceive a benefit in doing so (Longacre 1999). David Hurst Thomas (1986:84) suggests that a group of artisans with a CV of greater than 10 percent probably consists of one or more unrecognized subgroups. So variability greater than 6–10 percent should be explained by factors besides human or material limitations.

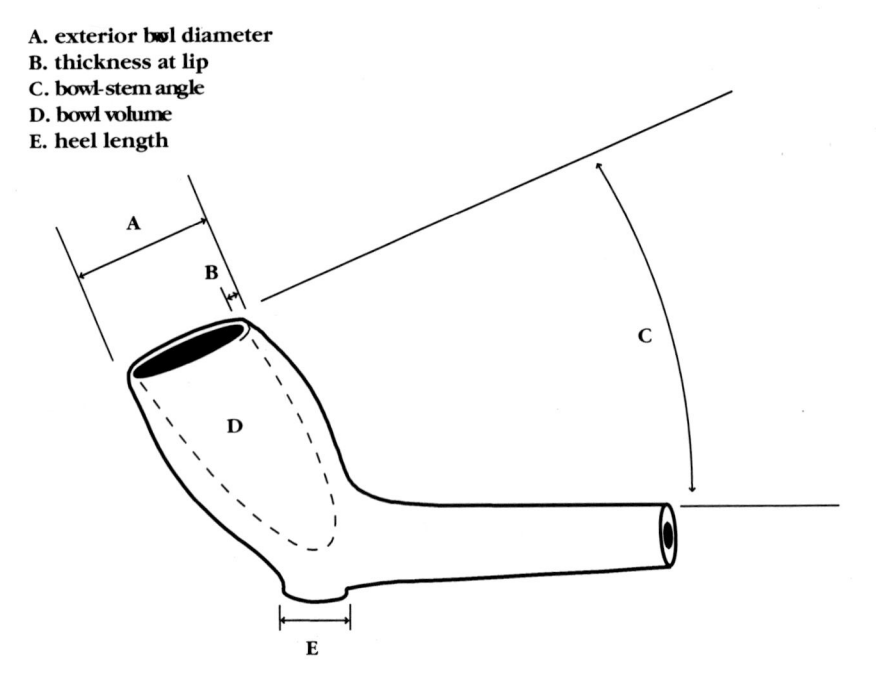

A. exterior bowl diameter
B. thickness at lip
C. bowl-stem angle
D. bowl volume
E. heel length

Figure 4.4 Measurements of pipe fragments discussed in this chapter. Explanations and a list of additional measurements may be found in Agbe-Davies (2004c). Illustration by J. E. Deetz.

For example, one common form of local pipe closely resembles some imported pipes of the same period, including evidence for manufacture in European-style molds (fig. 4.5). However, metric comparison quickly showed that this common form masked a certain degree of internal variation. When all pipes that could be identified as "belly bowls" with heels were measured, the size of the heel ranged quite widely (from 8.5 to 15.5 mm long). Statistical analysis revealed that the presence of this attribute alone was insufficient for identifying production groups (CV = 11.6 percent) and that even molded specimens as a class are internally heterogeneous (CV = 10.4 percent), pointing to the products of multiple molds in the combined assemblage. However, with the addition of the attribute of dentate bands at the juncture of the stem and bowl (as in fig. 4.3c), the range of variation reduced sharply (CV = 6.4 percent).

Further analyses of the data revealed that, first and foremost, the sites do not appear to represent random selections of a heterogeneous tradition (Agbe-Davies 2004a, 2004b, 2004c). If the pipe assemblages from each site were statistically the same, then there would be no point in trying

Social Aspects of the Tobacco Pipe Trade • 83

Figure 4.5 This fragment from Green Spring comes from a pipe that was made in a vertical half mold prior to being decorated with a stamp. The scar is still visible in this photograph of the heel. Photograph by A. S. Agbe-Davies

to identify different sources of pipes for particular sites and the exchange relationships that connected them. It was therefore quite important to establish whether the individual assemblages looked like samples randomly drawn from a single larger population of all local pipes circulating during that period, or whether the individual assemblages differed from one another and from the combined assemblage enough to suggest that the combined assemblage was actually an amalgam of several distinct groups (Agbe-Davies 2004c:252–262). Chi-square tests of nominal traits and analysis of variance (ANOVA) of metric traits provided the evidence for this determination. For example, mold scars were significantly more prevalent on pipe fragments from Green Spring and the combined Jamestown assemblages than was typical of the entire combined assemblage. Drummond's Field, Jamestown Structure 127, Port Anne, and Rich Neck had significantly fewer fragments with mold scars. Fragments with cores that appear to demonstrate incomplete oxidation are more common than normal at Port Anne and Jamestown Structures 100 and 127 (Agbe-Davies 2004c:Appendix V). Statistical comparison allows us to tell the difference between measurements that identify (and explain) significant variation between sites (e.g., bowl volume) and those that are irrelevant (e.g., bowl-stem angle and exterior bowl diameter at the lip).

Yet neither are the sites totally unique constellations of attributes. The same ANOVA statistic reveals that although the sites exhibit significant metric variation on most measures, this variation is only partially explained by assemblage attribution (Agbe-Davies 2004c:Table 7.6). Both metric and nominal data seem to eliminate the argument that individuals who made pipes did so exclusively for use by themselves or their immediate associates. Few styles or attributes were associated exclusively with individual sites or subsets of the combined assemblage, whether one considers proximity or contrasts urban Jamestown with rural plantation sites (Agbe-Davies 2006).

The intervention of labor-owners is one factor that might have shaped the movement of pipes from one settlement to another yet confounded the simple dichotomy between town and plantation styles or the likelihood for assemblages from neighboring sites to resemble one another. Could it be that the assemblages that we see were structured by the alliances and trade relationships maintained by colonial elites? Some sites with clear elite-level connections have quite similar pipe assemblages. For example, the pipe assemblages from both Green Spring and Jamestown have abundant mold scars, vertical bowl-forming marks (suggesting the use of a pipe engine), tooled lips, and round instead of square heels (this last is true only if Structures 127 and 100 are omitted). However, when compared systematically, elite social networks do not seem to have exerted a much greater force than geography.

Sites that were close together and owned by allied elites tended to share more attributes than those that were close and owned by antagonists. Yet ownership by friends (or even in some instances by the same individual) did not overcome the effects of distance (Agbe-Davies 2006:134). When pairs of assemblages coming from sites owned by "friends" are compared, they tend to share variables associated with pipe forming techniques, but they share fewer characteristics having to do with the clay itself, firing conditions, or decoration. A similar pattern holds for assemblages associated with sites that are close together but were owned by antagonists. So although residents of these sites obtained their pipes from makers using similar technologies, the pipes themselves probably came from different producers. When both elite networks and geography are taken into account, the sites that are nearest to each other share the most attributes, including attributes indicating that the similarity is due to more than the reproduction of popular or symbolic decorations (Agbe-Davies 2004c:312–317). But at the end of the day, it does not appear that pipe distribution was managed or directed according to the social networks that bound together land- and labor-owning elites. At most, elite antagonisms may have constricted opportunities for exchange of either pipes or ideas at distances that might otherwise have encouraged it.

A few assemblages consistently show evidence of more specialized pipe-making toolkits (isochrestic style) that more closely resemble contemporaneous pipes made in Europe (adjunct style). These traits show up most frequently in some of the Jamestown assemblages—especially Structure 144—and at Green Spring. These findings force us to consider in more detail the idea that the local pipe tradition was not a unitary phenomenon, requiring us to use techniques that allow for greater precision in the delineation and distribution of these varieties. And although I have not attempted to demonstrate whether the makers of these pipes were free or bound or from what continent their ancestors came, it bears noting that the trade in local pipes was theirs, not that of land- and labor-owning elites, which is saying something, considering the time and place in which they lived.

A New Emphasis on Trade?

The research strategy described above differs significantly from that of much previous work on local pipes, wherein analysts started by identifying co-occurring attributes, labeling clusters of attributes as "types," and then comparing the distribution of these types. Such an approach could be useful if one had a limited number of attributes or independent confirmation of the nature of the relationships among the attributes. Neither of these conditions currently holds true for the study of these artifacts. Likewise, the prior emphasis on bowl shape and decorative motif is useful if one wishes to characterize a cultural tradition or culture area, examine change over time, or decode symbolic meanings. However, such variables are less useful when attempting to isolate particular technological styles and thereby identify exchange relationships. Two recent studies have used decorative types in the pursuit of an understanding of the pipe trade. These results are now compared with the present analysis.

Al Luckenbach and Taft Kiser examined pipes from sites all along the western shore of the Chesapeake Bay and found that there is little typological overlap from one subregion to the other. "We contend that the regional variations of pipe makers (and perhaps their apprentices or later generations of related makers) are readily recognizable" (Luckenbach and Kiser 2006:162). In their article, they identify nine distinct manufacturers based on the decorative style of their pipes. Although such an exercise is critically important for standardizing descriptions of artifacts and facilitating communication among archaeologists, it cannot replace the kind of analysis described above if we wish to understand the exchange of local tobacco pipes.

Two of the types identified by Luckenbach and Kiser may serve as examples for the discussion here; both were identified in the assemblages in and around Jamestown that were used for the present study. "Bookbinder" pipes are made in a single-elbow bowl form with marbleized clay and intensively decorated with "elaborately cut rectangular wheel stamps" (Luckenbach and Kiser 2006:167; figs. 4.6a and 4.6b). The "Star Maker" produced pipes with slightly bulbous bowls and decorated them with 1) an eight-rayed star on the front and back of the bowl, 2) a star on the back only, 3) a star on the back with a panel on the bowl front, 4) parallel vertical lines and stamps on the back, or 5) "no decoration" (Luckenbach and Kiser 2006:170; fig. 4.6c).

The attributes used to identify the types do not allow for the sorting of fragmentary or ambiguous cases (for example, dentate decoration that may be a star or some other motif, a six-pointed star on the front of a bowl only, or the impressions of metal stamps on a belly bowl pipe). Tests for associations among the traits in the present assemblage reveal both random and significant associations. The association of marbled clay with the use of rolling metal stamps (as opposed to other decorative tools) is significant but not exclusive, so that one trait cannot be used as a proxy for another or as a reliable indicator of the presence of the given type. Likewise, single-elbow bowls are not significantly associated with rolling stamps in general, nor with the elaborate rectangular cut designs that are the hallmark of the "Bookbinder" pipes.[2]

The specificity of the types also limits their application to quantitative studies of real assemblages. The types are readily identified in archaeological collections, and Luckenbach and Kiser use the types' presence or absence to indicate exchange of a particular pipe maker's wares. The presence of many pipes of a given type is taken to indicate its production locale. However, when the criteria for the nine types they identify are applied to the present combined assemblage of nearly 5,000 pipe fragments, only thirteen specimens could be identified with a specific pipe maker. A more flexible application of the criteria yielded seventy-eight identifiable fragments. When only maker-associated fragments were included, a significant association with the sites in the present study emerged.[3] But the number of associated fragments is swamped by the larger dataset.

Finally, a strict application of the criteria for identification does not give us a meaningful way to discuss variants, such as the six rayed pipes in the collection, or a means to determine whether the distinction between six and

Social Aspects of the Tobacco Pipe Trade ❧ 87

Figures 4.6 Pipe fragments A and B from Rich Neck are of the type designated Bookbinder by Luckenbach and Kiser (2006). An unusual characteristic of this variant on the typical Star Maker pipe (from Drummond's Field) is that the star is inscribed within a square panel (C). Usually if a panel appears, it is on the opposite side of the bowl, facing away from the smoker. Photographs by A. S. Agbe-Davies.

eight rays is meaningful. A number of these problems seem to argue for the use of technological as opposed to decorative criteria for analyses because the former are more plentiful in the assemblages and less subject to imitation and therefore more indicative of individual style (that is, less likely to be decoupled from their indexical referent; see also Urban, chapter 10, and Doonan and Bauer, chapter 9, both this volume).

88 • Anna S. Agbe-Davies

A technique that acknowledges the significance of technological style and uses a modal as opposed to a typological approach (e.g., Agbe-Davies 2006) allows one to see the similarities *and* the differences between the "Bookbinder" pipes and the specimen depicted in figure 4.7. This rare imitation of the classic "Bookbinder" decorative grammar that clearly uses different tools and clays could offer significant insight to the circulation of ideas, symbols, and objects in the early colonial Chesapeake, provided we deploy techniques and methods that allow us to study it in all of its complexity.

Like Luckenbach and Kiser, J. Cameron Monroe and Seth Mallios (2004) approach the question of manufacture and distribution through types based on decorative style. Though the number and character of the individual categories are unspecified, the authors refer to a previous study that analyzed a set of assemblages into five decorative layouts and, maximally, eight handmade and one mold-made pipe form categories (Monroe 2002). The number of forms and decorative types present at each of thirteen sites was used to create an index of similarity[4] measure, with Jamestown having a value of one and the remaining sites lower values roughly corresponding to their distance from the town. "These observations strongly supported the likelihood that the Colono pipes on the James River were distributed outwards from Jamestown" (Monroe and Mallios 2004:73–74).

Whereas this conclusion may hold when considering formal and decorative variation, the technological variables tell a different story. The

Figure 4.7 The maker of this pipe, excavated at Green Spring, was clearly familiar with the conventions governing the creation of Bookbinder pipes (Luckenbach and Kiser 2006) and yet produced a novel version of that design. Photograph by A. S. Agbe-Davies.

Jamestown fragments in the present analysis[5] form a distinctive subset of the combined assemblage (see fig. 4.2 above). For example, mold scars were significantly more prevalent on the Jamestown fragments than in the combined assemblage. The Jamestown pipes were more likely to have heels. The fragments for which bowl-forming technology was evident were more likely to be formed using a plunging rather than a reaming tool. They were less likely to exhibit marks typical of cutting or scraping the clay before firing (Agbe-Davies 2004c:Appendix V). All of these characteristics do in fact speak to a more mechanized and streamlined production process. However, these are characteristics that *distinguish* the Jamestown fragments from outlying sites.

Although the pipes from nearby plantations may exhibit a pattern of decreasingly similar appearance, they seem to have very different production styles. According to Prudence Rice,

> The decorative or stylistic attribute system is more removed from direct inferences of production and more complex in terms of its interpretation. Stylistic and decorative data are extremely sensitive to a broad range of social-interactional phenomena....Unless the stylistic information can be related directly to the production process..., style as measured by diversity (unlike earlier correlation interaction analyses) does little to inform on productive location or organization. [Rice 1989:113]

From the technological variables, it appears that the Jamestown pipes were made under a different production regime than those recovered from several nearby plantations. Furthermore, previous testing has demonstrated that samples of complete and decorated specimens do not always best represent entire site assemblages (Agbe-Davies 2004b).

Monroe and Mallios's similarity index appears to capture not only similarity but richness, with Jamestown being the most rich of the assemblages. Although space (i.e., trading distance) might not explain the intersite differences among pipes, perhaps time does. Although the authors compared the indices against previously published site occupation spans (Emerson 1988:22) and found them to be unaffected by length of occupation, the possibility still exists that the date of occupation may be an influential factor. Figures 4.8a and 4.8b show that supplementing the dates in Emerson's summarizing chart with the details provided in his text and truncating the occupation date range so that the end date coincides with the likely end of local pipe production indicate a correlation between length of occupation and index value.[6] Graphing the initial or median date of occupation against

90 @ Anna S. Agbe-Davies

the indices of similarity produces a moderate and a weak negative correlation respectively (fig. 4.8c). This finding parallels an earlier discovery by Monroe (2002:29, 32) that the richness of both decorative layouts and pipe bowl

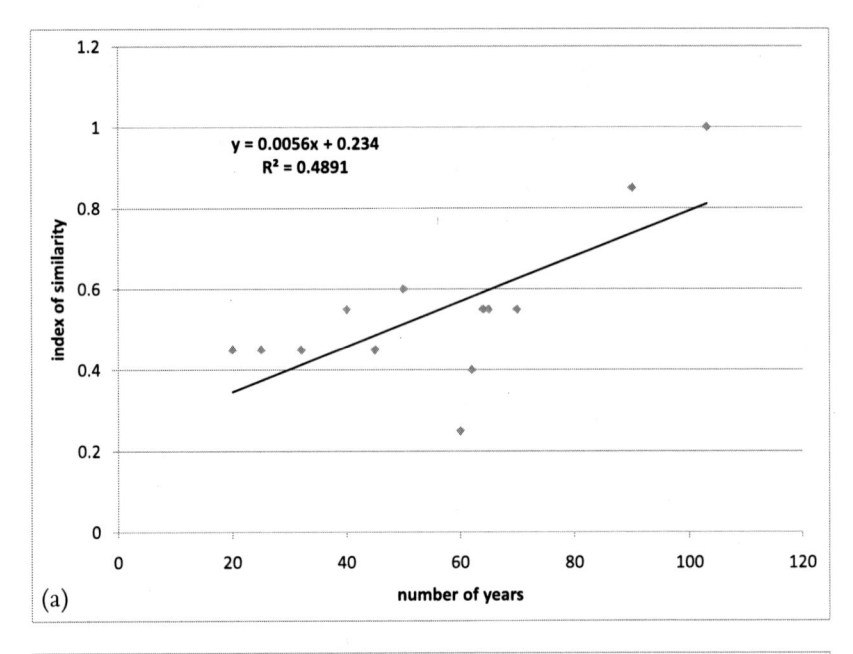

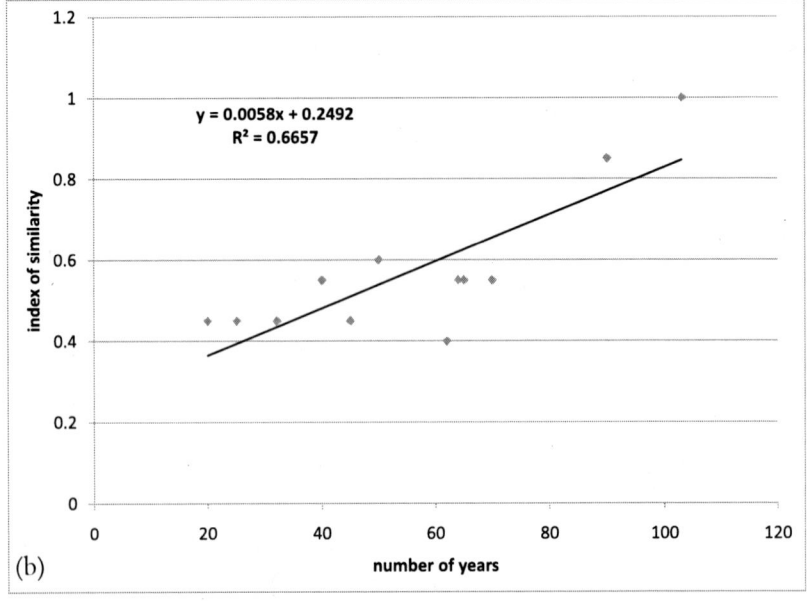

(a)

$y = 0.0056x + 0.234$
$R^2 = 0.4891$

index of similarity vs. number of years

(b)

$y = 0.0058x + 0.2492$
$R^2 = 0.6657$

index of similarity vs. number of years

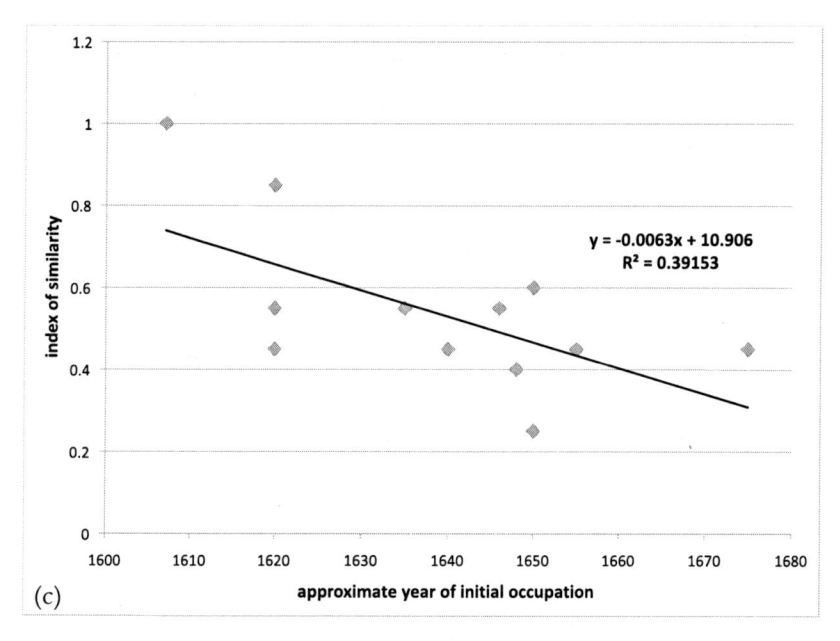

(c) [chart: index of similarity vs. approximate year of initial occupation; y = -0.0063x + 10.906; R² = 0.39153]

Figure 4.8 There is a positive correlation (a) between length of site occupation (adjusted from the dates reported in Emerson 1988:21–29 to reflect years of likely pipe production, rather than total site occupation span) and pipe assemblage index value (as presented in Monroe and Mallios [2004:73, Figure 2]); (b) this chart excludes one site, Bennett Farm, which is poorly dated and also has an unusually low index value (see note 6); (c) this chart shows the negative correlation between year of initial occupation and index value, suggesting that formal variability of the tradition may decrease over time.

forms declined over the course of the seventeenth century. If computed in a manner comparable to the similarity index, the first quarter of the century would have a value of .91, the last quarter, .55.

Fuller assessment of the contradictory evidence for and against Jamestown as a center for pipe distribution is hampered by the difference between presence/absence and quantitative analyses and also the fact that the assemblages used in the two studies (Agbe-Davies 2004c; Monroe and Mallios 2004) only partially overlap. Nevertheless, it seems that additional analysis is warranted before concluding that Jamestown was the distribution center for the pipes that are found on nearby plantations.

Conclusion

The focus of this research has been not trade for its own sake but using ideas about trade to make explicit the problem of the circulation of a particular class of goods and what that might tell us about social relations in the seventeenth-century Chesapeake. The investigations briefly outlined here have revealed that even though elites owned much of the labor in this society and used it to generate profits in the transatlantic *and* local economies, workers were not always alienated from the fruits of their labor. The minimal effect that elite social networks had on pipe exchange networks causes us to reconsider a picture (based primarily on elite texts) of a local economy totally controlled by labor-owners and dependent on imports for everyday necessities.

This view of the limits of elite power comes from a consideration of the pathways that pipes took from producers to consumers. This research also indirectly (and somewhat unintentionally) contributes to the ongoing debate regarding the racial groups to which the people who made these pipes (as well as the people who used them) belonged. These contributions have been achieved not by doing as many others have, comparing the decorations on the pipes to the symbolic repertoires of different groups who contributed to the polyethnic and polyracial society that was seventeenth-century Virginia, nor by viewing these artifacts themselves as symbols signaling difference from an imported (metropolitan, European) other. Rather, demonstrating that this tradition seems to have existed beyond the gaze of the labor-owning elite gives us more reason than ever to believe that this tradition is an index of the tastes, imperatives, and motives of the colony's large laboring class at a time when that group was increasingly being marked as a racialized other. Thus, attention to the contexts and control of exchange and an integration of the techniques of the processual paradigm with the thematic interests of its antithesis allow us new views on life in seventeenth-century Virginia and a greater appreciation of the extent (and limits) of the social dimensions of exchange.

Notes

1. I use the term *ethnicity* both deliberately and critically. See Agbe-Davies (2008, 2009, in press) for the problems of ethnicity and race in archaeology.
2. Marbled versus single colored clay in a two-by-two contingency table with rolling stamps versus other tools: $x^2 = 370.306$, $df = 1$, $p < 0.001$. Single-elbow versus other bowl shapes in a two-by-two contingency table with rolling stamps versus other tools: $x^2 = .006$, $df = 1$, $.9 < p < .95$, with Yates' correction, $x^2 = .029$, $.75 < p < .9$. Cut rectangular stamps versus other rolling stamps in a two-by-two contingency table with elbow bowls versus other bowl shapes: $x^2 = 1.918$, $df = 1$, $.1 < p < .25$, with Yates's correction, $x^2 = .553$, $.25 < p < .5$.
3. "Star Maker" pipes are prevalent at Green Spring, Drummond, and Page; "Bookbinder," "Broadneck" (which uses the same rolling stamp technology as

Bookbinder pipes but with a different design and bowl form), and "Faceted" pipes are more common at Port Anne and Rich Neck. Jamestown included all of the forms except for Broadneck. In a contingency table, the results were $x^2 = 66.443$, $df = 15$, $p < .001$.

4. Number of forms plus number of types, with the total divided by the number of types in the region (Monroe and Mallios 2004).

5. Structures 19, 26/27, 100, 112, 127 and 144, according to the numbering system on John Cotter's "Base Map" (1958).

6. Eppes Island/Cawsies Care, 1650–1700; Flowerdew Hundred, 1655–1700; Kingsmill, 1620–1710; Jamestown, 1607–1710; Green Spring, 1646–1710; Governor's Land, 1648–1710; Mathew's Manor, 1620–1652; Lightfoot, 1675–1700; Martin's Hundred, 1620–1690; Bennett Farm, 1650–1710; River Creek, 1640–1660; Knowles, 1620–1660; Chesopiean/Thorogood, 1635–1700 (Emerson 1988:21–29). These dates are best approximations based on associated datable artifacts and possible landowner affiliations. Bennett Farm and River Creek are described as "late seventeenth-century occupation[s]…incompletely investigated and documented at this time." The Knowles Collection is unprovenienced, and the Chesopiean/Thorogood site "is problematic due to disturbed stratigraphy…and lack of provenience information" (Emerson 1988:28). The index values taken from Monroe and Mallios (2004:73, Figure 2) are Eppes Island/Cawsies Care, .6; Flowerdew Hundred, .45; Kingsmill, .85; Jamestown, 1; Green Spring, .55; Governor's Land, .4; Mathew's Manor, .45; Lightfoot, .45; Martin's Hundred, .55; Bennett Farm, .25; River Creek, .45; Knowles, .55; Chesopiean/Thorogood, .5.

References

Agbe-Davies, Anna S.

2001 Thinking Outside the Box: New Avenues for Research for Locally Made Pipes. Paper Presented at the Annual Meeting of the Jamestown Conference, Jamestown, Virginia.

2004a Alternatives to Traditional Models for the Classification and Analysis of Pipes of the Early Colonial Chesapeake. Paper Presented at the 37th Annual Meeting of the Society for Historical Archaeology, St. Louis.

2004b The Production and Consumption of Smoking Pipes along the Tobacco Coast. In *Smoking and Culture: Recent Developments in the Archaeology of Smoking Pipes in Eastern North America*, edited by S. Rafferty and R. Mann, pp. 273–304. University of Tennessee Press, Knoxville.

2004c Up in Smoke: Pipe Production, Smoking, and Bacon's Rebellion. Unpublished PhD dissertation, Department of Anthropology, University of Pennsylvania.

2006 Alternatives to Traditional Models for the Classification and Analysis of Pipes of the Early Colonial Chesapeake. In *Dirt and Discussion: Methods, Methodology, and Interpretation in Historical Archaeology*, edited by S. Archer and K. Bartoy, pp. 115–140. Springer, New York.

Agbe-Davies, Anna S.
2008 "Critical Systematics" and the Archaeology of Race in 17th-Century Virginia. Paper Presented at the Interdisciplinary Archaeology Workshop, University of Chicago.
2009 Review of *Race and Practice in Archaeological Interpretation*, by Charles E. Orser, Jr. *Transforming Anthropology* 17(2):159–160.
2009 Review of *The Archaeology of Race and Racializaton in Historic America*, by Charles E. Orser, Jr. *American Antiquity*. 74(4):577.

Arnold, C. J.
1977 The Clay Tobacco-Pipe Industry: An Economic Study. In *Pottery and Commerce: Characterization and Trade in Roman and Later Ceramics*, edited by D. P. S. Peacock, pp. 313–336. Academic Press, London.

Atkinson, D. R., and Adrian Oswald
1969 *London Clay Tobacco Pipes*. Oxford University Press, Oxford.

Billings, Warren M.
1996 Sir William Berkeley and the Diversification of the Virginia Economy. *The Virginia Magazine of History and Biography* 104(4):433–454.

Binford, Lewis R.
1962 Archaeology as Anthropology. *American Antiquity* 28(2):217–225.

Blackman, M. James, Gil J. Stein, and Pamela B. Vandiver
1993 The Standardization Hypothesis and Ceramic Mass Production: Technological, Compositional, and Metric Indexes of Craft Specialization at Tell Leilan, Syria. *American Antiquity* 58(1):60–80.

Capone, Patricia, and Elinor Downs
2004 Red Clay Tobacco Pipes: A Petrographic Window into Seventeenth-Century Economics at Jamestown, Virginia, and New England. In *Smoking and Culture: Recent Developments in the Archaeology of Smoking Pipes in Eastern North America*, edited by S. Rafferty and R. Mann, pp. 305–316. University of Tennessee Press, Knoxville.

Chilton, Elizabeth S.
1999 One Size Fits All: Typology and Alternatives for Ceramic Research. In *Material Meanings: Critical Approaches to the Interpretation of Material Culture*, edited by E. S. Chilton, pp. 44–60. University of Utah Press, Salt Lake City.

Cotter, John L.
1958 *Archeological Excavations at Jamestown, Virginia*. National Park Service, U.S. Department of the Interior, Washington, DC.

Cox, C. Jane, Al Luckenbach, and David Gadsby
2005 Locally-Made Tobacco Pipes in the Colonial Chesapeake. Paper Presented at the 38 Annual Meeting of the Society for Historical Archaeology, York, UK.

Crass, David Colin
1988 The Clay Pipes from Green Spring Plantation (44 JC 9), Virginia. *Historical Archaeology* 22(1):83–97.

Davidson, Thomas E.

1995 The Virginia Earthenwares Project: Characterizing 17th-Century Earthenwares by Electronic Image Analysis. *Northeast Historical Archaeology* 24:51–64.

Deetz, James

1965 *The Dynamics of Stylistic Change in Arikara Ceramics*. University of Illinois Press, Urbana.

Eerkens, Jelmer W.

2000 Practice Makes within 5% of Perfect: Visual Perception, Motor Skills, and Memory in Artifact Variation. *Current Anthropology* 41(4):663–668.

Eerkens, Jelmer W., and Robert L. Bettinger

2001 Techniques for Assessing Standardization in Artifact Assemblages: Can We Scale Material Variability? *American Antiquity* 66(3):493–504.

Emerson, Matthew C.

1988 Decorated Clay Tobacco Pipes from the Chesapeake. Unpublished PhD dissertation, Department of Anthropology, University of California, Berkeley.

1999 African Inspirations in a New World Art and Artifact: Decorated Tobacco Pipes from the Chesapeake. In *I, Too, Am America: Studies in African-American Archaeology*, edited by T. A. Singleton, pp. 47–74. University Press of Virginia, Charlottesville.

Fleet, Beverly (editor)

1961 *Virginia Colonial Abstracts XXIII*: Westmoreland County, 1653–1657. Genealogical Publishing Co., Baltimore.

Galucci, Elizabeth Andersen, David Muraca, and Pegeen McLaughlin

1994 Identifying Producer-Client Relationships at the Bruton Heights Tile Kiln. Paper Presented at the 27th Annual Meeting of the Society for Historical Archaeology, Vancouver.

Harrington, J. C.

1951 Tobacco Pipes From Jamestown. *Quarterly Bulletin of the Archaeological Society of Virginia* 5(4):unpaginated.

Hegmon, Michelle

1992 Archaeological Research on Style. *Annual Review of Anthropology* 21:517–536.

Heite, Edward F.

1972 American-Made Pipes from the Camden Site. *Quarterly Bulletin of the Archeological Society of Virginia* 27:94–99.

Henry, Susan L.

1979 Terra-cotta Tobacco Pipes in 17th-Century Maryland and Virginia: A Preliminary Study. *Historical Archaeology* 13:14–37.

Hill, James N., and Joel Gunn (editors)

1977 *The Individual in Prehistory*. Academic Press, New York.

Hodder, Ian

1985 Postprocessual Archaeology. *Advances in Archaeological Method and Theory* 8:1–26.

Keane, Webb
2003 Semiotics and the Social Analysis of Material Things. *Language & Communication* 23:409–425.

Kelso, William M., and Beverly A. Straube
2004 *Jamestown Rediscovery, 1994–2004*. Association for the Preservation of Virginia Antiquities, Richmond.

Lechtman, Heather
1977 Style in Technology—Some Early Thoughts. In *Material Culture: Styles, Organization, and Dynamics of Technology*, edited by H. Lechtman and R. S. Merrill, pp. 3–20. West Press, New York.

Longacre, William A.
1999 Standardization and Specialization: What's the Link? In *Pottery and People: A Dynamic Interaction*, edited by G. M. Feinman and J. M. Skibo, pp. 59–80. University of Utah Press, Salt Lake City.

Luckenbach, Al, and C. Jane Cox
2002 Tobacco-Pipe Manufacturing in Early Maryland: The Swan Cove Site (ca. 1660–1669). In *The Clay Tobacco-Pipe in Anne Arundel County, Maryland (1650–1730)*, edited by A. Luckenbach, C. J. Cox, and J. Kille, pp. 46–63. Anne Arundel County's Lost Towns Project, Annapolis, Maryland.

Luckenbach, Al, and Taft Kiser
2006 Seventeenth-Century Tobacco Pipe Manufacturing in the Chesapeake Region: A Preliminary Delineation of Makers and Their Styles. In *Ceramics in America 2006*, edited by R. Hunter, pp. 160–177. University Press of New England, Hanover, New Hampshire.

MacCord, Howard A., Sr.
1969 Camden: A Postcontact Indian Site in Caroline County. *The Quarterly Bulletin of the Archeological Society of Virginia* 24(1):1–55.

Magoon, Dane T.
1999 "Chesapeake" Pipes and Uncritical Assumptions: A View from Northeastern North Carolina. *North Carolina Archaeology* 48:107–126.

McCartney, Martha W.
2000 *Documentary History of Jamestown Island: III. Biographies of Owners and Residents*. The Colonial Williamsburg Foundation. Colonial National Historical Park, National Park Service, Williamsburg, Virginia.

McCrery, Peter A.
1968 Two Pipes from Prince George County, Virginia. The Quarterly Bulletin of the Archeological Society of Virginia 23(1):37–38.

Metz, John, Jennifer Jones, Dwayne Pickett, and David Muraca
1998 *"Upon the Palisado" and Other Stories of Place from Bruton Heights*. The Dietz Press, Richmond.

Miller, Henry M.
1991 Tobacco Pipes from Pope's Fort, St. Mary's City, Maryland: An English Civil War Site on the American Frontier. In *The Archaeology of the Clay Tobacco Pipe: Chesapeake Bay*, edited by P. Davey and D. J. Pogue, pp. 73–88. BAR International Series 566. British Archaeological Reports, Oxford.

Mitchell, Vivienne
1983 The History of Nominy Plantation with Emphasis on the Clay Tobacco Pipes. *Historic Clay Tobacco Pipes* 2:3–38.

Monroe, J. Cameron
2002 *Negotiating African-American Ethnicity in the 17th-Century Chesapeake*. The Archaeology of the Clay Tobacco Pipe XVI, BAR International Series 1042. Archaeopress, Oxford.

Monroe, J. Cameron, and Seth W. Mallios
2004 A Seventeenth-Century Colonial Cottage Industry: New Evidence and a Dating Formula for Colono Tobacco Pipes in the Chesapeake. *Historical Archaeology* 38(2):68–82.

Moore, Peter
2000 Tilbury Fort: A Post-Medieval Fort and Its Inhabitants. *Post-Medieval Archaeology* 34:3–104.

Morgan, Edmund S.
1975 *American Slavery, American Freedom: The Ordeal of Colonial Virginia*. W. W. Norton & Company, New York.

Mouer, L. Daniel, Mary Ellen N. Hodges, Stephen R. Potter, Susan L. Henry Renaud, Ivor Noel Hume, Dennis J. Pogue, Martha W. McCartney, and Thomas E. Davidson
1999 Colonoware Pottery, Chesapeake Pipes, and "Uncritical Assumptions." In *I, Too, Am America: Studies in African-American Archaeology*, edited by T. A. Singleton, pp. 75–115. University Press of Virginia, Charlottesville, Virginia.

Neiman, Fraser D., and Julia A. King
1999 Who Smoked Chesapeake Pipes? Paper Presented at the 32nd Annual Meeting of the Society for Historical Archaeology, Salt Lake City.

Noël Hume, Audrey
1979 Clay Tobacco Pipes Excavated at Martin's Hundred, Virginia, 1976–1978. In *The Archaeology of the Clay Tobacco Pipe*, edited by P. Davey, pp. 3–36. BAR International Series Vol. 60. British Archaeological Reports, Oxford.

Oak-Rhind, Hugh
1980 Distribution of Clay Tobacco Pipes Round Their Place of Manufacture. In *The Archaeology of the Clay Tobacco Pipe, III Britain: The North and West*, edited by P. Davey, pp. 349–361. British Series Vol. 78. British Archaeological Reports, Oxford.

Orton, Clive, Paul Tyers, and Alan Vince
1993 *Pottery in Archaeology*. Cambridge University Press, Cambridge.

Oswald, Adrian
1975 *Clay Pipes for the Archaeologist*. BAR Vol. 14. British Archaeological Reports, Oxford.

Outlaw, Alain Charles, and Merry Abbitt Outlaw
2000 Governor's Land Archaeological District Records, Williamsburg, Virginia.

Peirce, Charles Sanders
1965 Division of Signs. In *Collected Papers of Charles Sanders Peirce*, edited by Charles Hartshorne and Paul Weiss, pp. 134–155. The Belknap Press, Cambridge, Massachusetts.

Rice, Prudence
1989 Ceramic Diversity, Production, and Use. In *Quantifying Diversity in Archaeology*, edited by R. D. Leonard and G. T. Jones, pp. 109–117. Cambridge University Press, Cambridge.

Rouse, Irving
1939 *Prehistory in Haiti: A Study in Method*. Yale University Publications in Anthropology Vol. 21. Yale University Press, New Haven, Connecticut.

Rutman, Darrett B., and Anita H. Rutman
1984 *A Place in Time: Middlesex County, Virginia 1650–1750*. W. W. Norton & Company, New York.

Sackett, James R.
1990 Style and Ethnicity in Archaeology: The Case for Isochrestism. In *The Uses of Style in Archaeology*, edited by M. W. Conkey and C. A. Hastorf, pp. 32–43. Cambridge University Press, Cambridge.

Sikes, Kathryn
2008 Stars as Social Space? Contextualising Chesapeake Star-motif Pipes. *Post-Medieval Archaeology* 42(1):75–103.

Smith, James M.
1981 The Pottery and Kiln of Green Spring: A Study in 17th Century Material Culture. Unpublished Master's thesis, Department of Anthropology, College of William and Mary.

Sprinkle, John
1992 Loyalists and Baconians: The Participants in Bacon's Rebellion in Virginia 1676–1677. Unpublished PhD Dissertation, Department of History, College of William and Mary.

Straube, Beverly
1995 The Colonial Potters of Tidewater Virginia. *Journal of Early Southern Decorative Arts* XXI(2):1–40.

Thomas, David Hurst
1986 *Refiguring Anthropology*. Waveland Press, Inc., Prospect Heights, Illinois.

Urban, Greg
2001 *Metaculture: How Culture Moves through the World*. University of Minnesota Press, Minneapolis.

Walker, Iain
1977 *Clay Tobacco Pipes, with Particular Reference to the Bristol Industry*. Parks Canada, Ottawa.

Weber, Max
1978 Types of Legitimate Domination. In *Economy and Society*, vol. 1, pp. 212–245. University of California Press, Berkeley.

CHAPTER 5

Arenas of Action: Trade as Power, Trade as Identity

Kenneth G. Kelly

The association of material goods with the expression of power has long been recognized in anthropological studies (DeMarrais et al. 1996; Schortman and Urban 1992; Thomas 1991). Particular categories of material culture, be they feathered cloaks, monumental architecture, prestige goods, or silk hats, communicate particular messages about the possession of power. Similarly, the lack of access to these sorts of goods may also demonstrate a lack of power. Whereas the first case, particularly when the prestige goods are exotic, may be more transparent to outsiders, the second case, in which such exotic prestige goods are absent, may be difficult to understand without an emic perspective. If a segment of society possesses something notable that the others do not and vice versa, it may be noticeable to the anthropologist and its role can then be theorized. The archaeologist working with historical documents, although not privileged to a truly emic perspective, nonetheless has at a minimum a historical record created by contemporary observers and the material record of archaeological remains to contrast with one another.

There is a long tradition of recognizing that the possession of particular kinds of material culture may convey power, and this chapter steps from that departure point to explore the idea that the manipulation of the circulation of material culture may describe power. Thus this chapter explores the idea that the *relationships* people engage in to obtain goods, or those actions that fall under the rubric of trade or exchange, may also be arenas in which social power is exercised and even created. Many of us are writing about the importance of trade, exchange, and other forms of negotiated social interaction as they relate to power, both the power *to* accomplish particular ends and the power *over* people (Rowlands 1987). This exploration of aspects of trade other than those related to the exchange or accumulation of goods sheds light on the social dimensions of trade that may otherwise remain obscure.

Frequently, in cultural situations that we describe as intercultural interaction (Schortman and Urban 1992), we see how new avenues of access, through trade and exchange, to material culture that has previously been rare, hard to get, or even unknown, have been a factor in sociopolitical evolution and the realignments in power relationships that necessarily ensue (Earle 2002; Renfrew 1975, 1986). The exploration of these events and the meanings assigned to them are heavily dependent on our understanding of the context. Historical archaeology, with its ability to describe rich contexts, is particularly well suited to these explorations. One ideal region in which to explore and contextualize the relationships between power, trade, and exchange and the formation of identities is the coast of West Africa during the several centuries of the Atlantic slave trade, when European traders and African nations came into prolonged and significant contact with each other. The rest of this chapter will investigate the social roles of exchange as they can been seen in the context of two hundred years of African-European interaction that took place in the Bight of Benin, the region known historically to European slave traders as the Slave Coast.

Introduction: Change and Realignment on the West African Coast

Coastal West African sociopolitical complexity has long been attributed, at least in part, to the role played by trade in the early interaction with Europeans (Kelly 2001; Law 1991; Monroe 2003, 2007; Polanyi 1966; Polanyi et al. 1957). The arrival of ship-borne European traders created new opportunities for polities that were previously at the distant ends of land-based trade networks, and allowed coastal groups to circumvent the existing relations of power and hierarchy. Coastal societies that had been oriented to fishing and salt extraction suddenly found themselves in a new role as middlemen or gatekeepers of trade entrepôts where products from the hinterland could be rerouted to the coast (Rivallain 1977; Ross 1987). Gold, ivory, pepper, and most notoriously, captives were new sources of wealth for coastal peoples (Law 1991).

Many have seen the setting of the slave trade on the coast of Africa as an almost textbook example of the world-system (Wallerstein 1974), in which European states or "cores" grew through the expansion of trade, in this case obtaining human capital in exchange for manufactured goods, and enmeshing dependant "peripheries" in a cycle of early capitalist dependency, foreshadowing the modern colonial and postcolonial world. However, a significant drawback of the world-system perspective, with its focus on the broader international and worldwide implications of trade, is that it tends to overlook the local actions, goals, perspectives, and meanings applied to the trade encounter by those directly participating in it (Kelly 1995; Schortman and Urban 1992). Although large-scale, *longue durée* processes (for example, the range of factors that eventually led to European colonial control over the region) can be seen operating on the Slave Coast, those Africans and Europeans who were engaged in trade and other social activities in the seventeenth, eighteenth, and early nineteenth century were not acting in the *longue durée* or with the hindsight it provides but in the shorter, human-scaled *événement* (Kelly 1997b). By turning our gaze away from the broad impersonal scales of inquiry required by the *longue durée* toward the shorter-term, actor-scaled way in which local polities and groups within them saw their involvement in commerce and interaction, anthropological insights into the ways that human groups make sense of encounters with others can be explored, and nuanced windows on complex historical issues such as the slave trade can be opened.

The origin and rise of the Hueda state fits within this framework very clearly. Broad world-system-wide developments impacted the Hueda and neighboring states as the demand for captives and consequently the slave trade grew in the seventeenth century. However, the specific ways in which groups within the Hueda polity and its successor state, Dahomey, chose to engage with those impacts are unique and show a distinct appraisal of the arenas of action. Hueda, located on the coast of present-day Bénin (fig. 5.1), became an important European trade destination about 1670, as European traders seeking new sources of captives for the blossoming slave trade began to trade with a coastal polity that took advantage of these new opportunities to split off from Allada, located in the interior. Allada had been a primary center of the seventeenth-century Bight of Benin region, although its control over neighboring groups was more of a tributary nature than a direct administration. In the mid-seventeenth century, as the demand for captive Africans for the plantations of the New World increased, trade interactions spread from the Gold Coast to regions of the West African coast where previously there had been little of interest or economic value to European trade. As Allada, 40 km inland, began to extract new varieties of trade goods and interactions through the profitable trade in captives, its tributaries along the coast, principally Hueda, realized that they were in better positions to

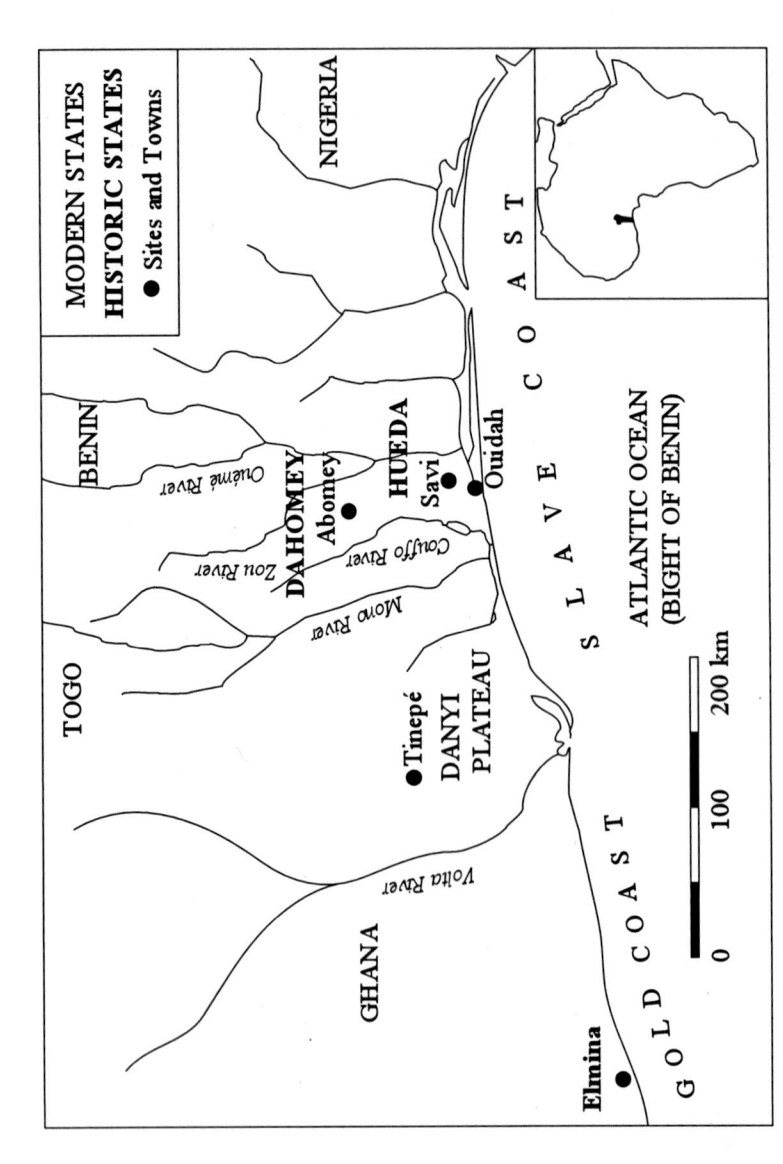

Figure 5.1 Map of Slave Coast region showing the locations of the Hueda and Dahomey polities and the sites of Savi and Ouidah. Map by the author.

control the trade passing through their territories and being negotiated on their own shores. By the 1670s, trade interactions were occurring in Hueda territory and no longer being brokered by Allada (Law 1991).

Moving forward in time nearly sixty years, we see that as the Atlantic trade developed and new wealth and opportunity spread to the interior beyond Allada from the middleman polities such as Hueda, interior polities sought more significant participation in and control of the trade. In particular, Dahomey, centered 100 km to the interior, demonstrated a renewal of this process, achieving its power and wealth and securing its political complexity in large part by usurping control over the trade that had been exercised by its rival, the Hueda (Monroe 2003, 2007; Ross 1987). Dahomey continued to be the primary polity on this section of the coast for nearly 175 years, until the French ultimately consolidated their colonial administration over the region just before the turn of the twentieth century.

It is easy to view this historical trajectory from the perspective that privileges trade as an engine of sociopolitical complexity, and to theorize the rise of Hueda and later Dahomey as examples of secondary state formation (Renfrew 1975). Indeed, there is an extensive literature that discusses the role that trade and exchange play in the centralization of social power and control and in the evolution of increasingly complex societies (Adams 1974; Brumfiel and Earle 1987; DeMarrais et al. 1996; Earle 2002; McIntosh 1999; Renfrew 1975, 1986; Sabloff and Lamberg-Karlovsky 1975; Schortman and Urban 1992, and so on). Yet trade and exchange, as well as the access to wealth they engender, serve other purposes as well as being agents and mobilizing forces for political complexity (Brumfiel and Earle 1987; Coquery-Vidrovitch 1969; McIntosh 1999). Beyond systemic influences on societies, the arenas of trade and exchange also serve immediate purposes within particular societies, as the wealth and prestige goods these activities bring are directly associated with exhibition of and maintenance of power relations and identity between individuals and groups (Blanton et al. 1996; Earle 1991:3; Stein 2002). This aspect of the interaction, associated with identity of trading people, is often overlooked in the archaeological study of trade but can be seen very clearly in several social arenas in Hueda and Dahomey (Kelly 1997b; Norman and Kelly 2004).

The Hueda Arena

We will first explore the social importance of interaction with outside groups and the role of that interaction in the development of identities among the Hueda. I argue that the Hueda, as relative latecomers to the bounty of the

Atlantic trade, were able to take advantage of accumulated knowledge about the trading relationships among neighboring polities (Kelly 1997a, 2002). The Hueda elite and commoners did not exist in a vacuum, unaware of what was going on elsewhere on the African coast. Indeed, European traders and explorers had visited the region in the early sixteenth century, before the slave trade developed, and continued to pass by the region through the next century and a half, although they did not establish permanent posts because the Slave Coast did not possess the resources desired at that time. Furthermore, the many ethnic and political groups throughout West Africa have long traditions of local and regional trade and interaction. Thus, Hueda people no doubt traveled east and west through the coastal lagoon system, and other coastal people as well as inland dwellers visited the Hueda area also. As astute observers of the consequences of exclusive alliance with specific European trading nations, the Hueda elite were aware of the costs of exclusivity. Instead, and in contrast to most other entrepôt polities engaged in the slave trade, the Hueda actively maintained trading relationships with multiple European trading partners at the same time. By preventing any single European trading partner from dictating the terms of trade (Hair et al. 1992; Law 1991; Van Dantzig 1978), Hueda were in a situation of power and control over the arena of exchange. Thus, direct Hueda control over European traders was an example of the power over others.

This power over Europeans was materialized in a variety of ways (cf. DeMarrais et al. 1996). The clearest, although by no means only, manifestation of this was the way the Hueda used the landscape to reinforce their direct control (Kelly 2002; Kelly and Norman 2007; Norman and Kelly 2004). Among a variety of distinct expressions of power, Hueda required all the European trading companies to have their establishments in the center of the capital town of Savi. Savi lay about 10 km inland, on the inland side of two lagoons that separated the traders from their source of power, the ships that brought European traders and their goods to the West African coast (fig. 5.2). Additionally, and also uniquely, the Hueda prohibited the construction of fortified European trading posts in Savi, insisting that the European lodges be unarmed and defenseless, and only eventually allowed the traders to secure their warehouses at Ouidah, halfway between the coast and Savi.

Historical archaeological research at the site of Savi has identified a series of features of the constructed landscape that show how the Hueda elite manipulated not only landscape features but also the traders, local people, and local elites within that landscape for social ends (Kelly 1997a; Norman 2008). The maps in figures 5.2 and 5.3 show some of these landscape elements,

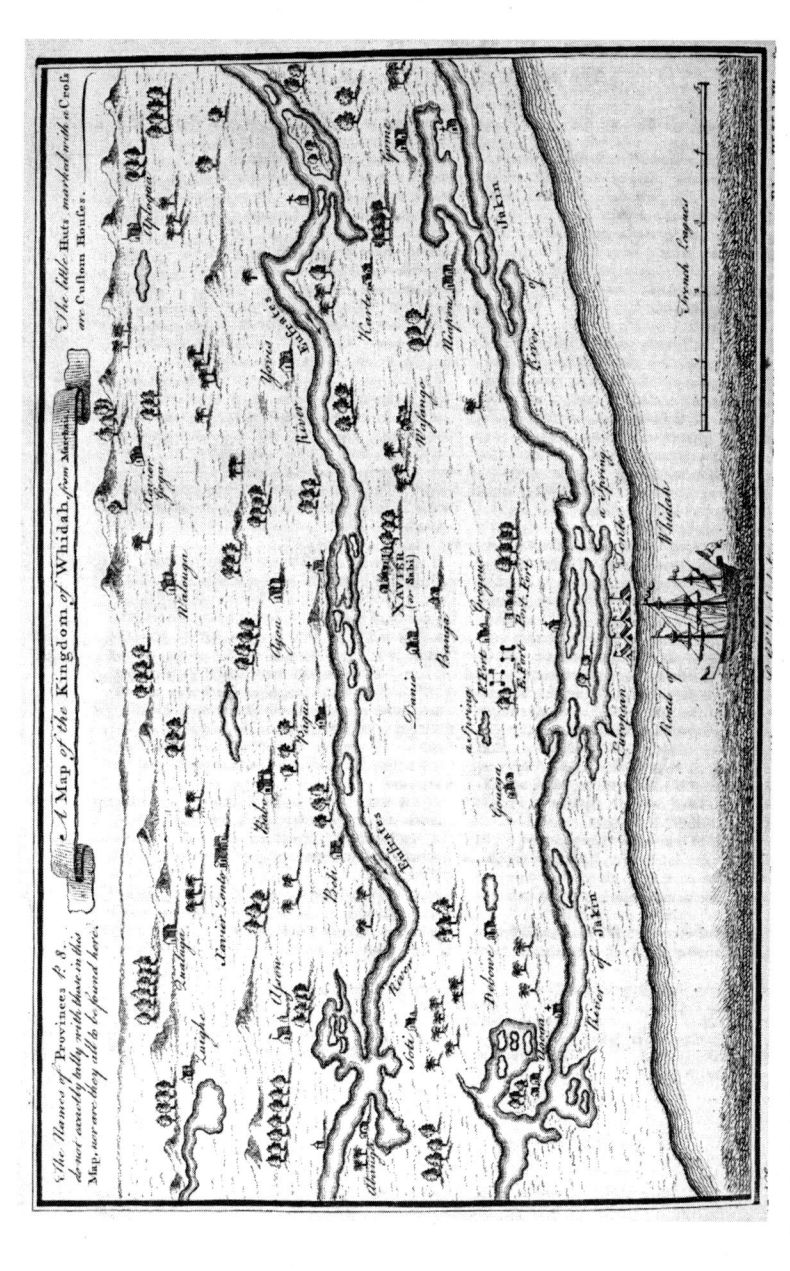

Figure 5.2 Period depiction of the location of Savi, inland from the coast along the Bight of Benin. From Thomas Astley, *A New General Collection of Voyages and Travels* (1746).

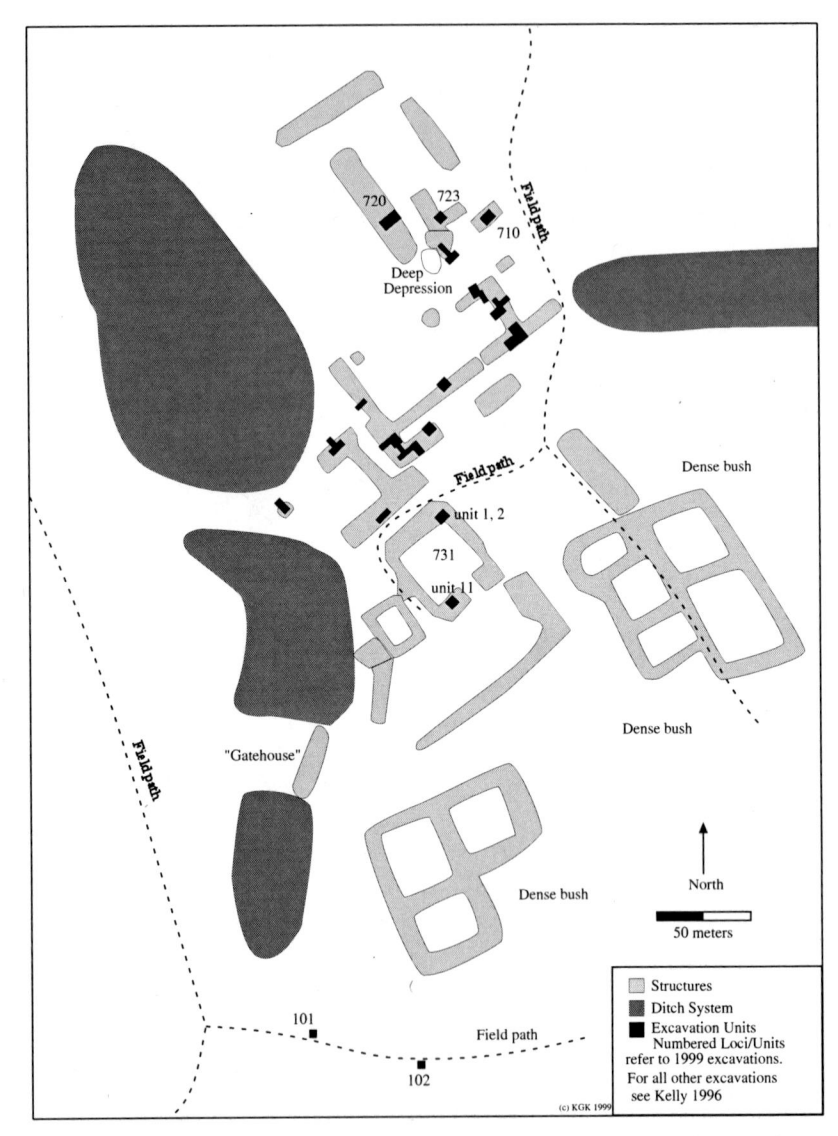

Figure 5.3 Map of archaeologically defined features in the central area of Savi. Map by the author.

including the lagoons, the site of Savi, and the archaeological features within it. What is more important, however, is to attempt to understand how this manipulation of people and landscape *felt* to individuals and groups, whether they were transients or residents in it. By creating a situation in which the European traders were continually placed at a disadvantage, the Hueda elite were able to engineer the trade setting to their advantage (Hair et al. 1992:644; Jones 1985:191; Van Dantzig 1978:180). Of course there were and are many ways of perceiving this arena of action, and by using a combination of travelers' accounts and archaeological data, we can view it from the general perspective of the European traders and get some idea of how their presence was used to social ends in ways they did and, and perhaps equally important, did not recognize (fig. 5.4).

When compared with the depictions of other trading establishments along the coast, which usually show European forts with bastioned walls bristling with cannon overlooking the sea roadsteads, where trading ships and warships ride at anchor, the few views of European structures in the principal Hueda towns are conspicuous in their lack of defensive posture (fig. 5.5). The location of the trading lodges, more than 10 km inland from one of the most dangerous landing spots on the West African coast, across several lagoons and far beyond sight of the trading ships, must have conveyed isolation and an unaccustomed degree of helplessness. Furthermore, the lodges were crowded in the center of a town in excess of 4 km in diameter and with a population of perhaps 20,000 people (Kelly 1995). Although in the center of the town, the lodges were not part of it. They were separated from the rest of the town, isolated by an extensive system of ditches and watchtowers. These ditches, as much as 5 m deep, were only bridged by a few causeways, and archaeological evidence suggests that these were controlled by gatehouses. At various points along the ditch system stood watchtower platforms that placed the European traders under constant surveillance.

In addition to using the landscape to place the European traders so that they would clearly recognize that they were not in charge, the Hueda elite used material culture to convey and symbolize relationships of power. Although they had brought their own building materials, the European trading lodges were built by the Hueda to conform to local custom for elite housing, with earthen walls and floors and thatched roofs (Kelly 1995:273–275, 277–78; see fig. 5.5). A letter written in 1705 describes the European attitudes in reference to the Dutch lodge at Savi: "Look at our lodge there! We could not compare it with anything better than a peasant's cow-stable and hovel..." (Van Dantzig 1978:letter 119). Bosman (1705:366) makes the point that the Hueda controlled the construction of buildings abundantly clear by writing, also in 1705, about "our lodging here, which the king caused to be built for me..."; a letter in 1709 stated that "the king is obliged, according to promises and agreements, to maintain the lodge..." (Van Dantzig 1978:letter 158). By providing the buildings, the Hueda elite denied the Europeans the opportunity to use their own architectural forms to control the region symbolically, as

Figure 5.4 Period depiction of the coronation of the king of Hueda in 1725. Note the privileged location of the European traders and how they appear to be placed on display. From Thomas Astley, *A New General Collection of Voyages and Travels* (1746).

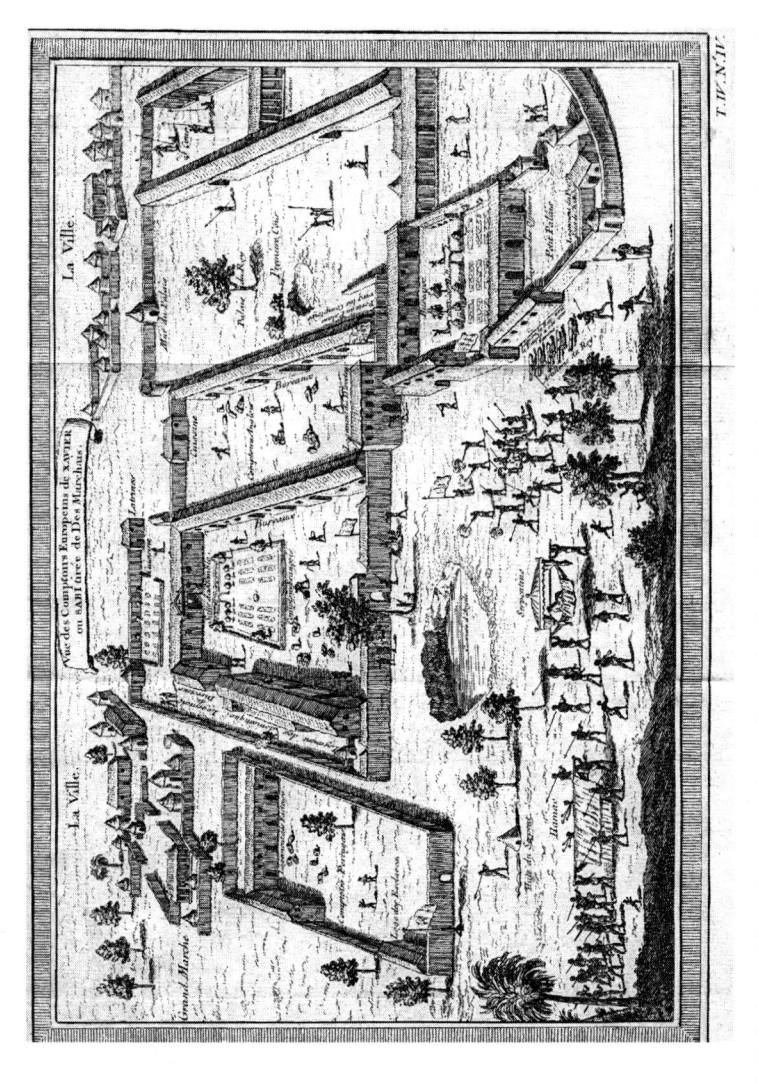

Figure 5.5 Period view of the palace complex and associated traders' lodges in the center of the town of Savi. Note both the lack of defensive measures and the conspicuous display of a number of European cannon outside the entrance to the palace. From J.-B. Labat, *Voyage du Chevalier des Marchais en Guinée, isles voisines et à Cayenne, fait en 1725, 1726 et 1727* (1731).

was clearly the case elsewhere along the coast, where European trade castles were erected to symbolize European control.

Additionally, the lodges at Savi were all situated adjacent to one another and literally incorporated into the palace complex of the Hueda king. The architecture of the Hueda palace, with massive buildings up to 100 m long arranged around spacious courtyards (see figs. 5.3 and 5.5), conveyed a sense of superiority. Although constructed of earth in the traditional manner, and therefore similar to the lodges provided to the Europeans, archaeological evidence recovered from the Hueda palace buildings shows the incorporation of European architectural elements, such as brick or tile floors and bricked archways on the doors (see Kelly 1995, 1997b for elaboration of this argument). These were built with building supplies imported by the Europeans for their use and confiscated by the Hueda elite for their own use. Thus when European traders met with Hueda officials, they were constantly reminded of their tenuous status and position. Not only were the European traders housed in inferior, unfortified quarters under the walls of the Hueda palace, but they were also confronted by the presence of an arsenal of cannons publicly displayed and used by the Hueda elite to demonstrate their power (see fig. 5.5). Probably without realizing exactly how, the European traders found themselves enmeshed in a system of symbolism that was using their presence and, importantly, the wealth opportunities they brought to express social relations and realities to other Europeans. Furthermore, and perhaps more importantly, the manipulation of the traders was materialized to others who also frequented the town of Savi and its important regional market. The Hueda elite used the European presence to communicate essential elements of status to their neighbors and rivals, posing the question of whether the traders or the trade were of primary importance. In fact, given the way the European traders were employed, their presence became a key aspect of Hueda identity.

The Hueda were adept at creating a system though which they signaled their unique status as a polity to their neighbors and residents expressly through the social meanings of their trade (Kelly 1997b). Other African visitors, whether from the slave source regions to the north or from the polities to the east and west along the lagoon system, were able to read clearly the symbolism of the way the European traders were manipulated and presented in the trade arena of the Savi palace and marketplace. Although the European traders were probably unaware of their role in this presentation of identity, it is highly likely that many of the behaviors and activities of the Hueda elite were easily read by other Africans. Nonetheless, there were certainly occasions when European traders were aware of their being used, such as when Bulfinch Lambe was seized by the King of Dahomey as security for an unpaid debt (Law 1990:218). Trader William Snelgrave may well have been aware of the uses to which European traders were put when he noted that on one occasion European traders in audience with the King were allowed to sit on chairs but on another occasion were made to use mats on the ground (Law 1990:223). Additionally, the seemingly irrational (from the European perspective) use of valuable weaponry not to wage war but as communicative material culture and the appropriation of building materials are but two of many examples of the Hueda elite incorporating trade items in ways that engaged their multivalency (Kelly 2002).

The Dahomean Arena

Proof of the efficacy of the Hueda presentation of the meanings they attached to the presence of the traders is demonstrated through the subsequent success that the Dahomey enjoyed when they decided to consolidate the trade system under their own political control. The Hueda elite became so enraptured with the cleverness of their own manipulation of the social significance of their exchange partners that they grew oblivious to the risks that their behaviors presented. They should have recognized the growing threat to their autonomy when their former overlords, at Allada, were conquered by Dahomey in 1724 as it expanded from its homeland to the north. The Hueda should have recognized that the power of their relationship with the Europeans was not invincible. But they did not—their identity was too wrapped up in who they thought they were, invincible, clever, and able to manipulate the trade arena to their distinct advantage. They overlooked the rising challenge to the north, and when Dahomey attacked Savi on March 9, 1727, the Hueda had not even posted a guard, so convinced were they of their power, in spite of considerable evidence of coming hostilities (Law 1990, 1991; Norman 2008).

The elite and bureaucracy of Dahomey, however, were not oblivious to the strategies that had been successful for the Hueda (see Monroe 2003 for a detailed discussion of the growth and power of the Dahomean bureaucratic court). The Dahomey elites were quick to see that their identity as a sovereign trading state was also intimately linked to the presence of European traders. Indeed, the degree to which Dahomey was fundamentally tied to the presence of Europeans is made clear by the iconography chosen as the principal symbol of conquering King Agadja. To this day the European sailing ship is associated with Agadja because it was he who brought the power of trade control to the Kingdom of Dahomey. Yet despite Dahomey's recognition of the fundamental role that Europeans played in their political and social survival, the new rulers also saw the dangers of being too tightly associated with the traders. Following the success of the Hueda, the Dahomey recognized the importance of prohibiting any single European nation from achieving a trading monopoly. The Dahomey also recognized the potential danger of inviting the European traders into their capital towns on the Abomey plateau in the interior and avoided it by confining the traders to the location of their warehouses between Savi and the sea in the town that became Ouidah. In a departure from the Hueda, the Dahomey chose not to incorporate the presence of European traders into the construction of their political identity in their capital. Instead, Europeans were very rarely permitted to travel to Abomey, although statecraft and other activities of the capital and the elite occasionally included Europeans in meaningful ways (Law 1991; Monroe 2003).

One example of the way that Dahomey incorporated Europeans into its social symbology was through the events known to Europeans as the Annual Customs (Law 1991). This ceremony, which included ritual processions, sacrifices, and above all, a great potlatch-like distribution of accumulated wealth, much of it in the form of goods brought by Europeans, was one of the key events of the ritual calendar and the only one in which a European presence played a significant role (fig. 5.6). During the course of the redistribution of wealth from a high platform to the masses thronging below, the European traders were invited to take places adjacent to the king of Dahomey and his assorted nobles. The Europeans probably thought that their presence on the dais with the king was a symbol of respect for them; however, if we think of their presence as similar to the way the Hueda manipulated the European traders and read it through the eyes of the African observers, then the manipulation of the traders by Dahomey becomes clear. The Europeans were being displayed as a prestige good, just like the silk cloaks and firearms used in ceremonies and the beads and other goods distributed to the masses.

A second example can be seen in the second half of the nineteenth century, when Europeans were beginning to establish missions and other church-related activities in the areas where they were economically involved and soon would be politically and administratively as well. When a Catholic church was built in Ouidah, the town to which Europeans and their trading activities were confined, it was situated with care between the compound of the Yovogan, the second highest-ranking Dahomey official, and the principal temple of one of the most important deities in the region. These two religious structures still exist today, locked in ideological combat in the center of Ouidah, with the site of the Yovogan (now the police station)

Figure 5.6 Period illustration of the Annual Customs in Abomey, capital of Dahomey. Note that the European traders are placed on display here, as they were nearly a century earlier in Savi (see fig. 5.4). From A. Dalzel, *The History of Dahomy, An Inland Kingdom of Africa* (1793).

directly north of the Catholic church, blocking access to the Dahomey interior and capital (Kelly 2002).

Conclusion: Looking out for Number One

This evidence of space, architecture, and proxemics at Savi and Ouidah over a two-hundred-year span clearly demonstrates that in the view of the Hueda and Dahomey elite, the Europeans who brought trade goods were as important a commodity as the goods themselves. Furthermore, the European trading presence was a commodity that was consumed by Hueda and Dahomey to exercise social power, as were the goods. European traders were obliged to participate in these exercises of social power but not necessarily in ways they fully understood. Yet the European traders had no choice but to put up with awkward circumstances of being defenseless and removed from the coast, because in their view the value of the trade was worth it. Clearly for the

Europeans, the trade in which they engaged with Dahomey and Hueda was motivated by economic gain, which was probably also the primary motive for their African partners. However, we must be careful to recognize that the trade encounter could also have significant social meanings not shared by both parties. By situating the participants in this interaction with a context closely informed by sources as varied as contemporary accounts, landscape, architecture, and material culture, archaeologists can tease out relationships between trade contacts and the creation and maintenance of identities that would otherwise remain obscure.

The arena of interaction engaged in by European and African traders on the West African coast was a complicated place, where relationships between individuals and groups were fraught with meanings, many of which were apparent to some or all of the various participants. However, this was also an arena in which many performed, often in ways they did not understand. What is clear from our perspective is that the process of exchange was a key element in the formation of the identities of the all the parties who took part, whether they knew it or not.

References

Adams, Robert McC.
1974 Anthropological Perspectives on Ancient Trade. *Current Anthropology* 15:239–258.

Blanton, Richard E., Gary M. Feinman, Stephen A. Kowalewski, and Peter N. Peregrine
1996 A Dual-Processual Theory for the Evolution of Mesoamerican Civilization. *Current Anthropology* 37(1):1–14.

Bosman, W.
1705 *A New and Accurate Description of the Coast of Guinea, Divided into the Gold, the Slave, and the Ivory Coasts*. J. Knapton, London.

Brumfiel, Elizabeth M., and Timothy K. Earle
1987 Specialization, Exchange, and Complex Societies: An Introduction. In *Specialization, Exchange, and Complex Societies*, edited by E. M. Brumfiel and T. K. Earle, pp. 1–9. Cambridge University Press, Cambridge.

Coquery-Vidrovitch, C.
1969 Recherches sur un mode de production africain. *La Pensée* 144:61–78.

DeMarrais, E., Luis Jaime Castillo, and Timothy Earle
1996 Ideology, Materialization, and Power Strategies. *Current Anthropology* 37(1):15–31.

Earle, Timothy
1991 Property Rights and the Evolution of Chiefdoms. In *Chiefdoms: Power, Economy, and Ideology*, edited by T. Earle, pp. 71–99. Cambridge University Press, Cambridge.

Earle, Timothy
2002 *Bronze Age Economics: The Beginnings of Political Economies*. Westview Press, Boulder, Colorado.

Hair, P., Adam Jones, and Robin Law (editors)
1992 *Barbot on Guinea: The Writings of Jean Barbot on West Africa 1678–1712*. Hakluyt Society, London.

Jones, Adam
1985 *Brandenburg Sources for West African History, 1680–1700*. Franz Steiner Verlag, Wiesbaden.

Kelly, Kenneth G.
1995 Transformation and Continuity in Savi, A West African Trade Town: An Archaeological Investigation of Culture Change on the Coast of Bénin during the 17th and 18th Centuries. Unpublished PhD Dissertation, Department of Anthropology, University of California, Los Angeles.
1997a Using Historically Informed Archaeology: Seventeenth and Eighteenth Century Hueda/European Interaction on the Coast of Bénin. *Journal of Archaeological Method and Theory* 4(3/4):353–366.
1997b The Archaeology of African-European Interaction: Investigating the Social Roles of Trade, Traders, and the Use of Space in the Seventeenth and Eighteenth Century Hueda Kingdom, Republic of Benin. *World Archaeology* 28(3):77–95.
2001 Change and Continuity in Coastal Bénin. In *West Africa During the Atlantic Slave Trade: Archaeological Perspectives*, edited by C. R. DeCorse, pp. 81–100. Leicester University Press, Leicester, UK.
2002 Indigenous Responses to Colonial Encounters on the West African Coast: Hueda and Dahomey from the 17th through 19th Centuries. In *The Archaeology of Colonialism*, edited by C. L. Lyons and J. Papadopoulos, pp. 96–120. Getty Research Institute, Los Angeles.

Kelly, Kenneth G., and Neil Norman
2007 Historical Archaeologies of Landscape in Atlantic Africa. In *Envisioning Landscape: Situations and Standpoints in Archaeology and Heritage*, edited by L. M. Dan Hicks and Graham Fairclough, pp. 172–193. Left Coast Press, Walnut Creek, California.

Law, Robin
1990 Further Light on Bulfinch Lambe and the "Emperor of Pawpaw": King Agaja of Dahomey's Letter to King George I of England, 1726. *History in Africa* 17:211–226.
1991 *The Slave Coast of West Africa, 1550–1750: The Impact of the Atlantic Slave Trade on an African Society*. Clarendon Press, Oxford.

McIntosh, Susan K.
1999 Pathways to Complexity: An African Perspective. In *Beyond Chiefdoms: Pathways to Complexity in Africa*, edited by Susan K. McIntosh, pp. 1–30. Cambridge University Press, Cambridge.

Monroe, J. Cameron
2003 The Dynamics of State Formation: The Archaeology and Ethnohistory of Pre-Colonial Dahomey. Unpublished PhD dissertation, Department of Anthropology. University of California, Los Angeles.

Monroe, J. Cameron
2007 Continuity, Revolution or Evolution on the Slave Coast of West Africa? Royal Architecture and Political Order in Precolonial Dahomey. *Journal of African History* 48:349–373.

Norman, Neil. L.
2008 An Archaeology of West African Atlanticization: Regional Analysis of the Huedan Palace Districts and Countryside (Bénin), 1650–1727. Unpublished PhD dissertation, Department of Anthropology. University of Virginia, Charlottesville.

Norman, Neil, and Kenneth G. Kelly
2004 Landscape Politics: The Serpent Ditch and the Rainbow in West Africa. *American Anthropologist* 106(1):98–110.

Polanyi, Karl
1966 *Dahomey and the Slave Trade: An Analysis of an Archaic Economy*. University of Washington Press, Seattle.

Polanyi, Karl, Conrad M. Arensberg, and Harry W. Pearson (editors)
1957 *Trade and Market in the Early Empires: Economies in History and Theory*. Henry Regnery Company, Chicago.

Renfrew, A. Colin
1975 Trade as Action at a Distance: Questions of Integration and Communication. In *Ancient Civilization and Trade*, edited by J. A. Sabloff and C. C. Lamberg-Karlovsky, pp. 3–60. University of New Mexico Press, Albuquerque.
1986 Introduction: Peer-Polity Interaction and Socio-Political Change. In *Peer-Polity Interaction and Socio-Political Change*, edited by C. Renfrew and J. F. Cherry, pp. 1–18. Cambridge University Press, Cambridge.

Rivallain, J.
1977 Le sel dans les villages côtiers et lagunaires du Bas Dahomey: Sa fabrication, sa place dans le circuit du sel africain. *West African Journal of Archaeology* 7:143–169.

Ross, D.
1987 The Dahomean Middleman System, 1727 – c. 1818. *Journal of African History* 28(3):357–375.

Rowlands, M.
1987 Power and Moral Order in Precolonial West-Central Africa. *Specialization, Exchange, and Social complexity*, edited by E. M. Brumfiel and Timothy K. Earle, pp. 52–63. Cambridge University Press, Cambridge.

Sabloff, Jeremy A., and C. C. Lamberg-Karlovsky (editors)
1975 *Ancient Civilization and Trade*. University of New Mexico Press, Albuquerque.

Schortman, Edward M., and Patricia A. Urban (editors)
1992 *Resources, Power, and Interregional Interaction*. Plenum Press, New York.

Stein, Gil J.
2002 From Passive Periphery to Active Agents: Emerging Perspectives in the Archaeology of Interregional Interaction. *American Anthropologist* 104(3):903–916.

Thomas, Nicholas
1991 *Entangled Objects: Exchange, Material Culture, and Colonialism in the Pacific*. Harvard University Press, Cambridge, Massachusetts.

Van Dantzig, A.
1978 *The Dutch and the Guinea Coast, 1674–1742: A Collection of Documents from the General State Archive at The Hague*. Ghana Academy of Arts and Sciences, Accra.

Wallerstein, Immanuel
1974 *Capitalist Agriculture and the Origins of the European World-Economy in the Sixteenth Century*. Academic Press, New York.

CHAPTER 6

Greeks and Phoenicians: Perceptions of Trade and Traders in the Early First Millennium BC

Susan Sherratt

If we are interested in trying to understand the social contexts of prehistoric trade and exchange, one of the most important aspects that has to be considered is the way in which traders (and the goods they traded) were perceived by those with whom they came in contact and by those who were the recipients (either directly or indirectly) of those traded goods.[1] This is a particularly important question in the context of long-distance maritime trade, involving encounters between people from different cultural backgrounds whose home bases were separated by long distances, in an environment in which most people did not travel. In cases in which such encounters took place with a modicum of regularity over a more or less prolonged stretch of time, we may expect the resulting relationships to have been dynamic rather than static (see Urban, chapter 10, this volume), with concomitant implications for changes in the perceptions involved. Thus, for instance, goods that may initially have seemed highly exotic and on that account valuable may eventually have come to be devalued, while increasing familiarity may have lessened the mystique of those who brought them, along with the credulity of their recipients.

Much of this dynamism will have depended on perceptions of the advantages or disadvantages of engaging with long-distance traders, not just at the level of individuals, groups, or whole communities but also within the context of changing perceptions of the norms and values of a wider world and the place of individuals, groups, and communities within it. For instance, the question of exploitation, often raised in the context of core-periphery relationships in a "world-systems" perspective, essentially comes down to one of relative perception: as long as a periphery does not think it is being exploited and sees only mutual advantage in exchanges with a core, from the former's point of view there is no exploitation. It is only once the periphery has adopted the economic and cultural values of the core that the possibility of a perception of exploitation can arise.

Unfortunately, however, these kinds of perceptions are not something that the archaeological record on its own can often shed light on directly, with the result that archaeologists are usually left to draw oblique, generalized—and often arguably rather crude and flat-footed—inferences from such limited types of information as the ways in which exotic objects or materials were deployed by recipient communities, the kinds of depositional contexts (deliberate or accidental) in which they are found, and the extent to which they seem to have had an effect on the material culture of the recipient society. Archaeologists do their best to elaborate theoretical models based on historical or ethnographic data culled from other times and places to help them interpret these sorts of archaeological observations. However, much of the time it comes down to a question of guessing not only about how exotic goods were perceived by recipient communities in prehistory but also more importantly about how the goods got there and who precisely brought them—factors that must in themselves have had a considerable effect on how they were received and the perceptions that surrounded them.

The Greek Early Iron Age (that is, the early centuries of the first millennium BC) offers an unusual opportunity to investigate some of these problems and to get beyond the impasse that they usually present in several ways: first of all, by drawing attention to the importance of perceptions where long-distance maritime trade or exchange was concerned; and second, by revealing just what a fundamental effect such perceptions—and the activities that gave rise to them—could have on the long-term construction of identities of whole societies and the way they viewed the outside world. This view of identity is based on the principle that conscious group identity is invariably dependent on contact and that increasingly sharply defined identities (both of one's own group and of those in relation to which it is defined) result from encounters on an increasing scale. Although this process can operate at a variety of different levels, it is often associated with specialized subgroups carrying out a specific economic role (for example, see Artzy 1998; Bauer 1998, 2006; cf. Sherratt and Sherratt 1998). A feeling of being locked into interaction with such a group on the part of others (particularly when the interaction is no longer seen as wholly advantageous) or economic competition with it can both harden the edges of the group's externally perceived identity and precipitate the definition of new identities that are defined quite specifically in relation to this perception.

The opportunity to examine this process more directly arises because in the case of the Greek Early Iron Age we are not solely reliant on the archaeological record but also have an ideologically powerful source through which to approach it, in the form of the Homeric epics, the *Iliad* and the *Odyssey*.[2] It is widely acknowledged that these epics, which were created or emerged in some sort of recognizable form roughly around the end of the eighth century BC, have a great deal to do with the process of creating and defining a new sense of collective Greek identity that can also be detected in various aspects of the archaeological record at that time (see, e.g., Nagy 1979:1–11; Osborne 1996:157; also Winter 1995; Sherratt 1996. The epics also formed the basis of Greek moral education from an early period).

Aspects of the archaeological record of the late eighth century that have a bearing on the definition of a new sense of collective Greek identity at one level or another include the introduction of the Greek alphabet; the foundation of politically motivated colonies in the central Mediterranean, in a zone which rapidly became well differentiated from that of earlier or contemporary Phoenician colonies; the growth of supraregional sanctuaries; activity in and around much earlier Mycenaean chamber tombs; a growing interest in the depiction of specific narrative scenes; and the possible foundation of hero cults. Of these, the last three, like the Homeric epics, are particularly relevant to the creation and formulation of the idea of a shared "past" (see, e.g., Sherratt 2003:237–238).

Given the epics' success in this respect, it is inconceivable that this past, though first and foremost a product of its own time, could simply have been invented out of nothing in the eighth century. Instead, like all successful and consensual pasts, it depended on containing what its audiences knew intuitively to be true through the inclusion of a composite buildup of inherited beliefs, values, and attitudes accumulated in popular consciousness over an extended period.

The aim of this paper is to look very briefly at one aspect of the Homeric epics that may be argued to have a particular bearing not only on the impetus behind the emergence of a collective sense of Greek identity in the later eighth century but also on the form that identity took, the particular view of the outside world that it entailed, and the "others" in relation to whom it was defined. Maritime trade and perceptions of particular kinds of traders and the goods they traded, as well as their general maritime activities, played a large part in this process, as I hope to show. Moreover, it is possible to trace some of the history of these perceptions through a combination of textual analysis and the judicious tracking of aspects of the archaeological record. In this way, these perceptions can probably be related to a more or less prolonged process of ethnogenesis—in this case, what might be termed the double genesis of Greeks and those whom Greeks called "Phoenicians."

Literary Perceptions of Phoenicians

It is well known that the name "Phoenician," as we know it, is an entirely Greek invention that is first encountered in this form in the Homeric epics. The people whom the historical Greeks called Phoenicians did not call themselves Phoenicians and very probably did not identify themselves collectively at all. They identified themselves as the inhabitants of individual cities (Sidon, Tyre, Byblos, Arvad, and so on; fig. 6.1), which is also predominantly how the Hebrew bible sees them. Although the word *phoinikios* appears on the Greek-language Linear B tablets of the fourteenth and thirteenth centuries BC (see Aura Jorro 1985, s.v. *po-ni-ki-ja* and so on), there is no indication that it is thought of as an ethnonym or even that it has any particular geographical reference. This means that, even though the earlier word is probably related etymologically, the first Greek use of "Phoenician" to refer to people probably dates to somewhere between 1200 and 700 BC. In fact, the word very likely does have something to do with the word *phoinix*, which is used quite liberally in the epics (as well as on the Linear B tablets) to denote the color red or purple; and it may well come from an association with the murex-dyed red or purple textiles that formed such an important industry in East Mediterranean coastal cities from at least the end of the second millennium. If so, it should probably remind us that such textiles may well have formed a conspicuous (but archaeologically invisible) component of the eastern manufactured products that reached the Aegean on eastern ships, possibly as early as the twelfth century BC.

In some respects we get a relatively clear picture of the people called Phoenicians in the epics (especially in the *Odyssey*), particularly their range of exclusively maritime-based activities of various sorts and their areas of operation. They are presented as maritime trampers, away from home for a year or more at a time.[3] On arrival in one place, they sell the goods they are carrying and then hang around until they have amassed a new cargo to take on and sell somewhere else. They act as convenient maritime taxi drivers, willing to pick up passengers; but they are also not averse to the odd act of kidnapping, slave dealing, theft, and even murder. We hear of them operating in the East Mediterranean, on the Levantine coast, in the Nile delta, and further west in Libya, as well as on Crete (where it is evidently quite easy

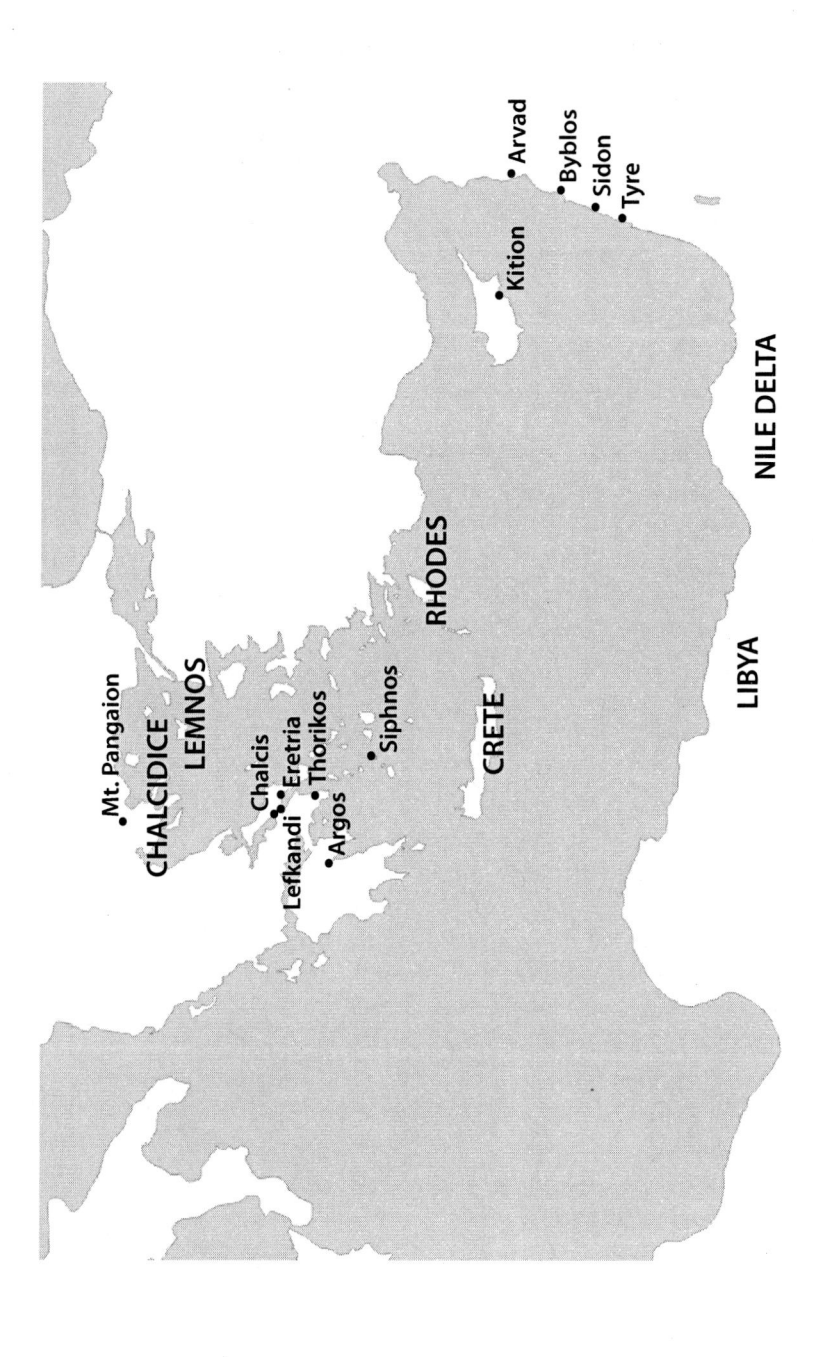

Figure 6.1 Map showing places mentioned in the text.

to pick up a Phoenician ship when needed), up the west coast of Greece, and in the northeastern Aegean.

In other respects, however, the picture of Phoenicians seems anomalous and contradictory. In some passages they are clearly regarded as the same as Sidonians (the inhabitants of Sidon); but in other passages they are clearly differentiated from them. Attitudes toward them, particularly in the *Odyssey*, also seem contradictory. Whereas the Phoenicians who seduce the Phoenician nurse of the baby Eumaios and successfully bribe her to help them kidnap him are portrayed as thorough rats (*Odyssey* xv.415–484), in other instances (particularly through the eyes of Odysseus, disguised as a Cretan), they are seen as admirable, at times well-meaning and honest, and—although not perhaps entirely to be trusted—useful to know and profitable to spend some time with. It also seems that these Homeric Phoenicians are among those characterized, at least by implication, as *allothrooi*—that is, speaking some other (i.e., non-Greek) language, or strictly speaking, "making other unintelligible noises," since the word *allothroos* has virtually the same meaning as the Greek word "barbarian" and has almost identical connotations of a language-focused distinction between those who think of themselves as Greeks and everyone else (Sherratt 2003).

One thing seems clear: the Greek invention of their own idiosyncratic term "Phoenician," like their earlier, second-millennium invention of the ethnonym "Cypriot" (*kyprios*), almost certainly means that Greek-speakers first encountered the people to whom they gave this name primarily and probably exclusively in Aegean waters. Moreover, some of the curious anomalies in terminology suggest that what we have in the epics is a composite picture of Phoenicians, incorporating different Greek perceptions of and attitudes toward the characters to whom they gave this name. These perceptions and attitudes accumulated in popular consciousness over a fairly long period and both contributed to and were determined by a developing Greek view of their own collective identity as much as by any objective reality in the East Mediterranean. The characterization of Phoenicians in the *Iliad*, for instance, as the carriers and traders of craft goods made by Sidonians, from whom in this case they are clearly differentiated,[4] suggests that, at one end of the chronological spectrum, the name "Phoenician" was probably first applied on the basis of the maritime activities of easterners in Aegean waters, rather than any real or precise knowledge of (or interest in) where they might have come from or who precisely they were. In this sense, it could as well have applied to any East Mediterranean mariners as to those whom they later recognized as Phoenicians.

Equally striking, however, is the complete absence in the epics of any mention of Tyrians or Tyre, one of the most active and powerful of the Phoenician cities, particularly from the mid-eleventh century BC onward, and the one most implicated in the westward expansion of Phoenician trade and colonization in the Mediterranean (Aubet 1993, 2000). This absence contrasts with the prominence of Sidonians and suggests that at some point (probably quite early in its use), the name "Phoenicians" may have come to be applied chiefly to the inhabitants of Tyre. If so, this naming is quite likely to have occurred when regular Tyrian maritime activity began to take off in the Aegean, probably from around the second half of the eleventh century and certainly no later than the tenth century, when by far the majority of the earliest Aegean pottery imports to the East Mediterranean can be seen to head straight for Tyre or Tyrian-dominated sites in the southern Levant (see, for example, Aubet 2000; Coldstream 1989, especially fig. 1a; Coldstream 1998).

The identification of Phoenicians with Sidonians seems to suggest a still later stage, probably no earlier than the eighth century BC, when the name was beginning to take on the meaning that it has in later Greek literature—that is, a single undifferentiated Phoenician people inhabiting a considerable chunk of the coastal Levant. Even more interesting and probably part of the same process is the introduction of the fictional concept of a "Phoenicia" as a distinct territorial homeland for the Phoenicians, which appears a couple of times in the *Odyssey* (iv.83; xiv.291). This development seems particularly significant in view of the role of the Homeric epics in helping to shape the idea of a single Greek people united by a single Greek language and occupying a single Greece or Hellas, all concepts that can already be detected in the epics in explicit or implicit symbolic form.

As far as the concept of a single Hellas, which appears fully fledged in the seventh-century writings of Hesiod (*Works and Days* 653), is concerned, we can glimpse it in the curious phrase *Hellas kai meson Argos* (something like "Hellas and Argos in the middle," although effectively untranslatable), which occurs several times in the *Odyssey* (i.344; iv.726, 816; xv.80) and is quite clearly intended to mean "all Greece," in the same way that Achaeans, Danaans, and sometimes also Argives are used interchangeably throughout the epics to mean "all Greeks." What seems to be at work in this implied symmetry is the simultaneous creation of a territorially based pan-Phoenicianism (in other words, a single Phoenician people, distinguished from Greeks by language and occupying a single territory called Phoenicia) and the idea of a territorially based panhellenism. To put it another way, these Homeric Phoenicians were the principal other in relation to whom a collective Greek identity was being created and defined.[5]

The Creation of a Stereotype

What is here involved, of course, are stereotypes; and, as needs no pointing out, there is nothing more widely accepted as true in popular consciousness than a stereotype, particularly if it is one made to seem even truer by an inherited accumulation of long-standing beliefs and attitudes. Stereotypes cannot just be invented out of nothing to suit some immediate contemporary purpose, whether this is political, social, literary, or whatever. They have to be based on what people are already conditioned to recognize intuitively. The roots behind the recent (nineteenth- and early twentieth-centuries) historical European stereotype of the wily and faintly sinister oriental trader (or, for that matter, the successful Semitic merchant)—the skillful hustler who could find and sell anything, even his grandmother, if it suited him—may have been diverse and complex in immediate historical terms. However, at least some of these roots originate in a stereotype that we can trace deep in antiquity: the Greek perceptions of Phoenicians that first become apparent in the Homeric epics and arguably also in the archaeological record of Greek interaction with the people of the eastern Mediterranean a few centuries earlier.

This correspondence between the epics and the archaeological record can be illustrated by focusing on some of the specific attributes of Phoenicians and the goods in which they deal in the epics and then looking briefly at how these relate to material actually found in the ground. For the most part, the epics do not tell us much about what their Phoenicians carry, except in the case of the silver krater of Sidonian workmanship that they bring to the island of Lemnos in the *Iliad* and, in the *Odyssey,* in the case of the amber and gold necklace in the cargo of the crew who abduct Eumaios and the golden goblets that his nurse snatches from his father's house as payment for her anticipated passage home with them (*Odyssey* xv.460, 469).

What the epics do tell us, however, is that the Phoenicians carry in their ships countless *athurmata*, a word that derives directly from the word "to play" and is clearly translatable elsewhere in the *Iliad* and *Odyssey* as children's "toys" or "playthings." In the context of Phoenician cargoes, the word is often translated as "trinkets"—and, indeed, this seems not a bad description of the countless faience beads and assorted faience novelties of East Mediterranean origin that are found, for instance, in late tenth- and early ninth-century graves in the cemeteries at Lefkandi on Euboea in the western Aegean (tables 6.1 and 6.2). These are among the objects of East Mediterranean origin that can be associated most plausibly with Phoenician (specifically, perhaps Tyrian) trading activity and that began to appear at sites

Table 6.1 Faience objects in Lefkandi tombs (data from Popham, Sackett, and Themesis 1979–1980; Popham and Lemos 1996).

Date	No. of tombs (including pyres)	No. of tombs with faience	Proportion of tombs with faience	Total faience	Vessels	Rings	Scarabs	Pendants	Beads	Faience objects as proportion of faience of all dates	Notional average of faience objects per tomb	Average of faience objects in tombs with faience
LPG–SPG I ca. 950–875 BC	82	18	21.9	17,360	10	3	2	4	17,341	73.9	212	964
SPG I–II ca. 900–850 BC	11	3	29.2	2,124	0	0	0	4	2,120	9	193	708
SPG II ca. 875–850 BC	21	3	14.2	2,651	0	0	0	1	2,650	11.2	126	883
SPG II–III ca. 875–825 BC	5	2	40	823	0	3	0	0	820	3.5	164	411
SPG III ca. 850–825 BC	11	4	36.3	527	1	0	1	1	524	2.2	48	131

Table 6.2 Rock crystal and amber in Lefkandi tombs (data from Popham, Sackett, and Themelis 1979–1980; Popham and Lemos 1996).

Date	No. of tombs (including pyres)	No. of tombs with rock crystal	Proportion of tombs with rock crystal	Total rock crystal	Beads	Other	Rock crystal objects as proportion of rock crystal of all dates	Notional average per tomb
LPG–SPG I ca. 950–875 BC	82	1	1.2	2	0	2	20	0.02
SPG I–II ca. 900–850 BC	11	0	0	0	0	0	0	0
SPG II ca. 875–850 BC	21	2	9.5	3	1	2	30	0.14
SPG II–III ca. 875–825 BC	5	0	0	0	0	0	0	0
SPG III ca. 850–825 BC	11	3	27.2	5	4	1	50	0.45

Date	No. of tombs (including pyres)	No. of tombs with amber	Proportion of tombs with amber	Total amber	Beads	Inlays	Other	Amber objects as proportion of amber of all dates	Notional average per tomb
LPG-SPG I ca. 950–875 BC	82	1	1.2	1	1	0	0	4.7	0.01
SPG I–II ca. 900–850 BC	11	1	9	4	4	0	0	19	0.36
SPG II ca. 875–850 BC	21	2	9.5	8	4	2	2	38	0.38
SPG II–III Ca. 875–825 BC	5	0	0	0	0	0	0	0	0
SPG III ca. 850–825 BC	11	3	29.2	8	6	0	2	38	0.72

in the Aegean (Rhodes, Crete, and the eastern Greek mainland) from the late eleventh century BC onwards, much the same time that the first Greek (Protogeometric) pottery appeared at Tyre and in areas of the Levant where Tyre was active (Bikai 2000; Coldstream 1998; Coldstream and Catling 1996:721; Hoffman 1997:19–108; Lemos 2002:226–228; Popham 1994).[6]

The appearance of eastern items in Greece and Greek items in the east followed a brief period in the early eleventh century when East Mediterranean objects seemed rare to nonexistent in Greece and there was little sign of active contact between the two areas. There seems little doubt that Tyrian activity in the Aegean area and subsequently further west was motivated mainly by the acquisition of silver, in which Greece is relatively rich. Silver resources that were certainly exploited in this period and earlier can be found on Siphnos in the Cyclades, in eastern Attica (at Thorikos/Laurion), and in the northern Aegean, around Mount Pangaion and the Chalcidice (for production of silver at Thorikos and Argos in the late eleventh to tenth centuries, see Snodgrass 1971:248, 290n34, 378). It seems no coincidence that the site of Lefkandi, which has yielded an impressive number of objects of East Mediterranean origin (including ones of faience, glass, metal, and ivory) between the later eleventh and ninth centuries BC (Popham et al. 1979–1980:217–226, 248–251; Popham and Lemos 1996:Plates 125(e), 132–135, 141–145), lies at a natural choke point on the main maritime route between the eastern Attic and northern Aegean silver sources. By the end of the tenth century, Tyrian ships were traveling as far as Huelva in southwest Spain, close to an area particularly rich in silver (González de Canales et al. 2006). During the ninth century, Tyre began the process of laying political claim to colonies in Cyprus (Kition) and the central Mediterranean (on Sardinia, in western Sicily and along the north African coast) to supply and secure its trade routes and protect them from the depredations or competition of others, including other Phoenician cities and, from the early eighth century, Greeks.

The greatest number and variety of these East Mediterranean faience objects are concentrated, in the Lefkandi cemeteries at least, in the later tenth and early ninth centuries, at a time when faience, while of no very great absolute value in the east, would seem to have carried considerable cachet in the western Aegean. Popham et al. (1979–1980) and Popham and Lemos (1996:Plate 141) present a selection of what can best be called faience novelties from late tenth- and early ninth-century tombs at Lefkandi. By the time the last phase of use of these cemeteries was reached in the second half of the ninth century BC, faience objects appeared in a greater proportion of graves but were fewer overall in comparative number and were reduced to the odd pendant, scarab, or necklace of small beads. By contrast, a higher proportion of later than earlier graves contained objects of imported rock crystal and amber (fig. 6.2). These latter (however they got there) suggest that by this time, the occupants of the cemetery were less easily impressed by what could be described as relatively cheap and cheerful man-made exotica and aspired instead to materials of commonly agreed value within a wider interregional economic exchange system—the nature of the value that amber clearly has in the epics, in which a material such as faience is not recognizably mentioned at all. The kinds of perceptions that lie behind this shift may well be encapsulated in the word *athurmata*: a realization that, in the past, the inhabitants of Aegean sites like Lefkandi had been fobbed off with what would be regarded as not much more than the equivalent of children's toys in their place of origin.

At this point, I want to look briefly at a duo of adjectives that are applied only to the Phoenicians in the *Odyssey*, regardless of whether the speaker in whose mouth these adjectives are put is more or less benign or openly hostile toward them. These words are, in the first place, *trōktēs*, and, in the second place, *polypaipalos* and its equivalent, *apatelia eidos*. The first of these, which is sometimes translated generally as "deceivers" or "greedy knaves," derives straight from the verb to "gnaw" and creates a wonderfully graphic impression of rodentlike behavior, conjuring up an image of rats in the grain store or something similar. Richmond Lattimore (1968:236), for example,

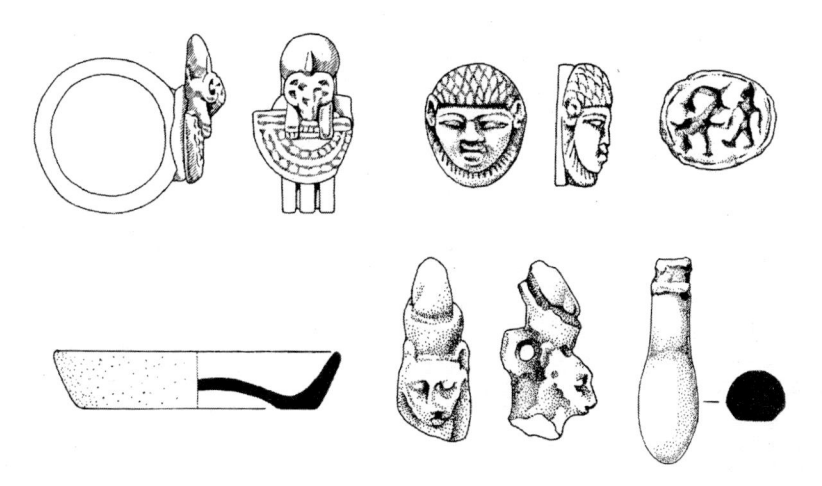

Figure 6.2 Assorted faience objects from Late Protogeometric and Sub-Protogeometric I tombs (c. 950–c.875 BC) in the Toumba cemetery at Lefkandi. After Popham and Lemos 1996, plate 135. Reproduced with permission of the British School at Athens.

translates the word very effectively as "a gnawer of other men's goods." Trōktēs, together with the other accompanying descriptions, which can be translated as "very subtle or crafty" and "skilled in deceit," add up to a very powerful stereotype of Phoenicians. It is a stereotype, moreover, that seems to have a very long life in Greek literature. In the first century BC, the historian Diodorus Siculus, describing early Phoenician activity in Spain in the quest for Spanish silver (which can certainly now be placed no later than the end of the tenth century), tells us: "The natives did not know how to use this metal. But the Phoenicians, experts in commerce, would buy the silver in exchange for some other small goods of little value. Consequently, taking the silver to Greece, Asia and all other peoples, the Phoenicians made great earnings" (Diodorus Siculus V:35). In addition, Diodorus (V:35, 4–5) tells us that the Phoenician merchants were so greedy that they went so far as to replace their lead anchors with silver ones in order to exploit the full carrying capacity of their ships. In this way stereotypes persist and feed on themselves.

Trade and Perceptions of Deception

I now turn to three objects from tenth- and ninth-century graves in Greece (again, as it happens, from Lefkandi) that raise some particularly interesting questions regarding how attitudes toward foreign traders may have developed over time as a result of greater familiarity with some of their practices. One is a bronze krater containing the cremated remains of a male that was found in the so-called Heroon building of mid-tenth century date (Popham et al.1993:87ff.). Another is a gold pendant found around the neck of a woman whose inhumed remains were found beside the cremated man (Popham et al. 1993:15–20). The third is a single plate from a suit of bronze scale armor, which was found in a ninth-century grave in the Skoubris cemetery and evidently last worn as a pendant (Popham et al. 1979–1980: 251, Plate 239[1]). These three items are especially interesting because all are of East Mediterranean origin and all were almost certainly antique or obsolete by the time they found their way into these graves.[7] Apart from the scale plate, which had long been divorced from the rest of the armor, none of them was in the best of condition by the time it was deposited. The rim and handles of the decorated bronze krater, regarded by H. W. Catling as a Cypriot product of perhaps no later than the twelfth century, had already broken in antiquity (Popham et al. 1993:87). Even more curious is the case of the granulated gold pendant, for which very precise parallels are to be found a millennium earlier in Babylonia around 2000 BC (Popham et al. 1993:15). It, too, is in a very damaged state. It has a large hole in its center that was quite clearly there when the pendant went into the ground (fig. 6.3).

Archaeologists are often tempted to label such objects as heirlooms, summoning up visions of their being passed from hand to hand down through the centuries or retained for many generations in the same family. However, it seems much more probable that these objects were already old and damaged by the time they came into the hands of their owners at Lefkandi. Moreover, given their nature and their probable age and state, it seems very likely that they had been removed comparatively recently from tombs somewhere in the East Mediterranean, possibly Cyprus, the Nile delta, or the Levant (perhaps some region like the Beka'a valley, where looted second-millennium tombs supplied a large number of objects for the international art market during the Lebanese civil war). There is, of course, a long and venerable history of tomb robbing in the east. There is clear evidence of it in Near Eastern texts; for example, in an Old Babylonian letter dating from the nineteenth century BC, a man called Adad-abum asks his father to get him a fine string of full beads to wear around his head: "If you have none

Figure 6.3 Gold pendant from female burial in the Heroon building at Lefkandi. From Popham, Touloupa, and Sackett 1982, plate XXIII:b. Reproduced with permission of the British School at Athens.

at hand," he says, "dig it out of the ground wherever such objects are found and send it to me. I want it very much" (Oppenheim 1968:87, quoted in Simpson 2000:6). During Egypt's Third Intermediate period (the period of the early first millennium with which we are particularly concerned), there is plentiful written evidence for illicit looting of tombs as a profitable way of gaining a livelihood (Phillips 1992). That Phoenicians took pains to guard against this sort of activity, probably because some of them engaged in it very successfully themselves, is indicated by the curses often set above the entrances to tombs, such as a ninth-century Phoenician inscription from Cyprus (the so-called Honeyman inscription), perhaps from the Tyrian colony at Kition, which warns of the terrible things that the gods will do to anyone who disturbs the tomb and its owner (Honeyman 1939:106–108n8, Figure 3; Masson and Sznycer 1972:13–20; Sznycer 1980:124).

The point is that anything plucked from a tomb in the East Mediterranean and sold or exchanged elsewhere was pure gain for the person who sold or exchanged it. Whatever it was exchanged for—drinking water, provisions, sex, safe anchorage or landing rights, humble clay pots, or valuable metalwork—the transaction was effectively getting something for nothing. One could compare it with the golden goblets stolen by Eumaios's Phoenician nurse in the *Odyssey* or with Diodorus Siculus's Phoenicians exchanging small objects of little value for Spanish silver. The objects found in early first-millennium Aegean graves, such as those at Lefkandi, suggest that these Homeric (and later Greek) perceptions were not just invented out of nothing.

I have no doubt that a man living in a mud-brick, thatched dwelling in the western Aegean who had a high opinion of his importance in his own community (as the occupant of the Lefkandi "Heroon" certainly had) would have been very glad to receive a large, exotic, fancily decorated bronze krater brought from far overseas and a gold pendant worked in a technique that few in his part of the world had seen and nobody could emulate. The metals, especially the gold, were valuable and worth having in themselves just as materials, and their exotic decorations would certainly have enhanced their value. However, even he could see that these objects had seen better days. No doubt they came accompanied by intriguing associations: This krater once belonged to the King of X, whose descendant Y sends it to his friend at Lefkandi as a present and token of his esteem" or "This pendant once adorned the neck of the royal daughter of Z and was damaged by a thunderbolt cast by the god who once tried to carry her off." It would be possible to have endless fun imagining the kind of stories that might be made up to explain such beaten up objects. However, there is a limit to how long this sort of thing could have gone on being repeated without the recipients rumbling that the true origin of such objects was rather more mundane and considerably less creditable than they once might have been willing to believe. This realization does not mean that they would necessarily have stopped being willing to acquire them, but it might well eventually have changed their perceptions of the characters and motives of those from whom they were acquired. It is easy to see how, in such circumstances, the stereotype of the dishonest but plausible spiv, the ratlike gnawer at the goods of others, could be born. Once the question of serious Greek competition in the kinds of commercial maritime activities carried out by these characters arose, the stereotypes built up gradually over the previous two or three centuries began to serve a very useful purpose.

Conclusion

The upper strata of nineteenth-century British society are often accused of modeling themselves on their own invented stereotype of the classical world, elaborated through their education system, including their idea that commerce, as opposed to landed wealth (or eventually the professions), was not inherently respectable (Wiener 1981).[8] However, this stereotype, which also resonated with attitudes that for historical reasons had characterized large parts of European society since the Middle Ages, was not so much invented as reinforced by more widespread acquaintance with classical writers themselves. The agrarian ideal, whereby a landed gentry was afforded the leisure to play its part in politics and administration and engage in the civilizing pursuit of art and literature, and which had at its core the moral desirability of the self-sufficiency of the well-regulated household economy, permeates the writings of classical authors from Hesiod to Pliny. At best, such perspectives ignored commercial trade and its profit motive as an irrelevant or epiphenomenal activity from the point of view of literate elites; at worst, they condemned it as a potentially corrosive social influence, despite the fact that trade was manifestly just as important to the economic prosperity of the ancient world as to Renaissance city–states or industrial Britain (Sherratt and Sherratt 1998). An antipathy to maritime trade at a purely ideological level can already be glimpsed in the late eighth century BC in Homer's openly ideal land of the Phaiakians, who are portrayed as in many ways the antithesis of his Phoenicians and even, at one point, of his Euboeans, who might equally be supposed to have had a reputation for engaging in maritime trade (*Odyssey* vii.321; see Sherratt 1996).[9]

It is tempting to conclude that the stereotype of untrustworthy, stop-at-nothing Phoenicians, which forms a striking part of their more complex portrayal in the *Odyssey*, played an important role in the early stages of construction of this ideology, as the other that helped shape and define a collective Greek identity, if only of the mind. Notions of self-identity, which exist above all in the mind and are often exploited in the rhetoric of local or regional power advantage, come about through encounters with others, frequently of an economic nature, and are molded by perceptions of such encounters and the circumstances in which they take place; but at every turning, the perceptions are likely to be sharpened and manipulated to create the necessary structural counterpoint.

One thinks here of the rhetoric of "yellow peril" versus "white devils" that characterized relations between Britain and China at the time of and after the nineteenth-century Opium Wars. Moral perspectives apart, this was a rhetoric based in international commercial advantage and its implications for domestic political power. Likewise, Phoenicians in Homer's epics are thus in part a Greek invention, created in the process of defining Greek identity. The rest is a series of perceptions formed by encounters initially in the Aegean and later central Mediterranean waters, hardened into stereotypes and determined not so much by any objective knowledge of Phoenicians in their own home setting but by the activities they were perceived to be engaged in and the implications these had for the growing sense of self-identity of those with whom they interacted. It seems that these activity-based perceptions had an actual grounding in the realities of maritime trade and other activities, even if this factuality was appreciated only gradually and in retrospect by those engaged in hardening their own identity in an increasingly competitive environment. These stereotypes serve to remind us that trade and exchange are not purely economic, and in this sense ideologically neutral, activities, but that economic, social, and ideological issues are closely intertwined. In particular, perceptions of the kinds of people traders are, what they deal in, and how they do it can be implicated in an integral manner in the construction of self-identity and the collective ideology of those with whom they trade.

The Greek Early Iron Age, though to all intents and purposes prehistoric, offers unusual opportunities for the study of such perceptions because of the Homeric epics. Much of the intuitive "memory" that supported the ideological content of the *Odyssey* and the *Iliad* must have roots in this earlier period. In most prehistoric periods, however, we have only the archaeological record to work on, and the question arises of how far we can get in uncovering the contexts of trade and exchange (let alone perceptions of traders) through this alone. In the case of the Lefkandi cemeteries, a certain amount of information can be garnered from diachronic changes in the types and quantities of exotic objects and materials and to some extent from observation of how some of these are deployed in comparison with their deployment in their areas of origin. Though notions of relative value are always very difficult to extract from the archaeological record alone, the decrease in concentrations of more or less mass-produced synthetic faience objects between the late tenth and later ninth centuries, with fewer objects distributed among a greater proportion of tombs, suggests that this material lost some of its value for display purposes among the burial communities of Lefkandi over this period. The observation that faience may have been supplemented over the same period by a slight increase in the exotic natural materials of rock crystal and amber, for which resources remained consistently restricted or far distant and whose limited supply ensured that they were universally regarded as valuable over a wide area, suggests a shift from esteem for exotic novelties for the sake mainly of their exotic nature within a local context and toward a concern for display based on materials of more intrinsically durable and widely recognized value.

In the case of eastern objects, such as the gold pendant and bronze krater from the Heroon burial and the bronze armor scale from one of the later Toumba tombs, their ages combined with their already damaged or (for the last of these) *déraciné* condition alert us to the probability that we are not here dealing with some romantic notion of heirlooms passed down from one indigenous generation to another but with items that had had a checkered history elsewhere, perhaps the most likely explanation being that they were robbed from tombs somewhere in the east. Although the materials of which these were made almost certainly represented durable value to both bringers and recipients, their widely differing ages, the obviously damaged condition of the pendant and krater, and the obscure significance of the single scale divorced from the rest of the armor (of a type unknown in the Aegean) would probably have demanded some inventive explanations on the part of their bringers that differed somewhat from the real ones, even if the objects were presented as outright gifts. What these explanations might have been we can only imagine, but it is quite likely that the items' desirability was enhanced by the provision of glamorous biographies or illustrious associations. Already in the archaeological record, without the aid of texts but with the exercise of a little imagination, we can glimpse some scope for deception or misrepresentation that may eventually have affected perceptions of those who brought them and their activities. It is all the more satisfying, therefore, that the stereotype of those whom the Greeks called Phoenicians should emerge in the *Odyssey* in the form of grasping and deceitful maritime traders whose holds were filled with stolen objects and worthless playthings.

I am not sure that one can extract any clear or simple methodological guidelines from the above, and certainly not ones of general or universal applicability. Each archaeological case in which uncovering the social contexts of trade and perceptions of traders and traded goods is an aim has to be taken on its own terms and looked at closely in whatever can be reconstructed of its own wider context. Archaeological interpretation—particularly where social or ideological aspects are concerned—is always going to be an art rather than a science, and if we want to bring alive those peculiarly human elements that otherwise elude us, we will always have to resort to a certain amount of imagination and tentative dramatic reconstruction. The approach is contingent and alert to the circumstantial, the method trial and error, and the test one of reasonable coherence. What this particular case study, with its additional text-based contribution, can show, however, is that something as nebulous as perception is nevertheless important and can have long-lasting implications for the way whole groups of people see themselves in relation to a wider world.

Notes

1. I offer no apology for using the words "trade" and "traders" in their commonly understood, vernacular sense, regardless of the type of trading mechanisms involved. I do so also regardless of the kind of distinction that anthropologists have often felt compelled to draw between "socially embedded" gift exchange and "disembedded" trade, since this seems to me an essentially artificial distinction. Any form of trade is invariably socially embedded in that it presupposes some sort of relationship between the parties concerned, and even the most profit-motivated of exchanges can be represented as gifts. One need only look, for instance, at the social contacts of those to whom the current British government, with its ostensible belief in allowing primacy to market forces, awards its most valuable contracts or at the gifts necessary for securing a business deal with certain foreign governments to realize how inextricably the social and commercial are often intertwined.
2. The *Iliad* is set in the tenth year of the war against Troy, initiated by a collective Greek expedition in which most regions of what we can recognize as historical Greece were involved, under the leadership of Agamemnon, King of Mycenae, to recover Helen, the wife of Agamemnon's brother Menelaos (King of Sparta) who had been abducted by Paris, a Trojan prince. Its central theme is the honor quarrel between the heroes Agamemnon and Achilles, which results in Achilles sulking in his tent and refusing to fight. It ends, eventually, in the heroic death of Achilles while avenging his friend Patroklos, who was killed while taking his place in battle. The *Odyssey* is set in the years after the successful sack of Troy

and concerns the adventures of another hero of the war, Odysseus, on his journey home to Ithaca—a journey that takes ten years. After wandering far and wide to both real and fantastic places, he returns home via the idealized land of Phaiakia to find his wife Penelope besieged by suitors who have consumed all his flocks and mistreated his son and servants. Using various disguises (in which he invariably represents himself as a Cretan), he reveals himself to some of his most trusted retainers. He defeats the suitors by means of a contest followed by a fight and reclaims his wife and kingdom. A good translation of the *Iliad* is that by Herbert Jordan (Norman, University of Oklahoma Press, 2008).
3. *Odyssey* xv.455–457 (translation R. Lattimore):

> and they [the Phoenicians], with their hollow ship, for the
> whole of a year remaining
> in our country, traded and piled up much substance.
> But when at last their hollow ship was loaded for sailing....

4. *Iliad* xxiii.743–4 concerns a silver mixing-bowl that surpassed all others in loveliness, "since skilled Sidonian craftsmen had wrought it well, and Phoenicians carried it over the misty face of the water and set it in the harbor."
5. For the Phoenicians as the "other" against which Greeks were defining their own collective identity in the later eighth century, see also Winter (1995).
6. For the earliest Levantine ceramic vessel and faience beads in the Early Iron Age Aegean, both from Early Protogeometric tombs at Lefkandi, see Popham et al. (1979–1980:114, 126, 347–348, 418, Plate 270b). For what is probably the earliest Greek Protogeometric fragment from Tyre, see Bikai (1976: plate XXXIX:20) in conjunction with Sherratt in press:n10.
7. For other possible examples of "antique" eastern metalwork deposited in the tombs at Lefkandi, see Carter 1998; Whitley 2002:225–226.
8. I remember my grandmother telling me that in the 1890s in Glasgow, a city built on mercantile enterprise, there were certain schools exclusively for the children of professional people that she, as the daughter of a merchant, would not have been able to attend.
9. In the eighth century BC, Euboean cities such as Chalcis and Eretria were foremost among those establishing trading posts in the central Mediterranean. By the end of the century, they were engaged in founding overtly political colonies in competition not only with Phoenicians, who had been operating in these waters since at least a century earlier, but also with other Greek cities, such as Corinth.

References

Artzy, M.
1998 Routes, Trade, Boats and "Nomads of the Sea." In *Res Maritimae: Cyprus and the Eastern Mediterranean from Prehistory to Late Antiquity*, edited by S. Swiny, R. L. Hohlfelder, and H. W. Swiny, pp. 439–448. Cyprus American Archaeological Research Institute Monograph 1. Scholars Press, Atlanta.

Aubet, M. E.
1993 *The Phoenicians and the West: Politics, Colonies and Trade*. Translated by M. Turton. Cambridge University Press, Cambridge.

Aubet, M. E.
2000 Aspects of Tyrian trade and colonization in the eastern Mediterranean. *Münstersche Beiträge zur antiken Handelsgeschichte* 19:70–120.

Aura Jorro, F.
1985 *Diccionario Micénico*. Instituto de Filología, Madrid.

Bauer, A.
1998 Cities of the Sea: Maritime Trade and the Origin of Philistine Settlement in the Early Iron Age Southern Levant. *Oxford Journal of Archaeology* 17:149–168.
2006 Maritime Interaction and Cultural Identity in the Bronze Age Black Sea. Unpublished PhD dissertation, Department of Anthropology, University of Pennsylvania.

Bikai, P. M.
1976 Tyre: Report of an Excavation, 1973–1974. Unpublished PhD dissertation, Graduate Theological Union.
2000 Phoenician Ceramics from the Greek Sanctuary. In *Kommos IV: The Greek Sanctuary*, edited by Joseph W. Shaw and Maria C. Shaw, pp. 302–312. Princeton University Press, Princeton, New Jersey.

Carter, J.
1998 Egyptian Bronze Jugs from Crete and Lefkandi. *Journal of Hellenic Studies* 118:172–177.

Coldstream, J. N.
1989 Early Greek Visitors to Cyprus and the Eastern Mediterranean. In *Cyprus and the East Mediterranean in the Iron Age: Proceedings of the Seventh British Museum Classical Colloquium*, edited by V. Tatton-Brown, pp. 90–96. London.
1998 The First Exchanges between Euboeans and Phoenicians: Who Took the Initiative? In *Mediterranean Peoples in Transition, Thirteenth to early Tenth Centuries* BCE, edited by S. Gitin, A. Mazar and E. Stern, 353–360. Israel Exploration Society, Jerusalem.

Coldstream, J. N., and H. W. Catling
1996 *Knossos North Cemetery, Early Greek Tombs*. British School at Athens Supplementary Volume 28. The British School at Athens, London.

González de Canales, F., L. Serrano, and J. Llompart
2006 The Pre-colonial Phoenician Emporium of Huelva, ca. 900–770 BC. *Bulletin Antieke Beschaving* 81:13–29.

Hoffman, G. L.
1997 *Imports and Immigrants: Near Eastern Contacts with Iron Age Crete*. University of Michigan Press, Ann Arbor.

Honeyman, A. M.
1939 The Phoenician Inscriptions of the Cyprus Museum. *Iraq* 6:103–108.

Lattimore, Richmond
1968 The Odyssey of Homer, translated with an introduction by Richmond Lattimore. New York: Harper & Row.

Lemos, I. S.
2002 *The Protogeometric Aegean: The Archaeology of the Late Eleventh and Tenth centuries* BC. Oxford University Press, Oxford.

Masson, O., and M. Sznycer
1972 *Recherches sur les Phéniciens à Chypre*. Droz, Paris.

Nagy, G.
1979 *The Best of the Achaeans: Concepts of the Hero in Archaic Greek Poetry*. Johns Hopkins University Press, Baltimore.

Oppenheim, A. L.
1968 *Letters from Mesopotamia*. University of Chicago Press, Chicago.

Osborne, R.
1996 *Greece in the Making, 1200–479* BC. Routledge, London.

Phillips, J.
1992 Tomb-robbers and Their Booty in Ancient Egypt. In *Death and Taxes in the Ancient Near East*, edited by S. E. Orel, pp. 157–192. E. Mellen Press, Lewiston, New York.

Popham, M. R.
1994 Precolonization: Early Greek Contact with the East. In *The Archaeology of Greek Colonisation*, edited by Gocha R. Tsetskhladze and Franco De Angelis, pp. 11–34. Oxford University School of Archaeology, Oxford.

Popham, M. R., P. G. Calligas, and L. H. Sackett
1993 *Lefkandi II: The Protogeometric Building at Toumba: Part 2, The Excavation, Architecture and Finds*. The British School at Athens, Athens.

Popham, M. R., and I. S. Lemos
1996 *Lefkandi III: The Early Iron Age Cemetery at Toumba. The Excavations of 1981 to 1994*. The British School at Athens, Athens.

Popham, M. R., L. H. Sackett, and P. G. Themelis (editors)
1979–1980 *Lefkandi I: The Iron Age Settlement and the Cemeteries*. The British School at Athens, London.

Popham, M.R., E. Touloupa, and L.H. Sackett
1982 The Hero of Lefkandi. *Antiquity* 56:169–174.

Sherratt, A., and S. Sherratt
1998 Small Worlds: Interaction and Identity in the Ancient Mediterranean. In *The Aegean and the Orient in the Second Millennium*, edited by E. H. Cline and D. Harris-Cline, pp. 329–342. Aegaeum 20. Université de Liège Histoire de la Grèce Antique/University of Texas at Austin Program in Aegean Scripts and Prehistory, Liège.

Sherratt, S.
1996 With Us but Not of Us: The Role of Crete in Homeric Epic. In *Minotaur and Centaur. Studies in the Archaeology of Crete and Euboea Presented to Mervyn Popham*, edited by D. Evely, I. S. Lemos and S. Sherratt, pp. 87–99. Tempus Reparatum, Oxford.
2003 Visible Writing: Questions of Script and Identity in Early Iron Age Greece and Cyprus. *Oxford Journal of Archaeology* 22:225–242.
Forthcoming The Ceramic Phenomenon of the Sea Peoples: An Overview. In *The Philistines and Other "Sea Peoples." Proceedings of an International Workshop in Memory of Prof. Moshe Dothan, 2001*, edited by M. Artzy, A. Killebrew, and G. Lehmann. Brill, Leiden.

Simpson, St. J.
2000 Observations on Early Iron Age Beads from Luristan. *Bead Study Trust Newsletter* 36: 6–10.

Snodgrass, A. M.
1971 *The Dark Age of Greece*. Edinburgh University Press, Edinburgh.

Sznycer, M.
1980 Salamine de Chypre et les Phéniciens. In *Salamine de Chypre: Histoire et archéologie. Colloque International CNRS, Lyon 1978*, edited by M. Yon, pp. 123–129. Éditions du Centre national de la recherche scientifique, Paris.

Whitley, J.
2002 Objects with Attitude: Biographical Facts and Fallacies in the Study of Late Bronze Age and Early Iron Age Warrior Graves. *Cambridge Archaeological Journal* 12:217–232.

Wiener, M. J.
1981 *English Culture and the Decline of the Industrial Spirit, 1850–1980*. Cambridge University Press, Cambridge.

Winter, I. J.
1995 Homer's Phoenicians: History, Ethnography or Literary Trope? In *The Ages of Homer: A Tribute to Emily Townsend Vermeule*, edited by J. B. Carter and S. P. Morris, pp. 247–271. University of Texas Press, Austin.

CHAPTER 7

Those Who Were Traded: African-Bahamian Archaeology and the Slave Trade

Laurie A. Wilkie and Paul Farnsworth

The scope of human suffering caused by the transatlantic slave trade makes it easy for us to ignore that this human misery was driven by the profit motive and consumer demand for particular types of people from different regions of the slave trade. Consumer demand for particular cultural and physical traits (see Gomez 1998; Higman 1984; Mullin 1992) ultimately played a large role in shaping regional demographics among enslaved and freed peoples in the New World and should not be ignored by archaeologists. As offensive as it is to our standards today, the reality is that for too long African people were a commodity—gathered as a resource, packaged for shipment, and presented for sale. They were advertised in newspapers and auctioned in the street. The people who purchased these human commodities had definite ideas about what constituted a good product. Age, sex, health, bodily appearance, and regional and ethnic origin (which buyers believed to indicate particular temperaments) were all factors considered by purchasers. These purchasing decisions have archaeological implications for our understandings of the diaspora and the construction of African American identities. It is a profoundly difficult, problematic—and for some areas, impossible—task to learn the geographic source of any particular enslaved population, yet as long as we ignore or deny this dimension of the slave trade, we will fail to develop fully the interpretive potential of African American archaeology.

In this chapter we explore two interconnected scales of trade in the Bahamas during the Loyalist period, 1784–1834. We examine the global and national trends and the preferences that shaped the demographics of the African slave trade to the Bahamas. Then, through an archaeological consideration of the consumer practices of enslaved households at William Wylly's Clifton Plantation, New Providence, Bahamas, we discuss how the dynamics of the slave trade shaped constructions of African identities in the New World.

We use the term *African* to denote the range of identities represented within the Bahamas. Among the enslaved and free black population of the Bahamas were African-born persons who lived in villages based on shared "tribal," "national," or "ethnic" identities (even today there are groups that self-identify by what they perceive to be their African ethnic origin). There were people who had been born in the American South and whose families had been there for generations before being relocated as part of the Loyalist migration. Each of these populations contributed to the first-generation Bahamian population. There were also people born in the Bahamas to Bahamian-born parents. This diverse population was united through the shared circumstance that they had been brought to and remained in the Bahamas because of the economic needs of their enslavers.

Work by historians like Michael Mullin (1992), Michael Gomez (1998), and most recently, Gwendolyn Midlo Hall (2006) has demonstrated that African peoples of the diaspora had strong opinions about one another. In the Bahamas, in parts of Nassau, as late as the twentieth century peoples who claimed Yoruba ancestry and those who claimed Congo ancestry intentionally avoided one another's communities. These particular communities are descendents of peoples brought to the islands as "spoils of war"—cargo bound for the Spanish colonies seized by the British after the end of the slave trade. They were able to separate themselves from one another and never endured the circumstances of enslavement. Such was not the case for enslaved peoples, who found themselves isolated on rural plantations with a plethora of cultural others. Whereas the population of the Bahamas was diverse, the southern planters who relocated from Georgia and the Carolinas brought with them certain expectations for their enslaved populations, including where people should originate. There were a few areas of the coast of Africa that contributed to the enslaved populations of the Bahamas, and a small number of slave traders who carried the captives there. Within any sizeable enslaved community, one would expect to encounter others with some sort of shared cultural experience. Therefore, the Bahamas, and particularly Clifton, a plantation occupied for only a generation, offer the opportunity to explore how African peoples brought together by global trade patterns sought to deal with one another.

Scholars have used the concepts of hybridity and double consciousness to look at the ways that African peoples move through white landscapes and deal with the contradictory challenges of creating postcolonial identities. We are co-opting these terms in this work, asking the reader to recognize the incredible cultural diversity that was the reality of the diaspora and the inherent tensions that any person would face in navigating those social terrains. By challenging the notion that enslaved populations were socially and politically homogenous, we offer the opportunity to explore ways that enslaved peoples sought to maintain multiple African identities simultaneously. In short, people could be Igbo and Bahamian, or Congo and Bahamian, or South Carolinian and Bahamian. Ultimately, we argue, it was consumer goods, obtained through formal and informal channels, that allowed for creative, ambiguous, and multilayered expressions of multiple and competing identities at Clifton.

Demographics

Many scholars of the African slave trade have attempted to document the demographics of the trade. This is an area of intense study by Africanists, who have used shipping and customs records, newspaper advertisements, colonial office records, and statistical models to attempt to construct the nature of the populations that moved between Africa and the New World. Records are not necessarily complete or complementary. What has been possible to construct are the broad contours and trends of the slave trade (e.g., Behrendt 1997; Curtin 1967, 1972, 1976; Eltis et al. 1999; Higman 1984; Iniakor 1976; Manning 1992; Richardson 1989).

It was once commonly believed that slave traders intentionally mixed peoples of different backgrounds and separated family members and persons who shared common languages. In other words, it was believed that traders exercised a "divide and conquer" approach toward enslaved Africans to ensure that they had no natural allies or affections among their fellow victims. Sustained study of regional trends in the slave trade, however, clearly demonstrates that this was not the case. Instead, slaveholders' knowledge of African peoples was based on a number of regional stereotypes that were expressed as preferences for peoples of particular backgrounds. Scholars such as Gomez (1998), Mullin (1992), Walsh (1997), and Hall (1992) have demonstrated that enslaved African peoples maintained distinct ethnic identities in the American South and Caribbean until the early nineteenth century. They were able to do so because of trends in the slave trade that led to people from particular regions of Africa being concentrated in particular slaveholding areas, with demonstrable cultural consequences. Although we agree with Mintz and Price (1976) that the impacts of enslavement were such that people could not replicate the whole of their social organization and experience on the community level, our foremost scale of social analysis in this study is the household. Community life may have been a product of collective cultural negotiation, but household life was a compromise between smaller numbers of persons. Through archaeology, we can look at the interplay between these two scales.

Although it may *not* be possible for an individual or a small group of individuals to replicate an entire social order, it *is* in their power to ensure that food is prepared in the proper way, that lived spaces are properly inhabited and maintained, that ancestors are remembered, and that family life maintains some sense of culturally prescribed order. The collective values and behaviors of households became the basis for the construction of communal social structures and values. It is at the household scale that archaeologists work. Indeed, Barry Higman (1998), in his study of Montpelier, Jamaica, and Leland Ferguson (1992), in his South Carolina research, have both demonstrated that understanding the geographic origins of enslaved people allows for greater nuance in archaeological interpretation. It is important to note that we are not advocating for a simple search for Africanisms á la Herskovits (1990). Instead, it is our contention that to understand how colonial and postcolonial identities are created, we must have a greater understanding of the social, political, and economic forces that brought peoples of particular backgrounds to a place. The social and cultural backgrounds of first-generation enslaved Africans informed their experiences of enslavement and ultimately were part of the raw material from which their senses of personhood were constructed.

In this study, we will be discussing one particular diasporic community, Clifton Plantation, located on New Providence, Bahamas. For the people of Clifton Plantation, village life was the main source of social interaction, and it is through a consideration of their household lives and community social relations that we can potentially see how trade, as both a shaper of the community's population and a means of self-expression, came into play. It is necessary, then, for us to look to the potential cultural sources of what came to be an African-Bahamian identity if we are to understand and illuminate practices at Clifton.

African-Bahamian Origins

Africans came to the Bahamas during the Loyalist period in three primary ways: they were brought as enslaved people from the Carolinas and Georgia by the Loyalists; they were brought from Africa to supply Loyalist plantations; they were seized from Spain as contraband by the British navy after the abolition of the slave trade in 1807 and apprenticed on the islands (Craton and Saunders 1992).

The slaves brought by the Loyalists to the Bahamas from the Carolinas and Georgia were likely to be drawn from a limited number of African regions (fig. 7.1): Senegambia, Windward Coast (specifically Sierra Leone), and Central Africa (Donnan 1931). Accompanying the remaining African-born component of the Loyalist slave population would have been their Creole children and grandchildren. Creoles came to the Bahamas with a sense of their African heritage. Archaeologists and ethnographers have demonstrated the rich influences of the Congo and Sierra Leone in the Carolinas and Georgia Sea Islands (Creel 1988; Ferguson 1992; Joyner 1984; Littlefield 1981).

To understand the African slave trade to the Bahamas during the Loyalist period, we used Eltis et al.'s 1999 database of the transatlantic slave trade, supplemented with information drawn from period Bahamian newspapers. The Transatlantic Slave Trade database includes entries for over 27,000 ships that brought slaves from Africa, and it accounts for at least 70 percent of the total slave trade, according to the compilers. A search of the database recovered a list of forty vessels whose primary port of disembarkation was in the Bahamas. These ships brought 9,560 enslaved people to the Bahamas between 1788 and 1807, when the British trade ended (table 7.1). It was possible to ascribe geographic origins to 6,277 persons (table 7.2). Of these, the majority were designated as from the Bight of Biafra (36.4 percent). After the Bight of Biafra, the next largest proportion of the population came from Sierra Leone (26.7 percent) or, more generically, the Windward Coast (4.1 percent). One additional ship carried persons from Sierra Leone but had also picked up slaves from the Gold Coast on the same journey. Central Africa accounted for 22.1 percent of the trade, distantly followed by Senegambia (6.6 percent).

When we compare the trade figures for the Bahamas with the broader British trade, as derived from Richardson's (1989) work (table 7.3), we see that peoples hailing from the Sierra Leone/Windward Coast of Africa were represented in greater numbers in the Bahamas than in the British trade overall. People from this area accounted for roughly 20.2 percent of the trade during the Loyalist period, but only 14.1 percent of the British trade overall.

Persons from Sierra Leone and Senegambia had been favored by Carolina slaveholders because of their expertise in rice cultivation. In addition, a number of visitors to the Sierra Leone region commented on the area's salt

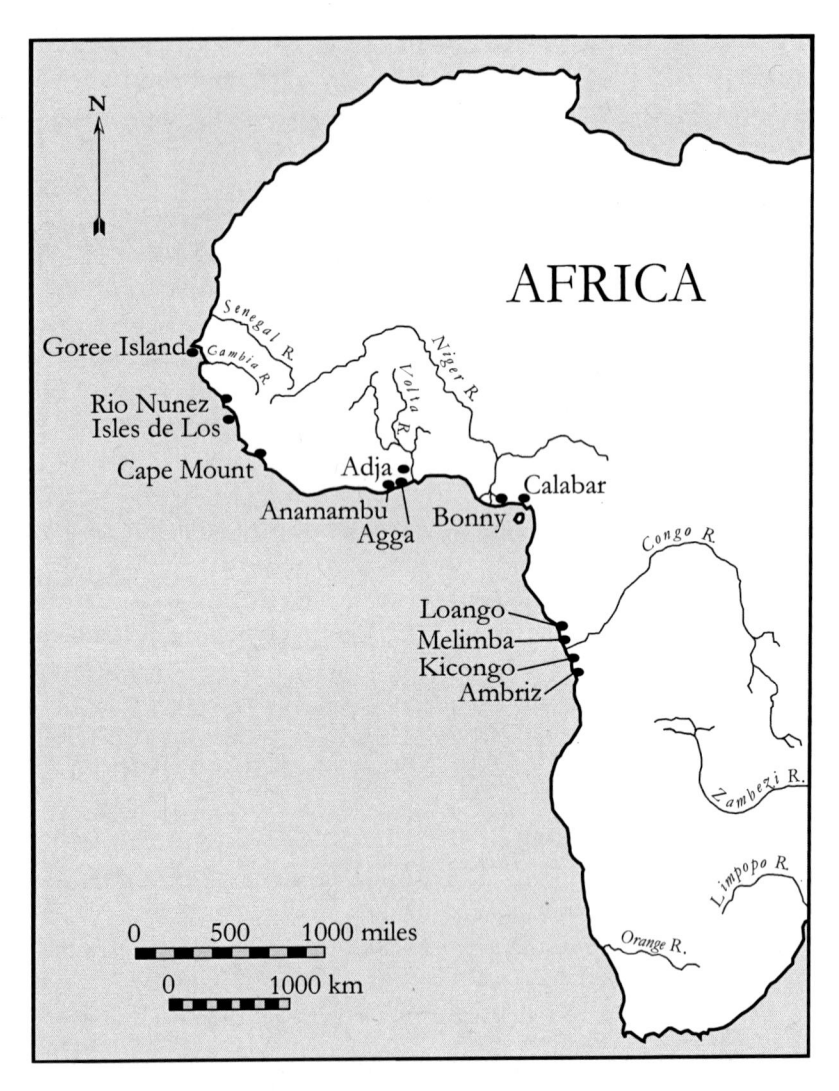

Figure 7.1 Major areas of the slave trade referred to in this paper and the ports from which Bahamas-bound enslaved Africans were brought. From Wilkie and Farnsworth 2005.

Table 7.1 Slave ships entering the Bahamas, 1788–1807. Data from Wilkie and Farnsworth 2005.

Year	Number of slave ships brought to Bahamas	Number of people brought	Identified geographic sources (not all ships identified source; other groups could be included)
1788	3	726	Windward, Angola
1789	1	72	Windward
1790	0	0	
1791	1	64	Windward
1792	1	210	Sierra Leone
1793	1	216	Sierra Leone
1794	0	0	
1795	1	247	Sierra Leone
1796	0	0	
1797	1	233	
1798	0	91	
1799	3	476	Senegambia, Windward, Gold Coast, Sierra Leone
1800	3	528	Sierra Leone
1801	4	1,066	Sierra Leone
1802	10	2,482	Bight of Biafra, Central Africa
1803	8	2,013	Bight of Biafra, Central Africa
1804	1	638	Sierra Leone
1805	1	341	Central Africa
1806	1	157	Senegambia
1807	0	0	
TOTAL		9,560	

150 • Laurie A. Wilkie and Paul Farnsworth

Table 7.2 Geographic origins of African slaves brought to the Bahamas, 1788–1807. Data from Wilkie and Farnsworth 2005.

African Source	Number of people landed in Bahamas	Percentage overall	Percent of population identified by region
Senegambia	413	4.3	6.6
Sierra Leone	1,674	17.5	26.7
Windward Coast	258	2.7	4.1
Gold Coast/Windward	259	2.7	4.1
Bight of Biafra	2,283	23.9	36.4
West/Central Africa	1,390	14.5	22.1
Unspecified	3,283	34.3	---

Table 7.3 The regional distribution of British slave exports from the west coast of Africa, 1780–1807 (compiled from Richardson 1989:Table 5).

	Senegambia	Sierra Leone	Gold Coast	Bight of Benin	Bight of Biafra	West Central Africa
Number of people imported	5,520	146,920	11,866	34,840	504,070	233,860
Percent of trade	.5	14.1	11.4	3.3	48.2	22.4

trade (e.g., Corry 1968 [1807]; Saugnier 1792). Senegambians were similarly skilled (Durand 1806). Although Loyalists may have gone to the Bahamas in hopes of developing sugar or cotton agriculture, salt-raking, particularly in the Turks and Caicos Islands and the southern Out (or Family) Islands, was the most stable economic opportunity.

The prevalence of "Angolans," many of whom, based on their ports of embarkation, were Congo, may also be the result of planters' continuing to engage in preferences formed while living in the American South (Creel 1988; Donnan 1931). The Igbo, who were shunned in Georgia and the Carolinas, did enter the Bahamas in large numbers in 1802 and 1803. By this time, most

Bahamian plantations had been abandoned and demand for on-island labor was low. The Igbo arrived at a time when most slaves were not being purchased for the work they could do for their owners but for their potential resale value in places like Havana, St. Augustine, and New Orleans (Wilkie and Farnsworth 2005). Yet for those plantations still supplementing their enslaved populations, by necessity of available supply, Igbo entered the Bahamian workforce.

Yet another source of Africans for the islands was people who had been destined to be sold in the Spanish colonies but had been seized by the British Navy and settled in the Bahamas. Most of the arrivals from the earliest of these ships were either enlisted in the British West India regiments or assigned as apprentices to planters who requested them (Craton and Saunders 1992). An important collective consequence of these demographic patterns was that, although their African origins may have been separated by a generation, transplanted Creole populations and newly enslaved Africans brought to the Bahamas could share geographic and potentially cultural heritages with one another. At the same time, any Bahamian plantation would have been a multiethnic community. Clifton was no different. Here, where court records and slave registers show that enslaved persons born in the American South lived with native-born enslaved individuals and apprenticed Africans, we can expect that peoples hailed from Sierra Leone, Senegambia, Benin, Congo and, the Gold Coast (Wilkie and Farnsworth 2005).

Archaeology

Clifton Plantation was developed around 1809 by William Wylly, attorney general of the Bahamas, who owned the plantation until his death in 1828, although most families were sold from the plantation in 1821. From 1996 to 2000, archaeological research was conducted at ten structures associated with the approximately seventy enslaved and apprenticed Africans who lived at Clifton. For this chapter, we want to look at just one aspect of the archaeological analysis—how the islands' demographic composition seems to have shaped consumer decision making among the people of Clifton.

The plantation was developed by Wylly as a social experiment, not as a wealth-producing enterprise. Wylly encouraged his enslaved people to be economically self-sufficient by providing them with several days a week for farming and transportation to the Nassau market and paying wages for the completion of extra tasks on the plantation. As we have detailed elsewhere (Wilkie and Farnsworth 2005), these circumstances gave enslaved people at Clifton an unusual degree of consumer autonomy, evidenced in both the diversity of goods contained within household assemblages and the inclusion of more luxury goods than ordinarily seen in enslaved families' assemblages (Wilkie and Farnsworth 1999).

In everyday life and practice, the people of Clifton created social relationships and institutions that united them as a community. Within that community, persons were defined and perceived according to their relationships with one another. It was this social self that could not be directly transplanted from Africa. The middle passage did rob individuals of the social selves they had been in Africa. Yet there is also the internal self to reckon with—the self that a person believes him- or herself to be, based on his or her memories and experiences. How did this sense of self-identity influence practice? How did individuals deal with the disjuncture between who they were and who they had become? How did past traditions influence new ones?

Scholars drawing on the work of W. E. B. DuBois have discussed how double vision or consciousness (Gilroy 1993; Gundaker 1998) has shaped the experiences of African peoples as they navigated racialized social landscapes. Such works focus on how actors constantly engaged in acts of social-cultural translation as they move through situations that place them in conflicting and contradictory social positions. We suggest that the people of Clifton may have experienced such a double consciousness, not just in regard to how they navigated through black/white discourses, but in a number of other dialogues as well—such as free versus enslaved and being both Bahamian and African. Hybridity theory posits that new identities are created when contradictory subject positions merge to become a new, third subject position. In the case of Clifton, we would suggest that through materiality, the new subject position of African-Bahamian was being negotiated—but not at the expense of other African identities.

Materiality at Clifton

Two aspects of African material culture that is reiterated by many Africanists are the vibrant creativity and innovation that continuously mark African cultural practice, whether in the performance of rituals or in the construction of material culture (e.g., Aniakor 1996; Ferme 2001). We see the collective aesthetic traditions of the diverse people who lived at Clifton as the potential universe of inspiration and knowledge that may have informed the construction of the material assemblages.

We will consider the artifacts from the perspective of how similar choices made by different households may indicate the creation of a Bahamian aesthetic generally shaped (but not dictated) by particular African aesthetic traditions. Because the slave registers reveal that there was a large number of African-born individuals among the people of Clifton, we cannot ignore the possibility that particular designs or symbols may have been consciously selected for their similarity to specific African motifs or symbols.

We will focus our discussion on the ceramic assemblages recovered from ten African houses at Clifton (fig. 7.2). Eight structures comprised the main enslaved people's village and housed married couples and their families. Two additional structures, known as the beach houses, appear to have been barracks-style housing for single persons. At several of these structures, only limited excavations (5 m^2) were conducted, and the resulting assemblages are too small to include in all of our analyses. However, significant excavations (a minimum of 20 m^2) were undertaken at seven of the structures (five in the village and both of the barracks) and warrant extended discussion. As we detail elsewhere, we want to assert first that the ceramic assemblages of the Clifton households are primarily the products of individual households' consumer decision making, not provisioning by the planter (Wilkie and Farnsworth 2005:252–257). As part of his reform initiatives, Wylly asserted that the people of Clifton should be encouraged to farm individual plots of land, raise animals, and have access to the Nassau market. Wylly's goals were not magnanimous. He accordingly reduced rations of maize, therefore cutting expenses at a money-losing plantation. A number of archival sources demonstrate that this policy was in place and acted on by the people of Clifton. In fact, the zeal with which trade opportunities were pursued was sometimes a source of frustration for Wylly. Faunal remains recovered from Clifton indicate that individuals were subsisting on foraged and hunted foods and not consuming marketable species or cuts of species. In such a way, the people of Clifton were maximizing the pecuniary return on their labors and maintaining a distinctly non-European diet (Wilkie and Farnsworth 2005). Indeed, a comparison of materials recovered from the houses at Clifton with those found at any other Loyalist period African site in the Bahamas demonstrates the greater abundance and value of materials found at Clifton (Wilkie and Farnsworth 1999).

In comparing the ceramic assemblages from the Clifton quarters, we were struck by the importance of factory-turned slipwares and hand-painted wares (table 7.4). These particular kinds of European ceramics bear structural similarities in form, decoration, and color palettes to pots, calabashes, and fabric designs popular among and common to the Congo, Benin, Windward, and Gold Coast peoples who are likely to have lived at Clifton (Wilkie and Farnsworth 2005:Figures 8.1 and 8.2). The popularity of these decorative

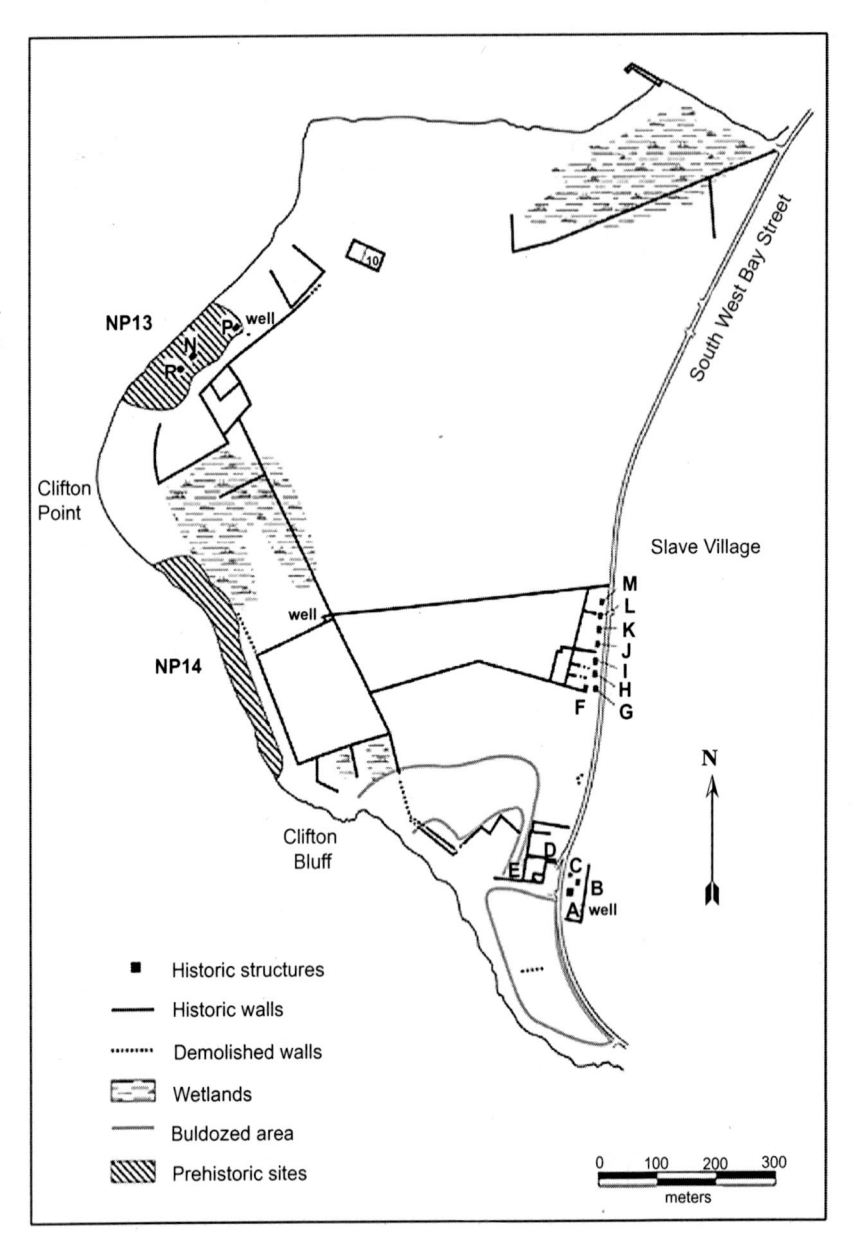

Figure 7.2 Locations of African housing at Clifton Plantation. From Wilkie and Farnsworth 2005.

types seems to us to be an expression of an emerging African-Bahamian

Table 7.4 Distribution of refined earthenware ceramics from Clifton by decorative type. Data from Wilkie and Farnsworth 2005.

Decorative Type	A Planter house %	F Slave house %	G Driver house %	H Slave house %	I Slave house %	L Slave house %	N Slave house %	P Slave house %
Plain	18.8	22.5	16.7	18.2	23.0	14.3	48.6	50.0
Shell-edged	25.0	10.0	18.5	10.9	19.2	21.4	21.6	10.0
Factory-turned slipwares	6.3	22.5	16.7	16.4	28.8	21.4	2.7	20.0
Sponged			1.9					
Embossed			1.9	1.8			2.7	
Hand-painted	18.8	22.5	24.0	43.6	11.5	32.1	21.6	
Gold leaf				1.8				10.0
Transfer-print	31.3	22.5	20.3	7.3	17.3	10.7	2.7	10.0

aesthetic. However, further consideration of individual household assemblages also demonstrates great diversity in specific pattern choices.

In his study of modern Igbo space, Chike Aniakor (1996:232–233) emphasizes the great variation and inventiveness that women express through their selection of household goods—including pottery. "Female household objects and associated architecture have intense variations in their stylistic range, primarily because most were accumulated over time from several different market sources…. In short, simple utilitarian household objects reveal a wide range of styles. These variations afford household objects an aesthetic base which amplifies the aesthetic/psychological bond between owner and object."

During the summer of 2000, we were able to reanalyze all of the ceramics recovered from Clifton specifically to identify patterns. This identification was achieved through the reconstruction of vessels and direct visual comparison of all vessels. If anything, this analysis was conservative in identifying distinct patterns. If we look at the ten Clifton households (including here the statistically small assemblages), we find that among the annular and hand-painted ceramics alone, there are twenty patterns repeated in at least two houses, but sixty-six patterns occur only in one household. At each of the houses with the largest ceramic assemblages, Loci G, H, I, and L, no more than that 52.3 percent of the assemblage overlaps with that of other households (table 7.5). In other words, for most of these houses, nearly half or more of the patterns used by the household were unique to that household. If we break this analysis down to look at overlap between households F, G, H, I, L, and P (the households that had assemblages containing ten vessels or more), we find that no two houses held any more than 33.3 percent of their patterns in common (table 7.6). In effect, the visual impression of the assemblages would have been of great diversity rather than similarity. The ceramic assemblages were somewhat unified across households by a tendency to select ceramics decorated in broadly similar ways (fig. 7.3). Within that generality, specific color preferences and pattern choices seem to have been more individualized by household. Some of these decorative motifs and designs were reminiscent of those of particular African ethnicities.

In their study of the maroons of Suriname, Price and Price (1999) found that women and men alike took great pride in being innovative in their artistic pursuits and valued creativity in the work of others. This preference results in ever-changing artistic fads and trends within and between vil-

Table 7.5 Overlap in hand-painted and factory-turned slipware ceramic patterns between each house and the overall community (★ = assemblage had five or fewer vessels for this analysis). Data from Wilkie and Farnsworth 2005.

Locus	Number of patterns unique to household	Number of patterns found in at least one other Clifton household	Number of vessels represented by overlapping patterns	Percentage of assemblage that overlaps with others
F	9	9	9	50.0
G	15	6	9	40.9
H	21	12	13	38.2
I	10	10	11	52.3
J★	1	0	0	0.0
K★	2	3	3	60.0
L	10	5	5	33.3
M★	0	2	2	100.0
N	8	1	1	11.1
P★	2	3	2	66.6

Table 7.6 Percentage of overlap in hand-painted and factory-turned slipware ceramic assemblages between each household (★ = five or fewer vessels comprised these assemblages; x represents a null). Data from Wilkie and Farnsworth 2005.

Locus	F	G	H	I	J	K	L	M	N	P
F	x	11.1	33.3	27.8	0	5.5	11.1	11.1	5.5	0
G	9.0	x	22.7	9.0	0	0	27.3	0	13.6	0
H	20.5	12.5	x	20.5	0	5.9	11.8	5.0	2.9	2.9
I	28.6	9.5	33.3	x	0	0	9.5	4.8	0	0
★J	0	0	0	0	x	0	0	0	0	0
★K	20.0	0	40.0	0	0	x	0	20	0	0
L	13.3	20.0	20.0	13.3	0	0	x	6.7	6.7	0
★M	100	0	50.0	50.0	0	50.0	50.0	x	0	0
N	11.1	11.1	11.1	0	0	0	11.1	0	x	0
★P	0	0	33.3	33.3	0	0	0	0	0	x

Figure 7.3 Examples of annular wares recovered from Loci G, H, and I in Clifton's village. From Wilkie and Farnsworth 2005.

lages. Although not of people's own manufacture, the ceramics and other consumer goods found within the village and beach houses at Clifton

Plantation were material expressions of people's labor and productivity—communicated in an African way.

The way that assemblages were constructed could further be seen as an expression of a person's creativity and personal sense of style. As the ceramics were used in the yards and viewed during communal food consumption, they were highly visible. As the people of Clifton became increasingly entrenched in the ways of Nassau's market—and perhaps created personal connections within the city that allowed access to different ceramic stocks—they would have become consumers increasingly aware of the monetary value of the goods. The display of ceramics within the village by different households would have been both a presentation of a person's style as well as his or her access to objects of wealth.

As discussed elsewhere, evidence suggests that Locus G (see fig. 7.2) was the driver's residence, occupied by Jack and Sue Eve (Wilkie and Farnsworth 1999, 2005). Both were African-born and resided in the cabin with their two children. In their assemblage, we believe that we see some evidence of how specific ethnic heritage could be communicated through European goods. Since we have discussed this evidence elsewhere (Wilkie and Farnsworth 1999, 2005), we will be brief. We found several elements of their assemblage that suggest a Central African or BaKongo cultural influence.

Other archaeologists and art historians have recounted in depth the importance in the diaspora of the image of the cross as a possible symbolic shorthand for the Bakongo cosmogram. In its original form, the Bakongo cosmogram is a circle quartered by an X, with smaller circles on the end of each arm of the X that represent the four movements of the sun, the cycle of life and death, and the annual progression of the seasons. Locus G contained an example of a hand-painted bowl that featured a design resembling a Bakongo cosmogram. On the broken sherd, the design is neatly centered and may have been curated after the bowl broke. A likeness of the cosmogram is also found along the border of three hand-painted bowls featuring a peacock feather design and on an engine-turned bowl. We have also argued that two examples of highly embossed pipes found at the driver's house depict the content of the cosmogram (Wilkie and Farnsworth 2005:279–280). These pipes feature a prominent beehive surrounded by flying bees and flowering vines. The beehive echoes the shape of African termite mounds, which in BaKongo belief are associated with the dead, whereas flying insects and birds are associated with the souls of the living. Thus, the interlocking of life and death is communicated through the pipe. In this context, the bird representations on the other hand-painted bowls take on greater meaning. Although we can suggest that the driver's assemblage includes spiritually charged, ethnically specific symbols, we also see another African expression of power in the assemblage. One of the greatest concentrations of gilt buttons at Clifton was associated with the driver's house (Wilkie and Farnsworth 2005). Gold is used to convey prestige and honor in many African contexts. Did the driver use gold buttons to emphasize his position of power? If so, the driver was using his cultural experiences as a means of communicating power in a way that would have been understood by planter and enslaved person alike.

Considering the whole village again, if we raise the possibility that the diversity of the respective households' ceramic assemblages conveyed beauty, creativity, wealth, and economic connectedness to their owners, how should we interpret instances where houses shared overlapping patterns? A number of circumstances can be envisioned that would lead to overlap in these assemblages. Perhaps households shared expenses in ceramic acquisition, buying larger lots of a particular vessel and pattern and then sharing the items between households. Perhaps some households actively emulated the materials of others.

We suspect much overlap between households is the result of the social connectedness of particular households with one another. Bahamians will often "share a pot" of food with neighbors, with the expectation that the courtesy will be returned at a later date (Eneas 1976). Informants have talked about taking a plate or bowl over to the other house to share food. The diversity of patterns used may even indicate that particular vessels and decorations were associated with particular household members, so that a person or household's bowl would be recognizable as such to others, though such an end could be achieved by marking bowls in other ways. For instance, the plain and shell-edged wares recovered from the planter kitchen and several of the enslaved people's cabins include several examples marked by an X scratched on their bottoms. We have interpreted these items as being marked to designate wares provided by Wylly (Wilkie and Farnsworth 2005). There are a diversity of beliefs related to health and spirituality throughout western and central Africa that, although arising from different cultural contexts, are similar in necessitating that one maintain control of one's own food, even when in the presence of friends and loved ones (see Wilkie and Farnsworth 2005:257–260 for further discussion).

It would be expected that vessels carried from one home to another might break from time to time. Within the quarters, a consideration of overlap in ceramic patterns between households suggests that factors in the distribution included more than just proximity to any particular yard. For instance, although the families who lived in the structures of F and G were living in closer proximity to one another than any other families, they had a limited amount of overlap between them—only one pattern. In contrast, Locus G had the greatest overlap with the household at Locus L, with six overlapping vessels (four patterns). This degree of overlap is visible even though Locus L has one of the smaller samples of ceramics recovered. The household at Locus G also shared three different patterns with its neighbors at Locus H (representing a five-vessel overlap). Do these connections between households represent ethnic, occupational, or age-related bonds between households? Clearly some households were more closely connected than others. Given that the house yards were discrete and intact middens, these distributions are not the result of taphonomic processes.

Given the ever-visible nature of life in the house yards of the village, household materials were always on display, always visible to be interpreted and evaluated by other families. The compilation of household assemblages was more than an action of static consensus-building within the community; it was also a means of continuously positioning and identifying oneself relative to others. Participation in the island economy and trade systems provided the people of Clifton with an important means of constructing both a broadly pan-African—that is, Bahamian—identity, as well as distinct sub-identities within their communities.

Conclusions

In this volume we have been challenged to think about trade as a social relation, not merely an economic one. For enslaved Africans, the shared social-cultural attitudes of the planter classes shaped where in the diaspora Africans were settled. Planters, the consumers of enslaved Africans, developed clear preferences for certain regions of Africa that would provide workers of the proper physical and mental nature. There were positive effects of these attitudes for enslaved peoples. Although the likelihood of family members or even village members being settled in the same area were remote, there was a strong likelihood that a person would encounter others who spoke the same or similar languages, shared familiar foodways, and held similar ideas about family, spiritual practice, household life, and aesthetics. There was the opportunity to build on shared commonalities while encountering new, baffling, and challenging situations. There was the possibility of maintaining a sense of one's humanity in dehumanizing circumstances.

Just as trade shaped the members of the enslaved people's social world, they in turn used trade as a means of both constructing new, shared identities and mediating between coexisting (and sometimes conflicting) identities in their communities. Just as enslaved and later freed Africans have had to maintain double consciousness to navigate safely through a multiracial world, they had to turn a similar binocular view toward interactions in their own multiethnic societies. Although European goods, like those found at Clifton, could be reinterpreted in pan-African ways that subverted European intentions, within the African community they could be infused with additional, multiple layers of meaning that were specific to particular subsets of the community. William Wylly, upon passing through the village of Clifton, would have been content, based on the abundance of English-manufactured goods being used, that his attempts to Europeanize his enslaved people were successful. Likewise, an African viewer might see in her own goods and those of her neighbor only the similarities in color and general design they shared, entirely missing specific patterns or motifs that communicated much more to other community members. Although the multiple layers of meaning that could infuse any object is dizzying to consider, in acknowledging the possibility, we can begin to recognize how trade and the acquisition of certain goods were socially constructive acts that allowed enslaved African peoples to define themselves and others.

References

Aniakor, Chike
1996 Household Objects and the Philosophy of Igbo Social Space. In *African Material Culture*, edited by M. J. Arnoldi, C. M. Geary, and K. L. Hardin, pp. 214–242. Indiana University Press, Bloomington.

Behrendt, Stephen D.
1997 The Annual Volume and Regional Distribution of the British Slave Trade, 1780–1807. *Journal of African History* 38:187–211.

Corry, Joseph
1968 [1807] *Observations upon the Windward Coast of Africa: The Religion, Character, Customs, etc. of the Natives.* Frank Cass & Co., Ltd., London.

Craton, Michael, and Gail Saunders
1992 *Islanders in the Stream.* University of Georgia Press, Athens.

Creel, Margaret Washington
1988 *"A Peculiar People": Slave Religion and Community-Culture among the Gullahs.* New York University Press, New York.

Curtin, Philip D.
1967 *Africa Remembered: Narratives by West Africans from the Era of the Slave Trade.* Johns Hopkins University Press, Baltimore, Maryland.
1972 *The Atlantic Slave Trade: A Census.* University of Wisconsin Press, Madison.
1976 Measuring the Atlantic Slave Trade Once Again: A Comment by Philip D. Curtin. *Journal of African History* XVII(4):595–627.

Donnan, Elizabeth

1931 *Documents Illustrative of the History of the Slave Trade to America. Volume II: The Eighteenth Century.* Carnegie Institution of Washington Publication No. 409. Carnegie Institution, Washington, DC.

Durand, Jean
1806 *Voyage to Senegal.* R. Phillips, London.

Eltis, David, Stephen Behrendt, David Richardson, and Herbert S. Klein
1999 *The Transatlantic Slave Trade.* Cambridge University Press, Cambridge.

Eneas, Cleveland W.
1976 *Bain Town.* Cleveland and Muriel Eneas, Nassau, Bahamas.

Ferguson, Leland
1992 *Uncommon Ground.* Smithsonian Institution Press, Washington, DC.

Ferme, Marianne
2001 *The Underneath of Things: Violence, History, and the Everyday in Sierra Leone.* University of California Press, Berkeley.

Gilroy, Paul
1993 *The Black Atlantic: Modernity and Double Consciousness.* Harvard University Press, Cambridge, Massachusetts.

Gomez, Michael
1998 *Exchanging our Country Marks: The Transformation of African Identities in the Colonial and Antebellum South.* University of North Carolina, Chapel Hill.

Gundaker, Grey
1998 *Signs of Diaspora/Diaspora of Signs.* Oxford University Press, New York.

Hall, Gwendolyn Midlo
1992 *Africans in Colonial Louisiana.* Louisiana State University Press, Baton Rouge.
2006 *Slavery and African Ethnicities in the Americas: Restoring the Links.* University of North Carolina Press, Chapel Hill.

Herskovits, Melville
1990 *The Myth of the Negro Past.* Beacon Press, Boston.

Higman, Barry
1994 *Slave Populations of the British Caribbean, 1807–1834.* Johns Hopkins University Press, Baltimore, Maryland.
1998 *Montpelier, Jamaica: A Plantation Community in Slavery and Freedom, 1739–1912.* University of the West Indies Press, Mona, Jamaica.

Joyner, Charles
1984 *Down by the Riverside: A South Carolina Slave Community.* University of Illinois Press, Urbana.

Littlefield, Daniel
1981 *Rice and Slaves: Ethnicity and the Slave Trade in Colonial South Carolina.* Louisiana State University Press, Baton Rouge.

Manning, Patrick
1992 The Slave Trade: The Formal Demography of a Global System. In *The Atlantic Slave Trade: Effects on Economies, Societies and Peoples in Africa, the Americas and Europe,* edited by Joseph E. Inikori and Stanley Engerman, pp. 117–145. Duke University Press, Durham.

Mintz, Sidney, and Richard Price
1976 *The Birth of African American Culture: An Anthropological Perspective*. Beacon Press, Boston.

Mullin, Michael
1992 *Africa in America: Slave Acculturation and Resistance in the American South and the British Caribbean, 1736–1831*. University of Illinois Press, Urbana.

Price, Sally, and Richard Price
1999 *Maroon Arts: Cultural Vitality in the African Diaspora*. Beacon Press, Boston.

Richardson, David
1989 Slave Exports from West and West-Central African, 1780–1810: New Estimates of Volume and Distribution. *Journal of African History* 30:1–22.

Saugnier, Mess
1792 *Voyages to the Coast of Africa*. G. G. J. and J. Robinson, London.

Walsh, Lorena
1997 *From Calabar to Carter's Grove: The History of a Virginia Slave Community*. University Press of Virginia, Charlottesville.

Wilkie, Laurie A., and Paul Farnsworth
1999 Trade and the Construction of Bahamian Identity: A Multiscalar Exploration. *International Journal of Historical Archaeology* 3(4):283–320.
2005 *Sampling Many Pots: The Archaeology of Memory and Tradition at a Bahamian Plantation*. University Press of Florida, Gainesville.

CHAPTER 8

Broads, Studs, and Broken Down Daddies: The Materiality of "Playing" in the Modern Penitentiary

Eleanor Conlin Casella

> *Ask any of the chickies in my Pen*
> *They'll tell you I'm the biggest Mother Hen*
> *I love them all, and all of them love me*
> *Because the system works, the system called*
> *Re-ci-pro-ci-ty.*
> —Matron Mamma Morton, Chicago, 2002

Within all penal institutions, networks of black market exchange circulate both limited resources and illicit luxuries throughout the inmate population. Material objects, kinship relations, and sexual encounters fuel these systems of illicit (or semi-sanctioned) distribution. Drawing from an international array of both scholarly studies and inmate accounts, this chapter explores the turbulent social dynamics produced through this "sub-rosa" economic system (Williams and Fish 1974). How do patterns of resistance, coercion, and collusion become materially communicated through the presence (or absence) of exchange relations? How are fictive kin created through material encounters? What are the sexual aspects of trade? Can the social world of the prison be understood as a basic exercise of exchange? This chapter comparatively explores the forms of trade that sustain sociality within the modern penitentiary.

Anthropological models of reciprocal gift exchange (Godelier 1999; Lévi-Strauss 1987 [1950]; Mauss 1990 [1950]; Strathern 1988; Weiner 1992) have linked the process of trade to the mobilization of power, influence, and social status. This study builds on such ethnographic literature by considering the material dynamics of trafficking—or those illegal and nonmonetary trade practices endemic to the modern carceral institution. Following Sahlins' classic model (1972), institutional "reciprocity" will be shown to operate in positive, neutrally balanced, and negative forms of material exchange, with the specific nature of these encounters determined by the degree of generosity between trade partners. Further, since trafficking is ultimately motivated by the fulfillment of desires, this study also explores how the sexual economy of prison trade actively forges specific power relations and social identities within the austere institutional environment.

On Keeping Sweet: Reciprocity and The Prison

> [The Admission Officer] really chewed out all the girls that came down today. One she demanded to know where her lipstick was, 'cause she had some on, and the girl didn't have it. So she said, "Don't think that I don't know your exchanging ways, you're not putting anything over on me." Why did she have to do that? So what, if one of the women out of the kindness of her heart did give her some lipstick, or they passes it around? .... Why do they want to strip us? To take away what makes us women? We have so little. And if any of them would have talked back and said, "It's none of your business where I got the lipstick," then she would have taken them right over to "the hole." There was nothing they could do, just had to take it, and that's what we have to do. We have to respect them and take it.... [Heffernan 1972:50–51]

Imprisonment has been described euphemistically by the British Home Office as "a painful experience." Since the 1950s, criminologists have analyzed and categorized these pains, with one formative study identifying "deprivations which attend the withdrawal of freedom, such as the lack of heterosexual relationships, isolation from the free community, [and] the withholding of goods and services" as three particularly damaging aspects of the experience (Sykes 1958:285). Another more recent study of male establishments noted that "the prisoner loses society's trust, the status of citizenship, and material possessions, which might constitute a large part of the individual's self-perception. The prisoner is figuratively 'castrated'" (Liebling 1999:285).

Drawing from adaptation models, many criminologists have identified constructive regimes that provide activity, opportunities for change, contact, and support—behavior patterns that help to ameliorate the worst aspects of prison life. Defined as "coping," these behaviors are actively undertaken "to help keep anguish and distress under control" (Liebling 1999:288; see also Gallo and Ruggiero 1991). Although recognized as always "partial, unstable and arduous" (Liebling 1996:288), these coping activities enable inmates to subvert the process of institutionalization (Goffman 1961:61–63). As the dangers of self-harming and suicide all too frequently accompany attempts to "go it alone" in prison, most inmates accept that everyday survival requires some form of sociality, some form of social support. To cope, one must trade.

In classic archaeological models (Polanyi 1957; Renfrew 1975; Sahlins 1972) issues of scale and distance are used to distinguish between trade (transactions that take place between social units) and exchange (transactions that occur within one social unit). But such traditional multiscalar anthropological models are difficult to apply to penal institutions—unique social worlds of incarceration and involuntary participation. As extensively debated in criminological literature, social units can be formed by locality (cell, dormitory, ward, penitentiary), affiliation (race, gang, religion, sexuality, fictive kinship group), aspiration (sobriety, rehabilitation, vocational training, leisure interest, education), and some complex intersection of these social forces (Heffernan 1972; Owen 1998; Rideau 1995; Tonry and Petersilia 1999; Wacquant 2001). Further, as movement into and out of the institutional environment is typically abrupt and involuntary, inmate sociality can appear opportunistic, transient, and superficial, thereby hindering the establishment or identification of cohesive units (Goffman 1961; Sykes 1958). Finally, the long-term maintenance of a sub-rosa economic system requires a degree of collusion by institutional staff, whether correctional officers, medical officers, administrators, or maintenance and educational staff. Thus within the modern correctional institute, trade inhabits the ambiguous spaces between inter- and intra-unit forms of resource distribution.

As classically argued by the French anthropologist Marcel Mauss, there are no free gifts (Mauss 1990 [1950]). In all nonmonetary forms of economy, the exchange of objects creates legal, moral, social, and sexual obligations. And it is this obscure web of obligations—of favors, duties, and extortions—that structures the black market world of the prison. In reciprocal economic systems, trade (or the giving of gifts) is crucially made up of three essential obligations: to give, to receive, and, after a period of time mutually deemed appropriate, to reciprocate (or counter-gift). Exchange thus forms a cycle of obligations, as counter-gifts themselves become gifts, thereby knitting together participants in a temporal as well as social relationship. Failure to engage with any of these obligations "is tantamount to declaring war; it is to reject the bond of alliance and commonality" (Mauss 1990 [1950]:13).

Access to or responsibility for a desired resource can therefore be highly stressful, as observed by British inmate and *Guardian* columnist Erwin James:

> This type of job [with access to prison commodities] attracts serious pressure from fellow prisoners. The hospital orderly, for instance, has to deal with people asking for needles. The reception orderly is pestered to access stored personal property. Those who work in the clothing-exchange store are badgered to provide new kit. Servery [meal hall] workers fare the worst as they face demands for extra or larger portions three times a day, every day of the week. A refusal is guaranteed to offend, and would be tantamount to an invitation to conflict, "What are you—a fucking screw?" Telling the supervising officer might seem like an option, but this would be the surest way to acquire a reputation as a grass. [James 2003:102]

Within British prisons, formal regulations acknowledge all three obligations of exchange. According to Rule 47 of the standard penal code, inmate offences against discipline include:

- Having in his cell or room, or in his possession, any unauthorized article, or attempting to obtain such an article;
- Delivering to or receiving from any person any unauthorized article;
- Selling or delivering to any other person, without permission, anything he is allowed to have only for his own use; and
- Taking improperly or being in unauthorized possession of any article belonging to another person or to a prison (BHO 1964).

It is, obviously, not just objects that enter into inmate exchange. Illicit information, craft knowledge, and access to communication (including "kites," or covert messages) all exist as potential valuables (Godelier 1999). However, it is the material dimensions of black market exchange that hold profound archaeological implications. Material signatures of the penal black market may include modifications to original institutional designs, such as the elaboration of perimeter walls, internal fencing, or the addition of surveillance towers or guard stations (Bush 2000; Casella 2007). For example, in his archaeological study of the Rhode Island State Prison (1835–1878), James Garman (2005:176) detailed a series of architectural features constructed to enhance institutional discipline within the early American penitentiary. Excavation of the prison yards revealed a series of undocumented stone cobble pathways "connecting the points of egress and ingress" between the main cellblock and workshop building. Consistently two feet wide, the paths would have been painstakingly constructed by inmate labor over a period of years. As a blatant demarcation of exterior space, these cobblestone features promoted both visual and auditory surveillance over inmate movement across the prison yard, thereby restricting opportunities for trafficking activities.

Similarly, artifact assemblages can also reveal the internal nature of illicit exchange, with extra rations, diverting luxuries, tokens of value, or discard stashes appearing within the institutional site (Bush 2000; Casella 2000, 2007; Wurtzburg and Hahn 1992). The Ross Female Factory (1847–1853) was a mid-nineteenth century British prison for female felons transported to the Australian penal colony of Van Diemen's Land (Tasmania). Excavation of the Solitary Cellblock recovered a substantial quantity of fragmentary prohibited materials from the earthen floors of individual cells, including coins, tobacco pipe fragments, and alcohol bottles (Casella 2001). Although official regulations documented an austere diet of bread and water, artifacts recovered from a stash pit located in the eastern cell in particular appeared to reflect black market trafficking within the colonial prison. Consisting of a white clay pipe stem, an olive glass bottle base, and bone fragments (*Ovis* sp.), this stash assemblage suggested that inmates under "separate treatment" ameliorated the worst deprivations of solitary confinement through some unauthorized mechanism of illicit exchange (Casella 2002). How would this system of resource distribution be configured?

Trafficking: Modes of Distribution

How does contraband move about the austere penitential landscape? The institutional black market is generally fed by the direct and cyclical exchange of favors, with trade tokens assuming a wide variety of forms. Stories of reciprocity pepper inmate accounts of daily life under incarceration: "I found out later that [Rinty] had persuaded George the video orderly to show the sci-fi thriller *Armageddon*, a treat Felix and his cartel of Trekkies could not resist. There's a rumour that George demanded a fee for the favour. But everyone's agreed—it was worth a phonecard" (James 2003:18).

Sahlins (1972) classically mapped reciprocity as a degree of generosity or altruism along a continuum of social distance—with positive reciprocity occurring between kin groups, balanced reciprocity amongst village or tribal members, and negative reciprocity occurring between intertribal competitors. However, all three forms of reciprocity simultaneously exist in tension within the institutional black market. The cyclical exchange of favors can be thus seen to reflect the complex, fluid, and situational relationships between those engaged in trade.

Family Life: Positive Reciprocity and Inmate Society

In an echo of Sahlins' model, sociological studies of inmate subcultures have linked patterns of altruism (or positive reciprocity) to the maintenance of fictive kinship groups within both male and female prisons. This literature has linked the social and emotional support roles of "mommy," "daddy," "child," "sibling," "husband," or "wife" within a "play-family" to such attributes as age, physical appearance, sexual identity, ethnic or socioeconomic background, and institutional experience (Foster 1975; Heffernan 1972). Ultimately, the situational yet clearly defined social roles become indicated by the degree of obligation to provide for or be provided for (Giallombardo 1966; Rideau 1995; Sykes 1958):

> Parents buy their children soda, powder, candy, and other items when they go to the canteen. Children also share whatever they buy with their parents, and often buy special items for them when they go off-campus. But the children are not exploited economically. When an economic need arises, the father—with the full knowledge of the wife—will "get a fox." This additional "woman" in the household provides the means whereby the economic problems of the family will be alleviated. [Giallombardo 1966:210]

Adherence to these inmate codes of kinship can relate to the length of institutional sentence (Tittle and Tittle 1964), the type of institutional facility involved (Wilson 1986), the strength of external familial bonds (Jones 1993; Zingraff and Zingraff 1980) and the influence of staff expectations (Kruttschnitt 1981).

The intricate operation of such positive reciprocity can be read from inmate accounts. One juvenile female inmate explained the obligation of generosity: "You share candy. It's like a family. You have an adopted mother that treats you like a daughter. It's like a regular family. If you're in room confinement, they'll slip issues, candy, gum, magazines and cigarettes under your door" (Giallombardo 1966:184). In his epic narrative of transportation to and escape from the penal settlements of French Guiana (Devil's Island) during the 1930s, Henri Charrière detailed how his inmate "brothers" similarly arranged for the delivery of contraband rations to his solitary cell:

> The corridor was being swept: it seemed to me the broom kept going a long while outside my cell. The bristles swished again and again against my door. I looked closely and I saw a scrap of white paper showing underneath....I pulled the paper in and unfolded it. It was a note written in phosphorescent ink. I waited for the screw to go by and then quickly I read,

> "Papi, from tomorrow there'll be five cigarettes and a coconut in your pot every day. Chew the coconut well when you eat it if you want it to do you good. Swallow the chewed meat.... Enclosed there's a bit of pencil lead. Any time you want anything, ask for it on the enclosed scrap of paper. When the sweeper rubs his broom against the door, scratch with your fingers. If he scratches, shove your paper under. Never pass the note unless he's answered your scratching. Put the bit of paper in your ear...and your pencil lead anywhere at the bottom of your cell wall. Thumbs up. Love. Ignace, Louis."
> [Charrière 1970: 273]

Sentenced to two years of solitary confinement, "Papillon" (as he was nicknamed) only survived the stark disciplinary conditions through the black market trade undertaken by his fictive kin.

Getting By: The Dynamics of Balanced Reciprocity

Other accounts of exchange systems would be characterized as balanced reciprocity under Sahlins' continuum model (1972). Serving to maintain the daily operation of the black market, these types of practices assist with the basic circulation of essential (yet limited) resources throughout the institution. In Esther Heffernan's sociological study of the Women's Reformatory at Occoquan, Virginia, one inmate patiently explained how to "make out."

> You can go it alone in here if you don't want anything. But otherwise you've *got* to have some kind of a bond. You've got to be one of them, but not too far. See this bra, well, this is from the sewing room. I make sandwiches, and get it sewed. Then I want it clean, so I gets contacts in the laundry. For a Sunday visit, I want a clean skirt. So, I bring a nice sandwich, mayonnaise and all the trimmings—'cause anything you don't get regular is a big thing in here—and I get a nice skirt. Nobody is going to check that it's not my number. You've got to have these things. If you go it alone, you've got nothing. But you've got to think all the time. You've got to wake up thinking and you've got to go to bed thinking. Of course, we've got a "kingpin" down here, but I don't mind. I can sell my sandwiches, and I tell the girls I won't pick up no kites [illicit messages] without being paid for it. Though I can't see why women stay up half the night in the toilet writing kites, and maybe going to the hole, for nothing. Now, if they were sending deodorant, or something like that, then I could see it. Now if a girl is really sick and not just that old complaining, I've always got cigarettes, and I'll buy her a pill. But only once. [Heffernan 1972:76]

Although not involving a correctional facility, Primo Levi's account of resource distribution amongst the dormitories of the Auschwitz concentration camp provides a similarly detailed example of balanced reciprocity under institutional confinement. While camp regulations prescribed the polishing of shoes every morning, none of the necessary provisions were allotted to the inmates. Instead, a semi-sanctioned barter system flourished:

> Those *Häftlinge* [prisoners]...who have the chance to fill their bowl with grease or machine-oil (or anything else: any blackish and greasy substance is considered suitable for the purpose), on their return to the camp in the evening, make a systematic tour of the huts until they find a *Blockältester* [hut leader] who has run out of the article and wants a fresh supply. In addition, every hut usually has its habitual supplier, who has been allotted a fixed daily recompense [of soup rations] on condition that he provides the grease every time that the reserve is about to run out. Every evening, beside the doors of the *Tagesräume* [kitchen], the groups of suppliers stand patiently around; on their feet for hours and hours in the rain or snow, they discuss excited matters relating to the fluctuation of prices and value. [Levi 1987 [1958]: 90]

In this example of balanced reciprocity, food rations serve as an internal currency—with known rates of exchange and regular networks of barter maintained by participants.

An equally important form of balanced exchange occurs as gaming practices. Marcel Mauss considered gambling a form of potlatch (an extension of the gift system), observing that the practice required an exchange of honor and social commitment in addition to material goods (Mauss 1990 [1950]:112n139). Providing temporary diversion and social engagement, gambling also enables the structured circulation of valued (yet limited) resources throughout the prison. Despite the ubiquitous prohibition of such activities within corrective institutions, they remain endemic to incarceration. Excavations at Hyde Park Barracks, an early nineteenth-century Australian accommodation depot for transported British felons, recovered a diverse assortment of tokens carved by male inmates out of a variety of available materials (fig. 8.1). Representing a range of interactive games, these gaming tokens indicate the enduring bonds of social interactions, amusing diversions, and reciprocal exchanges within the disciplinary environment.

Dice games appear particularly popular as method of gambling, perhaps because of the ease of concealment. Both contemporary inmate accounts and historic sources have detailed the construction of dice from a variety of materials, including papier-mâché made of damp toilet paper burnished into a cube and lacquered with sugary water or Kool-Aid (Angelo 2003:90–91), and "gutta-percha," or hardened eraser rubber carved into the appropriate shape and stained with india ink (Bush 2000:74). Archaeological examples of bone dice have been recovered during excavations of historic prisons such as the Old Baton Rouge Penitentiary in Louisiana (1835–1919) and the Walnut Street Prison in Philadelphia (1795–1835) (Casella 2007; Cotter et al. 1988; Wurtzburg and Hahn 1992). Evidence from the latter site suggests that inmates co-opted prison facilities and raw materials for covert manufacture, with bone dice and die blanks in various stages of manufacture recovered during excavation of the original prison workshops (Cotter et al. 1988:71). Since illicit production on such a scale would require some degree of collusion on the part of supervisory staff, the excavated assemblage could in turn suggest a semi-sanctioned acceptance of gambling as a mode of resource exchange within this early American prison.

Figure 8.1 Convict game tokens, Hyde Park Barracks, Sydney, Australia. *Left*: Assorted bone counters. *Upper right*: Blue transfer-printed earthenware token. *Bottom right*: Bone domino. Photograph by E. C. Casella.

Power and Possessions: On Negative Reciprocity

Finally, exchange cycles within penal institutions have been used to create "kingpins" and "slaves" tied by dependent and frequently violent relations of wealth and protection. Functioning as a type of negative reciprocity (Sahlins 1972), these modes of sub-rosa exchange require a competitive and defensive sociality. Revisiting his early analysis of a male institution, one sociologist observed that

> Most prisoners restrict their associations to a few other prisoners and withdraw from prison public life. A minority associates with gangs, gamble[s], buy[s] and sell[s] contraband commodities, and engage[s] in prison homosexual behavior. If they do so, however, they must act "tough" and be willing to live by the new code, that is, be ready to meet threats of violence with violence. [Irwin 1990 [1970]: vi]

As "cliques," "families," or organized, racially-affiliated gangs struggle to control the acquisition and distribution of valued resources, penitentiary trade can be seen to resemble the inter-tribal competition that Sahlins (1972) used to characterize negative reciprocity. Further, negative reciprocity can be seen to generate internal hierarchies within inmate society. Relations of black market exchange can be explicitly manipulated by individuals (kingpins) to achieve superior social status and material wealth within the prison—a form of negative reciprocity that Sahlins (1963) originally linked to the production of "big men" within Melanesian societies.

Entry into such prison exchange systems can frequently be involuntary, marked by the threat or actual experience of physical assault and rape. Like altruistic modes of exchange, some types of negative reciprocity can generate fictive kin relations, with personal protection bartered for various goods and services. In his article to the Louisiana State Penitentiary newspaper *The Angolite*, inmate Wilbert Rideau explained that

> [James] Dunn was fortunate, in that all his owner required of him was for him to be a good housewife. And he was. He'd wash and take care of his old man's clothing, fix the beds, prepare meals, bust pimples in his face and give him massages, and generally do all of the menial things needed doing. As with all other wives around the world, he'd also take care of his man's sexual needs....His old man had a dope habit and once, while not having enough money to get a "fix," he sold Dunn in exchange for two bags of heroin and the settlement of a hundred dollar debt. As a slave, his market value at the time was $150. "Two weeks later," Dunn recounts, "he bought me back because he was loving me." [Rideau 1995:145]

On the black market, people themselves become commodified—traded as material possessions within sub-rosa exchange cycles. Obviously, with questions of extortion, assault, protection, desire, and dependency plaguing most trade relations within the prison, distinctions between negative and altruistic reciprocity remain both situational and psychologically complicated.

Playing: The Sexual Economy of the Prison

> When they pass the basket
> Folks contribute to
> You put in for Mamma
> She'll put out for you.
> —Matron Mamma Morton, *Chicago*, 2002

Given the obvious social tensions and formal sanctions, *why* would inmates participate in the prison black market? Traditional criminological analyses (Heffernan 1972; Sykes 1958; Williams and Fish 1974) identify four generalized types of yearning or desire fulfilled through this reciprocal economy. According to these classic perspectives, the institutional black market satisfies various physiological cravings for food, personal safety, or sexual activity inadequately provided through official routes. Underground trade also supports a range of addictions, supplying contraband cigarettes, alcohol, and drugs for the right price. Trade networks and relations of obligation also create a form of reciprocal solidarity among inmate subgroups and between inmates and complicit members of the institutional staff. Finally, in parallel with anthropological understandings of gift exchange discussed previously, the mobilization of power, influence, and social status can also be seen effectively to fuel trade.

Nonetheless, Pierre Bourdieu (1998:76–79) recently adopted the concept of "libido" to describe the yearning that effectively fuels trade. People give, according to his model, in order to mobilize that powerful position of being owed a counter-gift. They are giving in the anticipation of receiving. Given the social context, Bourdieu's choice of the word libido seems particularly appropriate, because it encapsulates a sense of desire as both a material and a sexual yearning. In his original study, Marcel Mauss also recognized this delicate fusion of the objectified and the embodied, noting that "by giving one is giving *oneself*, and if one gives *oneself*, it is because one 'owes' *oneself*— one's person and one's goods—to others" (Mauss 1990 [1950]:46, emphasis in the original).

Variously glossed as "bulldogging," "playing," "being in the life," and "housekeeping," the same-sex conjugal relationships found within prison inmate populations demonstrate the interrelated values of objectified sexuality and sexualized materiality within the full cycle of gifting, receiving, and counter-gifting. Once free of his "old man," inmate James Dunn began to help young new arrivals learn the obligations that accompanied favors within Louisiana State Penitentiary: "If they needed money or items from the store, he would personally take them to the canteen and buy whatever they needed so as to prevent their borrowing things from guys who would later insist upon collecting their debt by turning them out [requiring submissive sexual acts]" (Rideau 1995:147).

For those convicts "playing house," specifically gendered roles sometimes appear socially related to the participants' form—and position—of reciprocity. One inmate participant in Esther Heffernan's study at Occoquan, Virginia, similarly described the fluid slippages between sexual and material libido:

> They get a person tangled up by giving them things on the bed, and then later when a girl makes canteen, they want everything. She's hooked then, and she gives and gives. To give you an example, a young girl in our dorm, came in all nice and quiet, and now she's all involved. She cried all yesterday morning, because she'd ordered an expensive negligee for a girl and the front office held it up because it was too expensive. Now she's already spent the money and can't get it. Spent everything on the girl. [Heffernan 1972:93]

In both male and female prisons, the person occupying the "butch" or masculine role typically appears to be in position of receiving material goods and reciprocating with sexual favors. Another interview from Heffernan's study of a women's institution related that "a girl comes in here and asks the family for 25 dollars, and goes and spends it on her 'husband,' buys 'him' clothes and canteen, and then when 'he's' got everything, 'he' goes off to another 'wife.' Some have a couple of 'wives,' and then it's called a 'stable,' and he's a 'stud'" (Heffernan 1972:93). The terms "sissy," "fox," "gal-boy," "punk," or "broad" have been recorded in both male and female prisons as equivalent terms for feminine-gendered inmates who are similarly "generous" with their number or range of conjugal relations (Sykes 1958; Giallombardo 1966). In a replication of heteronormative roles, such feminine-gendered inmates are expected to shop, both materially and sexually, for their husbands. As inmate Wilbert Rideau explained:

> Silky had two [gal-boys] and he kept them hustling. They produced around $600 income per month for him. After extracting what was needed to provide for their personal needs, the

> remainder was loaned out to other inmates at high interest rates or invested in illegal or black market enterprises that would turn a quick profit. Each month he was able to send four to five hundred dollars out of the prison to meet the [legal] expenses involved in his effort to secure his freedom. [Rideau 1995: 149]

Historical examples of such provisioning activities can also be found. At the Ross Female Factory of Van Diemen's Land (Tasmania), a letter in June 1850 from Superintendent Irvine to the Visiting Magistrate documented similar patterns of gift exchange:

> The most passionate appeals are frequently made by the women, as contra-distinguished [from] the pseudo-males, when they have suspected the last named parties of <u>infidelity</u> or fickleness; indeed an amount of jealousy seems to be aroused as [great as] possibly could be if an actual "male" was in question ... promises, & threats are alike lavished on the objects of their love, & they are habitually in the practice of making numerous presents to their "<u>lovers</u>", so that an individual who acts the infamous part of a pseudo male, is most <u>comfortably</u> provided for, by the presents bestowed, with every procurable luxury. [Archives Office of Tasmania, MM62/31/13859, emphasis in the original]

As previously noted, archaeological excavations at the Ross Factory site may have encountered a material signature of this sexual economy, with the greatest concentrations of illicit objects recovered from the earthen floors of the Solitary Cellblock (Casella 2000, 2002). As a place designed for the incarceration of particularly recalcitrant inmates, the Solitary Cells isolated those considered kingpins within the inmate society of Ross Factory—those, in other words, who would have been provided "with every procurable luxury."

Crucially, sociological studies indicate that not all positions of obligation within the inmate gift cycle hold equal status. If, according to Bourdieu, one gives to anticipate reciprocity, then participants are far more powerful during the period before the counter-gift than during the fulfillment of that obligation, as that trade merely begets a new and inverse obligation. Thus, it is better to be owed than to owe within the cycle. If the concept of libido refers to both material and sexual yearnings, it would follow that the enticement of desire, the prolonged flirtations and foreplay, could be far more lucrative than actual fulfillment of that desire. Further, the whole focus of the cycle is the anticipation, the *promise* of libido reciprocated, rather than the sexual or object exchange itself.

In the same letter of 1850, Superintendent Irvine of the Ross Female Factory noted that

> these young girls are in the habit of decorating themselves, cleaning themselves scrupulously, and making themselves as attractive as they can, before resorting to the "man-woman," if I may so style her, on whom they have bestowed their affections; I believe, a large proportion of the quarrels which too frequently occur amongst [the women]...are occasioned by, or take their rise from disagreements concerning the choice of a pseudo-male, or jealous feelings consequent on, some of these disgraceful transactions. To my certain knowledge several disputes have arisen here, from these causes, & there have been letters intercepted...which will prove the warmth & impetuosity of the feelings excited in women towards each other, when allied in such unholy bonds. [Archives Office of Tasmania, MM62/31/13859]

Perhaps this dynamic of anticipation serves to enhance the paramount status of "studs" within the black market economy of the prison. Receiving illicit material gifts in exchange for the promise of sexual fulfilment, these kingpin inmates are able to operate the gift cycle to their maximum benefit. In a study of the Federal Reformatory for Women in Alderson, West Virginia, Elizabeth Flynn similarly observed:

> The masculine partner dominated the relationship, demanding and getting service. Their clothes were washed and ironed for them, their rooms cleaned, presents made or bought, and commissary provided. I knew one girl who worked it like a racket, playing one admirer against another, while she laughed and told me privately of her true friend outside, to whom she would return. [Flynn 1963:160]

However, similar expressions of gendered identity do not necessarily mobilize an equivalent degree of socioeconomic status within prison exchange systems. In Heffernan's study (1972), female inmates carefully distinguished between those (somewhat heroic) studs who maintained an androgynous fusion between masculine and feminine traits and those who surpassed or overexerted the role by abandoning *all* material trappings of femininity. Referred to as "broken down daddies," the latter were portrayed as failed studs—socially isolated figures who, through their "abnormal" masculinity, could not entice inmate desires and had thereby failed to marshal a stable of broads or mobilize a network of resources. Within male institutions, equally careful distinctions are made between those who involuntarily participate in the sexual economy ("turn-outs," "gal-boys," or "bitches") and those who enthusiastically seek such reciprocity ("homos," "ladies," or "queens"). While gal-boys are generally reviled as exploitative possessions, queens may generate respect within inmate society, having earned an elevated status through their ability to manipulate prisoner libido:

> [It's] because of the definite power and influence they can wield over other prisoners, the feminine charm and grace they can utilize as a weapon to pit prisoners against each other, to foment jealousies and rivals. But...it depends upon the individual—she can be a lady or a whore. She can conduct herself where she don't create chaos, confusion or conflict, or she can constantly keep trouble stirred up. [Rideau 1995:161]

Thus, accounts by both inmates and criminologists demonstrate the complex intersections between conjugal relations and gendered status within the reciprocal economy of the prison. To survive this murky world is to entice the libido of one's fellow prisoners, to offer, in other words, the lure of material or embodied satisfaction.

Conclusions

Penal networks reveal the internal operation of a black market economy. These covert (and frequently semi-sanctioned) encounters create situational exchange relations, variously appearing in the form of altruistic reciprocity, forging bonds of mutuality amongst fictive kin; balanced reciprocity, circulating essential commodities throughout the institution; and negative reciprocity, generating violent and abusive relations between prisoners. Given the nature of trade within institutions of punishment, shadowy obligations of exchange appear to simultaneously articulate with dynamics of sexual activity. Through trafficking, prisoners repossess and recreate the sexual meanings of both illicit objects and their gendered internal relations. These illicit transactions enmesh them into social and temporal cycles of obligation and desire.

However, within these alternative inmate worlds, not all gendered roles can equally mobilize exchange. Those identified as studs, pseudomales, or queens benefit from the obligation to receive and extend that powerful position within the gift cycle by prolonging the promise of sexual fulfillment—the material flirtations and foreplay that precede sexual encounters and enhance the libido of fellow inmates. Nonetheless, theirs is a delicate identity, one accompanied by the danger of surpassing—of being too butch or girlie—and thereby risking social and material alienation.

In all nonmonetary societies, including the penitentiary, trade is undertaken to not only supply valued commodities but to mobilize social power, cultivate influence, and demonstrate status (Lévi-Strauss 1987 [1950]; Polanyi 1957; Weiner 1992). Whether transacted through objectified or embodied form, these economic encounters serve to identify inmates within the perpetual cycle of gifting, receiving, and reciprocating (Mauss 1990 [1950]; Godelier 1999). Further, considering the material life of these exchanges reveals reciprocity itself to be a complex social dynamic. Although traditional archaeological studies used questions of spatial distance and interpersonal altruism to characterize modes of reciprocity (Renfrew 1975; Sahlins 1972), such rigid distinctions cannot be applied to trade relations under incarceration. Rather, a fluid, situational, and simultaneous array of exchange relations can be seen to operate within the penal environment (Casella 2007). Ultimately, it is an obscure and pluralistic web of reciprocity—of competitions, favors, extortions, and obligations—that choreographs daily life within the austere institutional world of the modern prison.

References

Angelo
2003 *Prisoners' Inventions*. WhiteWalls, Inc., Chicago.

Bourdieu, Pierre
1998 *Practical Reason*. Polity Press, Cambridge.

British Home Office (BHO)
1964 *The Prison Rules*. Her Majesty's Stationary Office, London.

Bush, David R.
2000 Interpreting the Latrines of the Johnson's Island Civil War Military Prison. *Historical Archaeology* 34(1):62–78.

Casella, Eleanor Conlin
2000 'Doing Trade': a Sexual Economy of Nineteenth-Century Australian Convict Prisons. *World Archaeology* 32(2):209–221.
2001 To Watch or Restrain: Female Convict Prisons in 19th Century Tasmania, Australia. *International Journal of Historical Archaeology* 5(1):45–72.
2002 *Archaeology of The Ross Female Factory: Female Incarceration in Van Diemen's Land, Australia*. Records of the Queen Victoria Museum and Art Gallery, Volume 108. QVMAG Publications, Launceston (Tasmania).
2007 *The Archaeology of Institutional Confinement*. University of Florida Press, Gainesville.

Charrière, Henri
1970 *Papillon*. Panther Books, Ltd., St. Albans, United Kingdom.

Cotter, J. L., R. W. Moss, B. C. Gill, and J. Kim
1988 *The Walnut Street Prison Workshop*. The Athenæum of Philadelphia, Philadelphia.

Flynn, Elizabeth Gurley
1963 *The Alderson Story: My Life as a Political Prisoner.* International Publishers, New York.

Foster, Thomas W.
1975 Make-Believe Families: A Response of Women and Girls to the Deprivations of Imprisonment. *International Journal of Criminology and Penology* 3:71–78.

Gallo, Ermanno, and Vincenzo Ruggiero
1991 The Immaterial Prison: Custody as a Factory for the Manufacture of Handicaps *International Journal for the Sociology of Law* (19):273–291.

Garman, James C.
2005 *Detention Castles of Stone and Steel.* University of Tennessee Press, Knoxville.

Giallombardo, Rose
1966 *Society of Women.* Wiley, New York.

Godelier, Maurice
1999 *The Enigma of the Gift.* University of Chicago Press, Chicago.

Goffman, Erving
1961 *Asylums.* Anchor Books, New York.

Gregory, Chris A.
1982 *Gifts and Commodities.* Academic Press, London.

Heffernan, Esther
1972 *Making It In Prison.* Wiley-Interscience, New York.

Irwin, John
1990 [1970] *The Felon,* 2nd ed. University of California Press, Berkeley.

James, Erwin
2003 *A Life Inside: A Prisoner's Notebook.* Atlantic Books, London.

Jones, Richard S.
1993 Coping with Separation: Adaptive Responses of Women Prisoners. *Women and Criminal Justice* 5(1):71–97.

Kruttschnitt, Candace
1981 Prison Codes, Inmate Solidarity, and Women: A Reexamination. In *Comparing Female and Male Offenders,* edited by Marguerite Q. Warren, pp. 123–141. Sage Publications, Beverly Hills, California.

Levi, Primo
1987 [1958] *If This is a Man* and *The Truce.* Sphere Books, Ltd., London.

Lévi-Strauss, Claude
1987 [1950] *Introduction to the Work of Marcel Mauss.* Translated by Felicity Baker. Routledge and Kegan Paul, London.

Liebling, Alison
1999 Prison Suicide and Prisoner Coping. In *Prisons*, edited by Michael Tonry and Joan Petersilia, pp. 283–359. University of Chicago Press, Chicago.

Mauss, Marcel
1990 [1950] *The Gift.* W.W. Norton, New York.

Owen, Barbara A.
1998 *In the Mix: Struggle and Survival in a Women's Prison.* SUNY Press, New York.

Polanyi, Karl
1957 The Economy as an Instituted Process. In *Trade and Market in the Early Empires,* edited by K. Polanyi, C. Arensberg, and H. Pearson, pp. 243–270. Free Press and Falcon's Wing Press, Glencoe.

Renfrew, A. Colin
1975 Trade as Action at a Distance: Questions of Integration and Communication. In *Ancient Civilization and Trade,* edited by J. A. Sabloff and C. C. Lamberg-Karlovsky, pp. 3–59. University of New Mexico Press, Albuquerque.

Rideau, Wilbert
1995 Prison: The Sexual Jungle. In *The Wall Is Strong: Corrections in Louisiana,* 3rd ed., edited by Burk Foster, Wilbert Rideau, and Douglas Dennis, pp. 142–166. Center for Louisiana Studies, University of Southwestern Louisiana, Lafayette.

Sahlins, Marshall
1963 Poor Man, Rich Man, Big Man, Chief: Political Types in Melanesia and Polynesia. *Comparative Studies in Society and History* 5:285–300.
1972 *Stone Age Economics.* Aldine, New York.

Strathern, Marilyn
1988 *The Gender of the Gift.* University of California Press, Berkeley.

Sykes, Gresham M.
1958 *The Society of Captives.* Princeton University, Princeton, New Jersey.

Tittle, Charles R., and Drollene P. Tittle
1964 Social Organization of Prisoners. *Social Forces* 43(2):216–221.

Tonry, Michael, and Joan Petersilia
1999 *Prisons.* University of Chicago Press, Chicago.

Wacquant, Loïc
2001 Deadly Symbiosis: When Ghetto and Prison Meet and Mesh. In *Mass Imprisonment: Social Causes and Consequences,* edited by D. Garland, pp. 82–120. Sage Publishers, London.

Weiner, Annette B.
1992 *Inalienable Possessions.* University of California Press, Berkeley.

Williams, Virgil L., and Mary Fish
1974 *Convicts, Codes, and Contraband: The Prison Life of Men and Women.* Ballinger, Cambridge, Massachusetts.

Wilson, T. W.
1986 Gender Differences in the Inmate Code. *Canadian Journal of Criminology* 28(4): 397–405.

Wurtzburg, Susan, and Thurston H. Hahn III
1992 Hard Labor: A Cultural Resources Survey of the Old Louisiana State Penitentiary, Baton Rouge, Louisiana. Unpublished report by Coastal Environments Ltd., Baton Rouge, Louisiana.

Zingraff, M. and R. Zingraff
1980 Adaptation Patterns of Incarcerated Female Delinquents. *Juvenile and Family Court Journal* 31(2):35–47.

CHAPTER 9

Buying a Table in Erfelek: Socialities of Contact and Community in the Black Sea Region

Owen P. Doonan and Alexander A. Bauer

Buying a Table: An Archaeologist's Tale

The team was exhausted. After a hot morning surveying in the Sinop Midlands, we took a break for lunch in Erfelek, a local market town. Friday is market day in Erfelek, when people from all over the district come in for the kebab that the town is famous for. After lunch, we walked around the market and some team members admired a table in a junk shop window. An occupational hazard of working in this rarely visited area is that we attract attention wherever we go. The owner of the shop greeted us as a crowd gathered around.

Erfelek is a small administrative center in the forested midlands of Sinop, a promontory at the midpoint of the southern Black Sea coast in Turkey (fig. 9.1). The district has historically been sparsely populated and has an economy based on forest products, animal husbandry, and small-scale farming. Until very recently, the local economy has been almost totally self-sufficient. The town was transformed from an isolated settlement into an administrative center in the early 1970s. Paved roads and electricity were introduced at the same time, facilitating communications. At present Erfelek has a mixed monetary and barter-oriented economy, dependent largely on outside sources for manufactured goods and local sources for food (fig. 9.2). Most families have members living in large Turkish and European cities who contribute to the family income. All of our contacts

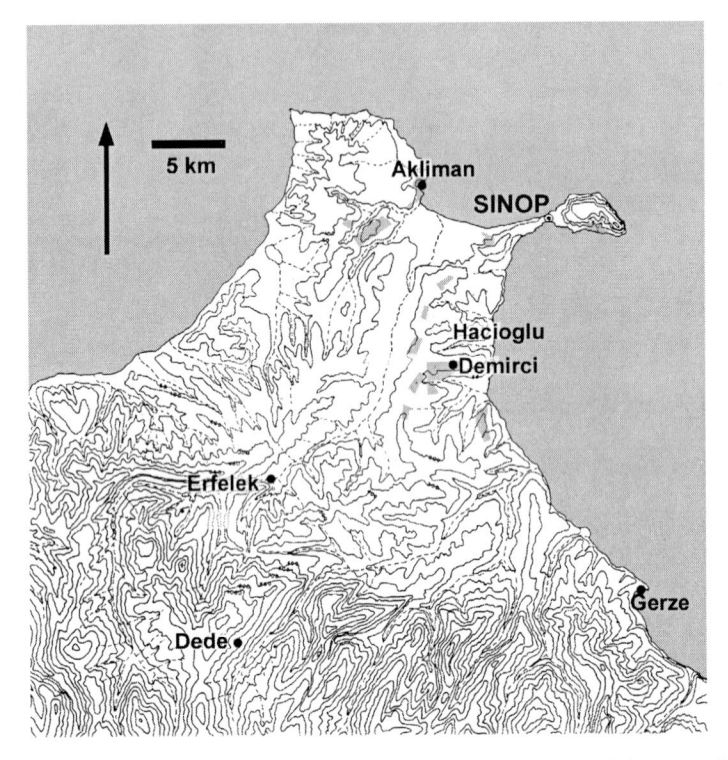

Figure 9.1 Map of the Sinop promontory, with major towns and sites mentioned in the text. Courtesy of the authors.

Figure 9.2 The cattle market in Erfelek, Turkey. Photograph by A. Bauer.

in Erfelek had previous experience doing business with outsiders, although their businesses were very small-scale and local in scope.

The process of buying a table illustrates the fundamentally social nature of trade and the chance and contingency that shape the interaction at every step. These qualities are particularly apparent in the initial engagement, in which two different economic cultures link. Turkoğlu, the owner of the shop (fig. 9.3) and a well-respected, conservative member of the community, expressed surprise and suspicion at our interest in the table. Why would we be interested in such a simple item? The table was about a meter across, low and round, carved from a single chestnut log. The workmanship was typical of Black Sea highland villages, where furnishings, vessels, and tools are nearly all fashioned of wood. We found this woodwork particularly appealing because of its long-standing tradition. The woodwork of this area has been praised from Classical Greek times onward. Turkoğlu explored the nature of our interest, bringing out an array of other items from his shop, from broken telephones to old undergarments. We, in turn, were shocked that he would offer us such items and said we were only interested in the table. A deal was struck and we departed. That was the first step in our engagement.

Nearly a year passed before our next visit to Erfelek. We returned on market day, and after lunch we spent an hour exploring the bazaar. Our

Figure 9.3 Junk shop window, Erfelek, Turkey. Photograph by A. Bauer.

friend's shop was shut, but while we were looking in the window, some men approached us. They led us to another shop, a small tourist agency run by Çorapçi, a rival of the junk shop owner. Inside, Çorapçi showed us several wooden items, but they did not appeal to us. He asked what sorts of things we were looking for and said he would have them the next week.

When we returned, Çorapçi offered us several beautiful wooden bowls at a very inflated price. We praised the quality of the merchandise but refused to pay his high asking price. He surprised us by offering the bowls as a gift, explaining that he had made a bet with a friend that we would buy them. This second interaction broadened the scope of our interaction with the community. We had become pawns in an ongoing rivalry between community leaders. Our skill in evaluating the worth of wooden bowls was tested by the tourist agent, who cemented our social relationship with the gift. Apparently, the contextual value of the bowls was a negotiation between our value for them as exotica and their local value as domestic implements. When we departed, we told the tourist agent we would return the following year and that we were interested in continuing our relationship. On our return, his shop was full of bowls and tables offered at a reasonable price. Our negotiations went smoothly because both parties had reached a consensus about the value of these items.

Two years passed before we returned to Erfelek. The tourist agent was friendly but expressed no interest in continuing to sell us anything. The junk shop had disappeared altogether. But when we encountered Turkoğlu, he suggested that he would be willing to collect many tables, provided we could buy them in bulk. We contacted a friend in who owns a handicraft shop in the city of Ankara, and the two struck a deal.

These latest stages of our negotiations shifted the context of interaction from the personal to interregional. Çorapçi, for his part, may have lost interest in our relationship because it was informal and unpredictable. The shift to a broader geographic and social context entailed the establishment of a more formal protocol between parties and implied the potential for continuous, long-term engagement. Interestingly, the impetus for moving the relationship to more formal terms came from the local agent, in contrast to the expectations of classic core-periphery models. The proposal to produce goods emerged out of the relationship between two parties, and in this case a third party enabled the actualization of a productive relationship. All engagements in this process were conditioned by chance, yet these independent interests intersected to create a relationship that satisfied each party.

We tell this story not to try to draw a direct analogy—such a claim would be simplistic at best and at any rate is epistemologically unfounded. Rather, we wish to use it to illustrate how archaeological studies that ignore the social dimensions of trade miss much of the richness and subtlety of human action and thus may not provide adequate explanations of past social processes.

Lessons from Erfelek: The Importance of Scale, Context, and Agency in Trade Relationships

Recent archaeological theorizing has virtually ignored trade as a subject of study, in spite of its emphasis on other social aspects of the past. Yet some of the most significant contributions of postprocessual archaeology have brought to the forefront the more subtle aspects of social interaction that have often been obscured by universalizing models. Our experiences interacting with merchants in a Turkish town over the course of our conducting an archaeological survey in the region illustrate the fundamentally social nature of trade. Using the story of our encounter as a point of departure, we highlight three areas in which the problems raised by the postprocessual critique might enrich the study of trade as a social phenomenon: scale, context, and agency. We then discuss how such insights about trade relationships lead to a richer and more sophisticated approach to understanding the Sinop region's history.

As discussed in the opening chapters in this volume, trade studies have a long history in archaeology, but recent years have witnessed diminishing interest in the topic, with contemporary concerns over meaning and practice coming to dominate archaeological discourse. Although there is no reason to believe that trade world not fit with these perspectives, the subject's close association with positivist processual models may make it seem less interesting or amenable to contemporary approaches. But as this volume asserts, is this lack of interest not just another case of throwing out the baby with the bathwater? Undoubtedly there are social aspects of the practice of trade that have been overlooked; for one thing, we must recognize that it is fundamentally a social act. And if we accept that trade is a social phenomenon, then its study can be enriched by many elements of the postprocessual critique. After all, some of the most significant contributions of postprocessual archaeology have been to bring to the forefront the more subtle aspects of social interaction that have often been obscured by universalizing models.

The Erfelek story highlights the complex and contingent nature of trade relationships, their establishment, and their transformation over time. Rather than developing and operating in the linear way that many positivist models suggest, the relationships are distinctly nonlinear and play out in different arenas, at different scales, and with different agendas. As a result, many of the contributions made by the postprocessual critique have salience for understanding the interactions we experienced in Erfelek.

In this chapter, we would like to highlight three themes of contemporary interest brought out by the Erfelek story that directly affect how archaeologists deal with trade in the past: problems of scale, context, and agency. The recognition of these themes as important for understanding the social dynamics of trade has in turn informed our approach to the archaeology of the Sinop region (in which modern-day Erfelek is situated) from the prehistoric period to the present. Cultural interaction and influence across the maritime space of the Black Sea is one of the long-term defining features of the region and its cultural identity (Doonan 2004b, 2007; Bauer 2006a, forthcoming). In our ongoing work there, we have envisioned a project that identifies the multiple ways in which culture moves among individuals, communities, and regions and the ways in which those players both actively shape and are shaped by the circulation of cultural elements, both tangible objects and intangible ideas and practices involving those objects. Following a discussion of the three concepts of scale, context, and agency, we will present three short archaeological cases from the Sinop region. The first two illustrate how recognizing the social dimensions of interaction we describe here enables us to develop a richer understanding of the archaeology of Sinop, and the third shows how those insights may be applied to a more fragmentary prehistoric case in order to explore dynamics that would elude more traditional approaches.

Scale

When archaeologists think of scale in relation to trade, we most commonly are referring to geographic scale or to the volume of goods or transfer of value. Recent explorations of scale have raised our awareness that it is an arbitrary analytical unit, particularly with respect to complex interactions (Mathieu and Scott 2004). Multi-sited frameworks of research have recently been applied to ethnographies of complex phenomena like diaspora formation and globalization that are mapped over diverse geographies and can be traced at multiple scales (Agbe-Davies 2009; Appadurai 1990; Doonan 2004a; Marcus 1995; Shami 2000). One of the strengths of multi-sited studies is that attention is focused as much or more on the links between sites as the sites themselves. Sites are thus chosen based on their potential for illuminating these links as much as for their inherent interest.

Table 9.1 Modes of interaction implicated in the Erfelek experience.

Context of relationship	Locus	Points of rupture or negotiation
Local	House Gatherings Markets Local shop	• Competition for local social/political influence • Access to sources, customers • Generalized, balanced reciprocity
Local-visitor	Local shop	• Value negotiated between local utilitarianism and external exoticism • Formality of the relationship dependent on mutual fulfillment of expectations • Balanced reciprocity
Local-professional	Local shop Telephone	• Value based on supply and demand • Relationship dependent on trust, volume, and regularity • Negative reciprocity
Professional	Urban shop	• Value based on broader market considerations • Negative reciprocity

We might identify four scales of interaction operative in the parable related above, each of which differs from the others in terms of the terms of reciprocity, geographic scale, and economic scale, and each of which is sited differently (table 9.1). First, exchange between locals can take place in many settings, including houses, social gatherings, markets of various types, and shops. Second, interactions between outsiders and locals take place primarily in shops and markets. Third, the interactions between the urban professional and local merchants take place mostly over the telephone, although the initial agreement was followed by a personal visit to the village. Fourth, the urban professional then sells the items to foreign and Turkish customers in his shop hundreds of miles away. In order to understand the process of trade and its roles in a community, it is necessary to take into account these multiple scales and the different spatial contexts in which they operate.

Scale is also important when we consider the shifting contexts of exchange. One of the problems with Braudel's (1972 [1949]) multiscalar model is that he does not adequately address how the scales interact. World-systems models, too, often gloss over multi-sited and multiscalar aspects of trade (Knapp and Cherry 1994). Thus, how are we to understand the shifts among them? We must take into account the differing social factors that are apparent when analyzing highly formal versus more opportunistic exchange, or low volumes versus high volumes of goods involving the transfer of value that can also be socially transformative. Although we are aware that our story cannot be used uncritically, one of the most interesting things about the Erfelek experience is that we witnessed the shifting scales in practice. And our experience raises the point that scale shifts may not only be chance occurrences but may also involve different agents who are in conflict with one another. Thus on an intersocietal level, what may appear to be a single mode of interaction may be quite variable and even a source of conflict within the community.

Context and Meaning

Any given trade interaction occurs within a unique context, and a central contribution of the postprocessual critique was to illustrate the ways in which meanings are context dependent (Hodder 1987; Hodder et al. 1995; Bauer 2002). Studies of trade that emphasize the large-scale processes obscure the roles of contingency and context by focusing on macro trends. Moreover, the contexts of interaction can play an important role in a trade relationship, particularly at its establishment, as well as at scalar shifts. The human relationships that constitute trade are fickle—people do not act within a system but within a matrix of community and individual goals. Participants can choose to shift the scale of interaction or drop out for any number of reasons. Others can engage or compete for control of an advantageous situation; for example, Çorapçi the tourist agent (whom we would expect to be most savvy in dealing with outsiders) chose to drop out and Türkoğlu elected to shift to a more intensive scale of exchange.

Examining context also helps us to understand more fully how the objects at the center of exchange relationships acquire and convey meaning to the participants involved. As Urban (chapter 10, this volume) describes, objects that are exchanged in moments of interaction between two actors are imbued with a host of meanings, many of which are specific to that interactive context. At the same time, however, even those meanings that seem singular and contingent to that particular moment may often be part of larger chains of meaning that build on prior experiences and set the stage for later ones. When Çorapçi offered us the bowls as a gift after we had refused to pay his high price, that was not simply a gift or acknowledgment of our savvy bargaining skills but expressed both his relationship with another person in his community (as he acknowledged when he gave them to us), as well as his hope to build new relationships with us.

Multiple meanings may thus operate simultaneously and on different scales in a single engagement, and archaeologists must be prepared to articulate and interrogate these possibilities. Transformations in the meanings of a local product from junk to export is the result when conflicting value systems are brought into harmony through the negotiation of value between two or more contexts. But as Appadurai (1986) and others (e.g., Bloch and Parry 1989; Fotiadis 1999; Kopytoff 1986) have pointed out, the oppositional categories of utilitarian and symbolic meanings are not our only interpretive options. On the contrary, meanings that are *indexical*, or result from spatio-temporal associations, may be the most important ones for understanding social relations (Keane 2006; Parmentier 1997; Preucel 2006; Preucel and Bauer 2001; see also Agbe-Davies, chapter 4, this volume; Urban, chapter 10, this volume).

Agency

A third contribution of recent social theories in archaeology is represented by the emergence of agent-oriented perspectives (Dobres 2000; Dobres and Robb 2000, 2005; Johnson 1989). Actor-oriented models may focus on decision making and competition between agents for prestige and in this way fit nicely with the growing trend of looking at and modeling social processes in the past. Particularly relevant to our work on maritime trade and the exchange of information in the Black Sea, McGlade and McGlade's (1989) study of fishing communities might serve as a good example of how various community agents affect the adoption and transformation of innovative ideas.

Focusing on agents helps us appreciate the role of the individual in interpreting and shaping his or her world in both context-specific and scalar ways, thus intersecting with the two previous themes highlighted by the Erfelek story. In this sense, the agent *is* the context of knowledge production. The meanings of things are constituted through the subjectivity of active agents and are communicated, reproduced, and transformed through social encounters among those agents. At the same time, agency is related to identity, both at the scale of community and among communities (Joyce and Lopiparo 2005). By considering agency at the individual level, we can problematize the role of communities in constituting the social identities of agents, as well as the ways in which communities themselves are both sites and agents of social action. In noncoercive situations, how might the community instigate and shape the practice of trade? Certainly, individuals act on their own, but as we saw from our encounter in Erfelek, they are also performing within and in response to their communities.

Trade is an action that requires the participation of multiple agents. A focus on the agent forces us to address questions regarding the choices of trade items and what meanings those items had for the different participants. Moreover, it also requires us to look "beyond the material" (Renfrew 1993b:5) and consider the role of trade in establishing and maintaining social relations among individuals and groups.

Exploring the Social Nature of Trade in the Black Sea: Three Cases from Sinop, Turkey

Trading Among the Milesian Colonial Community

Discussions of the nature of the Greek economy and trade often start with the debate between "primitivists," who view the Greek economy as essentially household based, and "modernists," who view the Greek economy as more like the emerging market economies in early modern Europe (see discussion in Morris et al. 2007). Moses Finley (1985) reoriented the terms of the debate by clarifying the structure of economic practice. Following Polanyi's (1957) substantivist model of exchange (but challenging Polanyi's conclusions about the Greek economy), Finley emphasized the socially embedded nature of Greek exchange and the critical role of citizen status and land ownership in restraining the development of more modern market exchange practices. The powerful influence of Finley's model can distort the very different conditions and practices in contexts far from Athens (Morris et al. 2007, citing Hopkins 1983). Competitive reciprocal exchange dominated great markets like the Athenian agora. Buying and selling between strangers, however, often involved deception and negotiation, as we saw in the story that serves as the catalyst for this discussion. Bargaining and cheating in Greek markets are known from a number of ancient sources (Aristophanes *Pax* 1197–1264; *Acharnians* 867–958; Athenaeus *Deipnosophistai* 3.76d; also see discussion in Möller 2007). Consider the following passage from Athenaeus of Naukratis, *Deipnosophists* (iii.10):

> Alexis also says in his "Cauldron"
> And why now need we speak of people who
> Sell every day their figs in close pack'd baskets
> And constantly do place those figs below
> Which are hard and bad; but on top they range
> The ripe and beautiful fruit. And then a comrade,

As if he'd bought the basket, gives the price;
The seller putting in his mouth the coin,
Sells wild figs while he swears he's selling good ones...[1]

The case of Sinope (modern Sinop) offers an important contrast to Athens in the nature of the port and its evolving relationship with non-Greek neighbors in its hinterland. Sinope was one of dozens of colonies founded by Miletus in the Black Sea (fig. 9.4). In fact, it was the earliest on the south coast, founded in the third quarter of the seventh century BC according to presently available evidence. Sinope in turn founded a handful of its own colonies along the Anatolian Black Sea littoral to create a trade system that integrated coastal control points with the metal-rich mountains and river systems of the southeastern interior. Profits derived from the management of overseas trade through its colonies sustained the port of Sinope perhaps as late as the early fourth century (Doonan 2004b), at which time the port was cut off from its colonial holdings by the aggressions of a renegade Persian governor named Datames. There is very little evidence of Greek engagement with the Sinope hinterland before the second quarter of the fourth century BC (Doonan 2004b), and given the profitability of the community's overseas arrangements, there may have been little impetus to develop agricultural territories or economic partnerships with the interior. Citizens were most likely not agricultural landowners, and we can imagine a freewheeling economy in which wealth was largely invested in ships and cargoes.

Soon after Datames' aggressions, however, Greek ceramics began to appear with much greater frequency in the hinterland, first on the headland of Boztepe and in nearby coastal valleys (Doonan 2004b). It appears that some of these settlements and industrial areas were partially or largely inhabited by Greeks, whereas others were primarily indigenous. One source of potential difficulty may have been the initial negotiations between Greeks and local non-Greeks as trading partners in the hinterland.

In developing an approach to investigate emerging exchange and production processes in the Sinop promontory and identify shifting relationships such as those in the fourth century, the Sinop Regional Archaeological Project is particularly concerned with the early emergence of coastal communities that served to integrate the port with the productive hinterland and its rich resources. The contexts of landscape monuments like burial tumuli are carefully studied and may suggest efforts by those in the new coastal settlements to establish a mythical "middle ground" that connects outside settlers to a local history by associating their own burial mounds with pre-existing mounded settlements (Doonan 2009). Other evidence, such as a predominance of distinctive black-sand tempered ceramic pastes produced

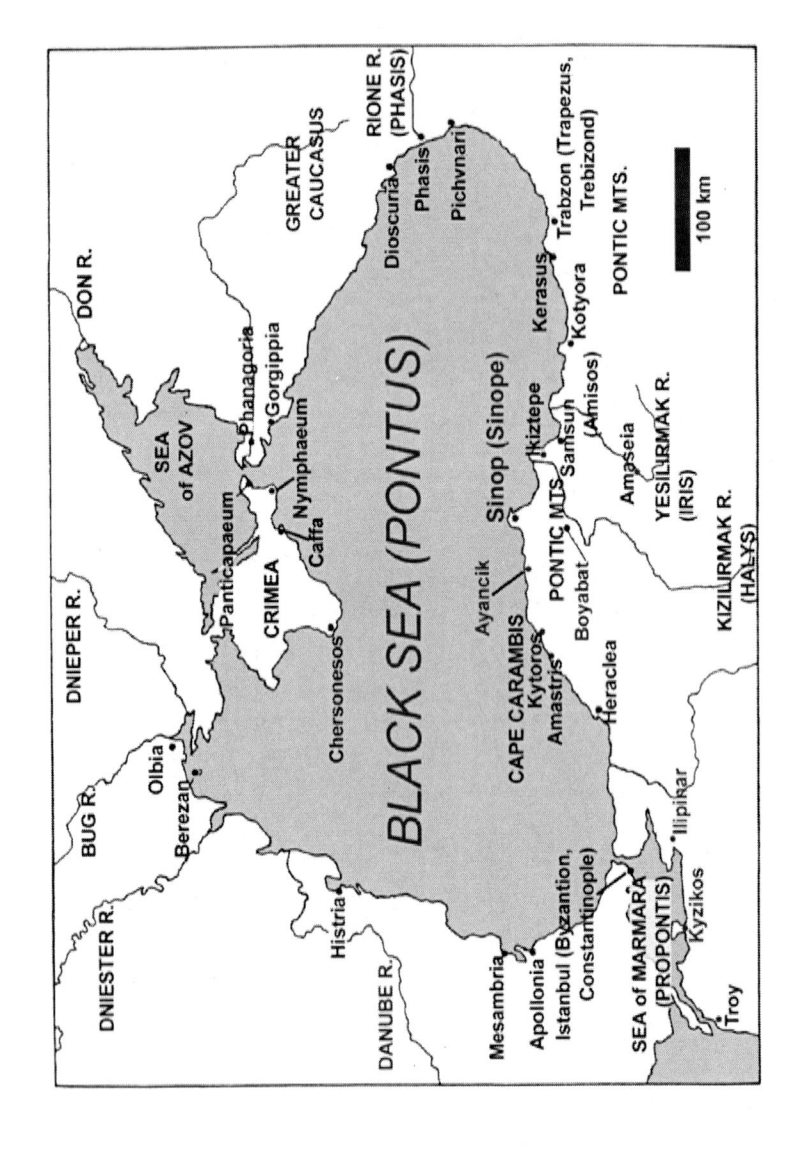

Figure 9.4 Map of significant archaeological sites in the Black Sea, showing Sinop (Classical Sinope) at the midpoint along the southern coast. Map by O. Doonan.

in the suburbs of the town in certain locations, may point to the establishment of close partnerships with secondary ports along the coast. The sampling strategy of the survey and our analysis of ceramic finds are designed in part to identify changing patterns of settlement and artifact distribution that point to changing relationships between Sinope and its hinterland (Doonan 2004a; Doonan and Bauer 2005). By collaborating with projects at Sinopean and Milesian colonies around the Black Sea, we hope to extend our understanding to Sinope's overseas foreland as well (Doonan 2006).

Tale of the Polish Merchants

Our second case study concerns a group of Polish merchants who landed at Sinop in 1576 or 1577 laden with silver, gold, and luxury cloth (Faroqhi 1984:66–69). When they landed, they had contact with a group of merchants from the inland town of Tokat who offered to guide them through the mountains. They were spending the night in a private home in the mountains when a group of *medrese* (theological seminary) students from Sinop, in collaboration with local authorities, ambushed and killed them, taking their goods. Subsequent investigations shed light on the extensive connections of the conspirators, including an *emin* (official bureaucrat) and a military commander in Sinop, a judge in the nearby town of Durağan, and a military commander in Kastamonu. It became clear that within only a few days of the incident, the Polish merchants' goods had been circulated among merchants in several towns spread over hundreds of kilometers.

As this event illustrates, communications across the Sinop landscape could be easy or difficult, depending on who one was and what one was trying to transport. Clearly, these students and local officials were integrated into an extensive network spread across northern and central Anatolia. In the context of weak state authority, outsiders attempting to circumvent this network were vulnerable to grave threats (Doonan 2004b).

This image of organized chaos in the mountains can be better understood by looking at recent ethnographic and ethnohistorical research in eastern Black Sea Turkey. Bellér-Hann and Hann's (2001) studies in this area examined the organization of markets (*pazars*) and their impact on regional cultural and economic integration. Building a dynamic model to bridge Polanyi's (1957) broader concept of "mode of integration," they investigate the processes (modes) of integration between city and countryside from Ottoman through contemporary times. From Ottoman times onward there is good documentation of periodic markets, normally held weekly in towns

196 • Owen P. Doonan and Alexander A. Bauer

and villages throughout the region. Villagers, often women, would bring surplus produce and animals to the designated location to exchange for refined or finished goods (flour, sugar, and so on). Personal, ethnic, and familial ties were vitally important in determining who would trade with whom and in such matters as the extension of credit (Bellér-Hann and Hann 2001:68–69). Ethnicities traceable in the hinterland of Sinop include various Turks, Greeks, Armenians, Circassians, Georgians, Laz, and others. These distinct subgroups were spread out in a patchwork of small villages and hamlets over the landscape (fig. 9.5). Meeker (2002) has noted a geographic component to the ethnic and familial networks in the eastern Black Sea. An interlocking checkerboard of ethnically distinctive microcommunities, sometimes allies, sometimes rivals, covered the ridges and valleys from the mountaintops to the sea. These social discontinuities created considerable friction, restricting movement through the countryside. Negotiating this complex social map would be particularly challenging for outsiders. At the same time, extensive social networks, aided at times by government institutions, afforded rapid movement of information and goods across vast areas.

The Sinop Regional Archaeological Project has conducted extensive surveys in the mountainous regions of Sinop and has recently begun systematic

Figure 9.5 Cautious hospitality at Sarıboğ a village in the mountains of Sinop. Photograph by O. Doonan.

research around the village of Sorkum. Results to date are preliminary, but they reinforce the general impression from historical sources that the region was isolated and underpopulated. Widely spaced Ottoman mosques have been recorded in Sorkum and Dedekoy, each near likely mountain crossings (fig. 9.6). Ibn Battutah and Hamilton traveled through these mountains in the thirteenth and nineteenth centuries, respectively. Each commented on the severely underdeveloped communications infrastructure of the Sinop mountain hinterland in contrast to the beauty and sophistication of the port. Our survey in the highlands works hand in hand with ethnohistorical and archival research to piece together what system of hamlets, *hans* (inns), pazars, and mosques there was in this difficult terrain (Doonan et al. 2001; Doonan and Bauer 2005).

Following the Fishes in the Bronze Age?

The kinds of relationships described in the previous case studies make clear that in many cases social processes govern interaction. How can this insight be used to inform and enrich a model for the prehistoric pattern in the Black Sea, which might otherwise be explained exclusively in ecological, technological, or demographic terms, as is typical for cases lacking a rich textual

Figure 9.6 The sixteenth-century wooden mosque at Dedeköy, Sinop Province. Photograph O. Doonan.

record? For one, this insight may encourage us to contemplate interpretive options—and methods to investigate them—not usually considered for prehistoric cases. In the Early Bronze Age Black Sea (particularly between ca. 3000 and 2500 BC), there is evidence of an emerging cultural cohesiveness across the region, manifest in material culture similarities among specifically coastal groups that appear at this time. In spite of these similarities, however, there is little evidence for the relocation of people or objects—signifying "migration" or "trade"— to explain the pattern. This is where the insights of the previous cases and the Erfelek story may be particularly helpful, as they illustrate how relationships may develop out of informal and even seasonal interactions.

One possible catalyst for such interaction lies in the Black Sea itself: the sea has long been a great resource for fish, and the seasonal spawning patterns of its many species (such as the anchovy; see fig. 9.7) require that fishermen exploit different parts of the sea at different times of year. Although sailing technology was not likely employed in the Black Sea until the Iron Age, fishermen following coastlines would have come into contact with one another and, as they do today, would likely have shared knowledge (to a variable extent) about the status of resources they sought. Such social relationships, as Urban points out in chapter 10 here, allow "bits" of culture to move from person to person in each encounter and may thus over time facilitate the development of new social forms. In this way, interaction may be understood as a virtual space forming the basis of a new social community that becomes real as its participants—the people actually moving and doing the interacting—communicate with each other and develop a shared cultural tradition across the contexts of that interaction (fig. 9.8).

To test this idea, the pottery technology of several of the coastal regions— the primary sample from Sinop, Turkey, and comparative samples from southern Ukraine and the northwest Caucasus— were analyzed in order to identify whether a shared pottery-making tradition developed during the Bronze Age as a result of the communication and knowledge sharing typical of a more integrated and interacting community (Bauer 2006a, 2008). Since technology is closely related to the identities of communities, studying it provides a productive way to investigate the development of such social relations in the past (Agbe-Davies, chapter 4, this volume; Lemonnier 1976, 1992; Stark 1998). Repeated and patterned ways of making pottery, such as the tempering, forming, firing, and finishing of vessels, may be considered social "habits" (Peirce 1992:334–351), and the appearance of habits unique to but shared among Black Sea communities may suggest that information

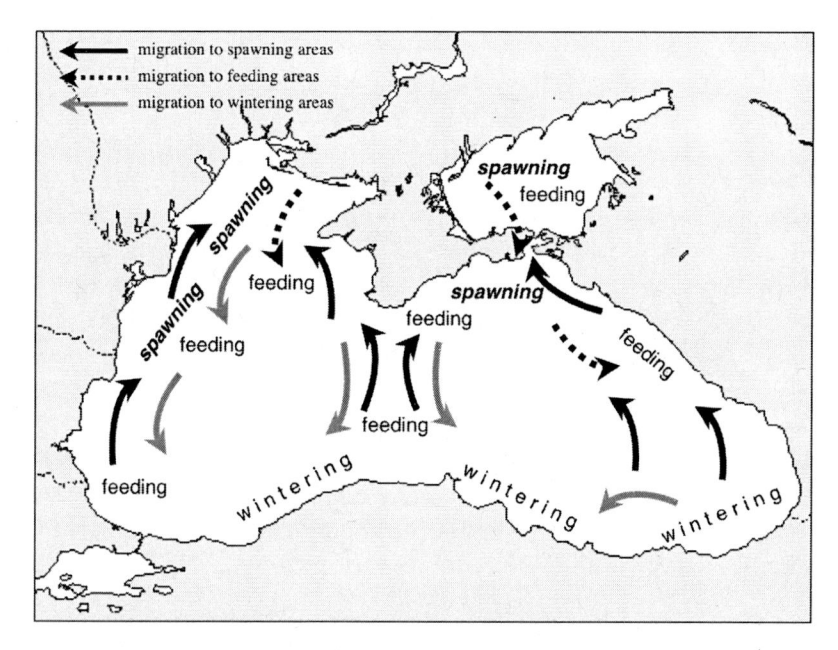

Figure 9.7 Map of Black Sea anchovy (*hamsi*) migration patterns (adapted from a map by I. L. Levkovich-Maslyuk, Department of Cartography and Geoinformatics, Faculty of Geography, Moscow State University, available at http://www.blacksea-web.net/maps/content7.htm, accessed November 5, 2009.

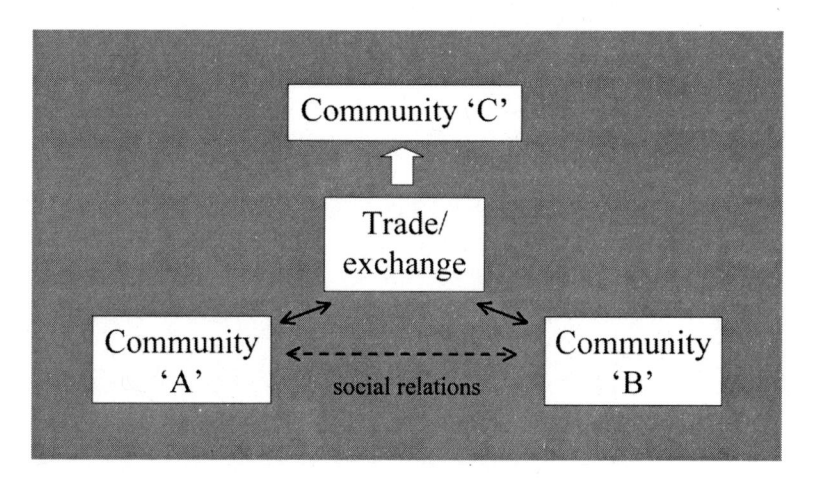

Figure 9.8 Trade as mediation. Communities A and B are themselves constituted and maintained by social relations as effected by trade and the exchange of ideas, services, people, and things. Community C represents the new social forms that are emergent out of those relationships (Bauer forthcoming).

was being exchanged and even that broader social bonds were forming on some level (see also Dietler and Herbich 1998).

Using a nested strategy of macroscopic and microscopic analytical techniques, we found that the study of the pottery from Sinop and other Black Sea coastal regions revealed a distinct pattern in which both the forming and finishing methods used in the pottery manufacture of these areas differed from that of their inland counterparts (Bauer 2006a, 2006b, 2008, forthcoming). In Sinop, the pottery consisted of dark burnished wares that were hand built even as areas of central Anatolia turned to wheelmaking after 3000 BC. In the northwest Caucasus, clear discontinuities were identified in all stages of the pottery-making process between the coastal Novosvobodnaya and Dolmen traditions and those of the more inland (and well-established) Maikop ones. And in the assemblages from the Usatovo group of the Lower Dniester Valley in southeastern Ukraine, the use of shell temper (likely related to the coastal situation of these communities), the forms of vessels made, and the finishing and decorative techniques employed all represent practices unknown in the inland communities thought to be the cultural antecedents of the people of this group. What is even more compelling is that the patterns noted as distinctive in all of these regions share an abundance of features with each other.

This emergence of particular ways of forming, firing, and finishing pots that were specific to the coastal regions and yet similar in a range of communities around the Black Sea attests to increasingly shared habits among Black Sea communities, a conclusion reinforced by similar technology-focused work done independently on the metals of the region (Chernykh 1992; Chernykh et al. 2002). How to interpret these patterns when faced with a lack of clear evidence for trade or population movements remains difficult, and this situation is where the interpretive possibilities suggested by the Erfelek experience and the other cases described here may be particularly helpful. These cases illustrate that interaction need not be intensive nor marked exclusively by the appearance of trade materials. Relationships may develop in ways that are both more contingent and ephemeral, and so while it is still possible that there were objects in circulation there— including perhaps products not easily preserved archaeologically—it is also possible that social relations across the region developed out of interpersonal encounters such as those that might have occurred among fishermen following the mobile resources the sea provided. The lesson here is that investigation into the early Black Sea (and, in fact, all archaeological cases) must thus consider and seek to test a range of alternative mechanisms for interaction.

Conclusion

Anthropologists have long been considered exchange to be a social practice that establishes and maintains social relations within and among social groups (Lévi-Strauss 1969 [1947]; Mauss 1990 [1950]). Trade may not only be an important mechanism for the exchange of materials but may also facilitate the spread of ideas and other aspects of culture. In archaeology, this characteristic of trade as facilitator was first raised by Wobst (1977) and is often cited in reference to the spread of technological or stylistic innovations. A more recent conceptualization suggests that culture itself is locatable within contexts of social interaction and discourse (e.g., Urban 1996). This view would suggest that trade and communication may themselves engender new cultural forms that have trade at their center. In her analysis of early Iron Age Mediterranean trade, for example, Susan Sherratt (1998) suggests that the decentralized trading activities of a heterogeneous merchant class resulted in the development of cultural practices and institutions that were specific to that group. These practices, though arising from specifically mercantile activities, appear now in the archaeological record as would the traces of any other culture group.

Our experience in Erfelek served as a reminder that such practices and new social forms have human relationships at their heart and often emerge out of highly localized and contingent interactions and events. And as quickly as such relationships can arise, they may be transformed or undermined by new participants and circumstances. This insight has in turn influenced our approach to the Sinop landscape, in which we draw on and synthesize (where possible) historical, ethnohistorical, and archaeological data to expand our interpretive possibilities and develop a richer understanding of the region.

Such an approach implies an important shift to *communication* rather than *trade* as the proper object of inquiry in studies of interregional relationships. Moreover, there is also a renewed appreciation for the different scales involved: we are dealing with interaction among social groups, but also between individuals. Any new studies must attempt to address the tremendous variability of experiences and scales involved. In one of the few recent discussions of trade, Renfrew (1993:9) remarks that "if we seek to gain an insight into the range of interactions, it is more important to do so under the rubric of 'interaction' than of 'trade,' since the underlying motivation and functional role may not primarily be the acquisition of goods." The social act of travel and meeting may be an equally strong motivation. As Greg Urban (1996:162) asks, "Is it exchange, or the idea of exchange, that binds? Must commerce take place, or is it sufficient to believe in the idea of commerce?"

It is time we try to move beyond a strict materialist analysis of trade. To play on a well-worn archaeological phrase, we might say, "trade is social or it is nothing."

Note

1. Athenaeus of Naukratis, *The Deipnosophists, or, Banquet of the Learned Athenaeus*, Vol. I. Translated by Charles D. Yonge. London: Harry Bohn, 1854. Electronic document, http://digital.library.wisc.edu/1711.dl/Literature.AthV1, November 9, 2009.

References

Agbe-Davies, Anna S.
2009 Scales of Analysis and Scales of Value at Bush Hill House, Barbados. *The International Journal of Historical Archaeology* 13(1):112–126.

Appadurai, Arjun
1986 Introduction: Commodities and the Politics of Value. In *The Social Life of Things: Commodities in Cultural Perspective*, edited by A. Appadurai, pp. 3–63. Cambridge University Press, Cambridge.
1990 Disjuncture and Difference in the Global Cultural Economy. *Public Culture* 2:1–24.

Bauer, Alexander A.
2002 Is What You See All You Get? Recognizing Meaning in Archaeology. *Journal of Social Archaeology* 2:37–52.
2006a Fluid Communities: Interaction and Emergence in the Bronze Age Black Sea. Unpublished PhD dissertation, Department of Anthropology, University of Pennsylvania.
2006b *Between* the Steppe and the Sown: Prehistoric Sinop and Inter-regional Interaction along the Black Sea Coast. In *Beyond the Steppe and the Sown*, edited by David L. Peterson, Laura M. Popova, and Adam T. Smith, pp. 225–246. Brill, Leiden.
2008 Import, Imitation, and Communication: Pottery Style, Technology, and Coastal Contact in the Early Bronze Age Black Sea. In *"Import" and "Imitation": Methodical and Practical Problems with an Archaeological Key Concept*, edited by Peter Biehl and Yuri Rassamakin, pp. 89–104. Schriften des Zentrums für Archäologie und Kulturgeschichte des Schwarzmeerraumes Band 11. Beier & Beran, Langenweißbach, Germany.
Forthcoming The Near East, Europe, and the "Routes" of Community in the Early Bronze Age Black Sea. In *Interweaving Worlds: Systemic Interactions in Eurasia, 7th to 1st millennia* BC, edited by Toby Wilkinson, Susan Sherratt, and John Bennet. Oxbow, Oxford.

Bellér-Hann, Ildikó, and Christopher M. Hann
2001 *Turkish Region: State, Market and Social Identities on the East Black Sea Coast*. School of American Research Press, Santa Fe, New Mexico.

Bloch, Maurice, and Jonathan Parry
1989 Introduction: Money and the Morality of Exchange. In *Money and the Morality of Exchange*, edited by Jonathan Parry and Maurice Bloch, pp. 1– 32. Cambridge University Press, Cambridge.

Braudel, Fernand
1972 [1949] *The Mediterranean and the Mediterranean World in the Age of Phillip II*. Translated by Siân Reynolds. 2 vols. Collins, London.

Chernykh, Evgeny N.
1992 *Ancient Metallurgy in the USSR: The Early Metal Age*. Cambridge University Press, Cambridge.

Chernykh, Evgeny N., Ludmila I. Avilova, Lubov B. Orlovskaya, and Sergey V. Kuzminykh
2002 Metallurgiya v Tsircumpontiiskom arealy: Ot edinstva k raspady. *Rossiiskaia Arkheologiia* 1:5–23.

Dietler Michael, and Ingrid Herbich
1998 *Habitus*, Techniques, Style: An Integrated Approach to the Social Understanding of Material Culture and Boundaries. In *The Archaeology of Social Boundaries*, edited by M. T. Stark, 232–263. Smithsonian Institution Press, Washington, DC.

Dobres, Marcia-Anne
2000 *Technology and Social Agency: Outlining a Practice Framework for Archaeology*. Blackwell, Oxford.

Dobres, Marcia-Anne, and John Robb (editors)
2000 *Agency in Archaeology*. Routledge, London.
2005 "Doing Agency": Introductory Remarks on Methodology. *Journal of Archaeological Method and Theory* 12:159–166.

Doonan, O. P.
2004a Sampling Sinop: Putting Together the Pieces of a Fragmented Landscape. In *Mediterranean Archaeological Landscapes: Current Issues*, edited by Effie F. Athanassopoulis and Luann Wandsnider, pp. 37–54. University of Pennsylvania Press, Philadelphia.
2004b *Sinop Landscapes: Exploring Connection in a Black Sea Hinterland*. University Museum, Philadelphia.
2006 Exploring Community in the Hinterland of a Black Sea Port. In *Surveying the Greek Chora: The Black Sea Region in a Comparative Perspective*, edited by P. Guldager Bilde and V. Stolba, pp. 47–58. Danish National Research Foundation Centre for Black Sea Studies, Aarhus.
2007 New Evidence for the Emergence of a Maritime Black Sea Economy. In *The Black Sea Flood Question: Changes in Coastline, Climate, and Human Settlement*, edited by V. Yanko-Hombach, A. S. Gilbert, N. Panin, and P. Dolukhanov, pp. 697–710. Springer, Dortrecht, Netherlands.
2009 Tumuli and the Creation of a Middle Ground in the Hinterland of Greek Sinope. Paper presented at the Tumulus as Sema conference, Koç University, Istanbul.

Doonan, Owen, and Alexander Bauer
2005 Sinop Province Archaeological Project: Report on the 2003 Field Season. *Araştırma Sonuçları Toplantısı* (Ankara) XXII:275–284.

Doonan, Owen P., Alex Gantos, Fredrik Hiebert, Mark Besonen, and Ali Yaycioglu
2001 Sinop Hinterlandi Sistematik Yüzey Araştırması, 1999 (Sinop Hinterland Systematic Survey, 1999). *Araştırma Sonuçları Toplantısı* (Ankara) XVIII:137–148.

Faroqhi, Suraiya
1984 *Towns and Townsmen of Ottoman Anatolia: Trade, Crafts, and Food Production in an Urban Setting, 1520–1650*. Cambridge University Press, Cambridge.

Finley, Moses
1985 *The Ancient Economy*. Hogarth, London.

Fotiadis, Michael
1999 Comparability, Equivalency, and Contestation. In *Material Symbols: Culture and Economy in Prehistory*, edited by John E. Robb, pp. 385–398. Southern Illinois University, Carbondale Occasional Paper Vol. 26. Center for Archaeological Investigations, Carbondale, Illinois.

Hodder, Ian (editor)
1987 *The Archaeology of Contextual Meanings*. Cambridge University Press, Cambridge.

Hodder, Ian, Michael Shanks, Alexandra Alexandri, Victor Buchli, John Carman, Jonathan Last, and Gavin Lucas (editors)
1995 *Interpreting Archaeology: Finding Meaning in the Past*. Routledge, London.

Hopkins, Keith
1983 Introduction. In *Trade and Famine in Classical Antiquity*, edited by Peter Garnsey and C. R. Whittaker, pp. ix–xxv. Cambridge University Press, Cambridge.

Johnson, Matthew H.
1989 Conceptions of Agency in Archaeological Interpretation. *Journal of Anthropological Archaeology* 8:189–211.

Joyce, Rosemary A., and Jeanne Lopiparo
2005 PostScript: Doing Agency in Archaeology. *Journal of Archaeological Method and Theory* 12:365–374.

Keane, Webb
2006 Signs Are Not the Garb of Meaning: On the Social Analysis of Material Things. In *Materiality*, edited by Daniel Miller, pp. 182–205. Duke University Press, Durham, North Carolina.

Knapp, A. Bernard, and John F. Cherry
1994 *Provenience Studies and Bronze Age Cyprus*. Prehistory Press, Madison, Wisconsin.

Kopytoff, Igor
1986 The Cultural Biography of Things: Commoditization as Process. In *The Social Life of Things: Commodities in Cultural Perspective*, edited by Arjun Appadurai, pp. 64–91. Cambridge University Press, Cambridge.

Lemonnier, Pierre
1976 La description des *Chaînes Opératiores*: Contribution à l'analyse des systèmes techniques. *Techniques et Culture* 1:100–151.
1992 *Elements for an Anthropology of Technology*. University of Michigan Press, Ann Arbor.

Lévi-Strauss, Claude
1969 [1947] *The Elementary Structures of Kinship*. Rev. ed. Translated by James Harle Bell, John Richard von Sturmer, and Rodney Needham, editor. Beacon Press, Boston.

Marcus, George E.
1995 Ethnography in/of the World System: The Emergence of Multi-Sited Ethnography. *Annual Review of Anthropology* 24:95–117.

Mathieu, James R., and Rachel E. Scott (editors)
2004 *Exploring the Role of Analytical Scale in Archaeological Interpretation.* Archaeopress, Oxford.

Mauss, Marcel
1990 [1950] *The Gift.* Translated by W. D. Halls. W. W. Norton, New York.

McGlade, James, and Jacqueline M. McGlade
1989 Modelling the Innovative Component of Social Change. In *What's New? A Closer Look at the Process of Innovation*, edited by Sander E. van der Leeuw and Robin Torrence, pp. 281–299. Unwin Hyman, London.

Meeker, Michael
2002 *A Nation of Empire: The Ottoman Legacy of Turkish Modernity.* University of California Press, Berkeley.

Möller, Astrid
2007 Classical Greece: Distribution. In *The Cambridge Economic History of the Greco-Roman World*, edited by Walter Scheidel, Ian Morris, and Richard P. Saller, pp. 362–384. Cambridge University Press, Cambridge.

Morris, Ian, Richard P. Saller, and Walter Scheidel
2007 Introduction. In *The Cambridge Economic History of the Greco-Roman World*, edited by Walter Scheidel, Ian Morris, and Richard P. Saller, pp. 1–12. Cambridge University Press, Cambridge.

Parmentier, Richard J.
1997 The Pragmatic Semiotics of Cultures. *Semiotica* 116(1):1–115.

Peirce, Charles Sanders
1992 *The Essential Peirce: Selected Philosophical Writings,* Vol. 1 (1867–1893). Indiana University Press, Bloomington.

Polanyi, Karl
1957 The Economy as Instituted Process. In *Trade and Market in the Early Empires*, edited by Karl Polanyi, Conrad M. Arensberg, and Harry W. Pearson, pp. 243–270. Free Press, Glencoe, Illinois.

Preucel, Robert W.
2006 *Archaeological Semiotics.* Blackwell, Oxford.

Preucel, Robert W., and Alexander A. Bauer
2001 Archaeological Pragmatics. *Norwegian Archaeological Review* 34:85–96.

Renfrew, A. Colin
1993 Trade Beyond the Material. In *Trade and Exchange in Prehistoric Europe*, edited by C. Scarre and F. Healy, pp. 5–16. Oxbow Monographs Vol. 33. Oxbow, Oxford.

Shami, Seteney
2000 Prehistories of Globalization: Circassian Identity in Motion. *Public Culture* 12:177–204.

Sherratt, Susan
1998 "Sea Peoples" and the Economic Structure of the Late Second Millennium in the Eastern Mediterranean. In *Mediterranean Peoples in Transition: Thirteenth to Early*

Tenth Century BCE, edited by Seymour Gitin, Amihai Mazar, and Ephraim Stern, pp. 292–313. Israel Exploration Society, Jerusalem.

Stark, Miriam T. (editor)
1998 *The Archaeology of Social Boundaries.* Smithsonian Institution Press, Washington, DC.

Urban, Greg
1996 *Metaphysical Community.* University of Texas Press, Austin.

Wobst, H. Martin
1977 Stylistic Behavior and Information Exchange. In *Papers for the Director: Research Essays in Honor of James B. Griffin*, edited by Charles E. Cleland, pp. 317–342. Museum of Anthropology, Anthropological Papers, Vol. 61. University of Michigan Press, Ann Arbor.

CHAPTER 10

Objects, Social Relations, and Cultural Motion
Greg Urban

My thoughts have been turning ever more these days to what Susan Sherratt (chapter 6, this volume) tells us the ancient Greeks dubbed *athurmata*—"trinkets," little things, cheap things, largely interchangeable. Phoenician traders carried them around the Mediterranean three thousand years ago, and they kindled a certain fascination, at least for a period of time, for the local folks with whom the Phoenicians traded. If one can take *athurmata* to mean more generally objects that are typically (though by no means always) small, that are largely intersubstitutable, and that are relatively easy to replicate, my question here is: what role do they play in the motion of culture and in the establishment or maintenance of social relationships? I am also interested in what might be called, based on a spurious morphological segmentation, the *thurmata* of life—objects that are typically big, more likely to be unique, and generally harder to replicate, such as sport-utility vehicles (or SUVs), *thurmata* of the middle and upper middle classes in the United States during the last decade.

I propose in this chapter to develop the idea of an *athurmata* to *thurmata* (or, for short, *thurmatic*) continuum and to explore its relationship to the motion of culture and social relations. One way that I have characterized this continuum is in terms of size of object—small to large—but in actuality only a loose correlation exists between size and the continuum I have in mind. To be sure, I am interested in the quantitative scaling of objects, but the key variable is not size but rather ease or difficulty in replication, that is, ease or difficulty in producing another object that for practical purposes is regarded as the same as another one.

A good example of an object that falls far toward the thurmatic end of the continuum might be a medieval European cathedral. It is relatively thurmatic not just because of its size but also because of the difficulty in replicating it. Chartres Cathedral, located near Paris, is a good example. It was built on the site of an older cathedral largely destroyed by fire in 1194 AD. Construction of the new cathedral began that year, and, according to Malcolm Miller (1991:10), "most of [it] was completed by 1223," just about three decades later. When construction began, "people gathered voluntarily in the quarries at Berchères and, in thousands, praying and chanting, dragged carts laden with stone a distance of five miles to the building site" (Miller 1991:9).

The degree of difficulty of replication is measured by both the time it takes and the number of people required—decades and thousands of people, in the case of a medieval cathedral. The cathedral might be contrasted, in this quantitative regard, with relatively athurmatic objects, such as the quickly made ceramic pots manufactured in an indigenous community in southern Brazil during the time I conducted ethnographic field research there in the 1970s and 1980s. The pots are often the work of one individual, not hundreds or thousands, in contrast to the medieval cathedral. And the production period can be measured in hours and days, including gathering of the materials (clay mud from the river bed), shaping, and firing (without kiln), rather than decades, as in the case of the medieval cathedral. It might be added that pots constructed in this fashion tended to be short-lived, cracking frequently even during the manufacturing process. In this regard, they are different from pots manufactured using techniques such as straining the clay mud, shaping on potting wheels, glazing, and firing in kilns. Of course, in relationship to still more athurmatic objects, even the simple ceramic pots may seem thurmatic.

I propose in this chapter to sketch in broad outline how objects differently situated along a thurmatic continuum differentially figure in cultural motion and how in turn that cultural motion is linked to social relations. Social relations are the conduits through which culture flows, and tangible physical objects—as vehicles for the transmission of culture—move through those conduits. Exchange relations of the sort found typically in trade are social relations of a special kind. Although they may be traditional, as in the case of trading partners between whom a relationship exists prior to the moment of a present trade, exchange relations can also be brought into existence or transformed through the exchange process. Exchange relations of the latter sort—emergent relations—depend on the attractive force of the objects exchanged. And attraction, in the case of objects, as I propose to argue, has something to do with the position of the objects along the thurmatic continuum. For this reason, exchange of cultural objects is a key place to look for linkages between cultural motion, broadly construed, and social change, including large-scale, epochal change.

Objects and Cultural Motion

I regard culture as *intangible*—one cannot see it, touch it, taste it, smell it. It consists in abstract patterns and meanings. This may surprise readers, since I opened this chapter with a discussion of physical objects, trinkets, SUVs, ceramic pots, medieval cathedrals, and the like. The linking proposition is this: Whereas culture itself is abstract, in order for it to move through space and time, in order for it, in other words, to be socially learned, socially transmitted, passed from one actor (whether individual or group) to another, it must be deposited, however fleetingly, in perceptible objects. Things—whether *athurmata* or *thurmata*, whether accessible through visual, tactile, auditory, gustatory, or olfactory pathways—are indispensible for the motion of culture. This process is depicted in figure 10.1.

To be able to transmit a pattern, Object 1 has to be an exemplar of a pattern,[1] one of a potentially infinite number of such objects that are essentially alike for practical purposes. This pattern is what we find in the case of language and discourse and culturally recognizable behaviors such as gestures more generally. A child growing up in a language learns words as general patterns of sound by being exposed to multiple instances or objects in the present sense. One utterance of the word "mom," whose sound form might be represented phonetically as [mam], is one object. The object, in turn, is an exemplar of the general form or element, that is, the word as a sound shape. All of the exemplars of the sound shape [mam] are essentially alike for practical purposes of language learning, even though careful scrutiny will show the distinctiveness of any given exemplar vis-à-vis all of the others.

Visible objects like ceramic pots and cathedrals have a different temporality than sound objects, and their uniqueness may be, for that reason, more readily apparent. The Chartres Cathedral remains visible to this day, nearly 800 years after "most of [it] was completed," and it is certainly architecturally distinctive—no other cathedral is exactly like it. Yet it too represents an object of a specific general type (or what I am calling a "cultural element"): the cathedral. One can immediately recognize its similarity to other such objects by examining its external form, for example, its footprint or floor plan. Figure 10.2 shows the floor plans of four different cathedrals. The features of the floor plan are familiar to anyone with even a passing

```
                    ┌  Object n
                    │
      Element 1    ┤   ...
                    │
                    │  Object 2
                    └  Object 1
                  ↗           ↘
              A  ·················→  B
```

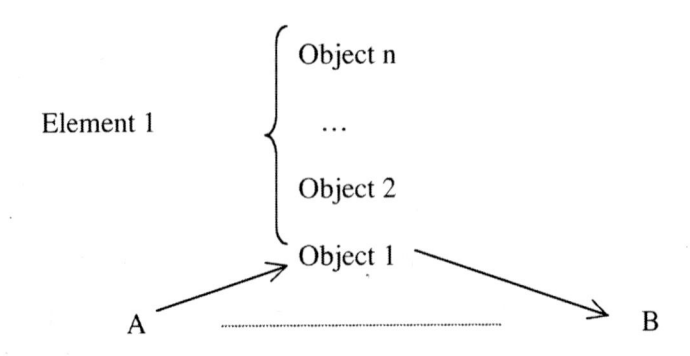

Figure 10.1 Social relationships, objects, and cultural motion. A and B are actors (individuals or groups) in a social relationship. The objects 1 through *n* are exemplars or carriers of a cultural element that is itself abstract. The movement of culture occurs when the element moves. For the element to move, objects must appear at the interface between A and B, although this appearance does not mean, necessarily, that giving or exchange takes place. Courtesy of the author.

acquaintance with this class of objects and scarcely require explication—the shape of the cross, its long access with an entry way at one end, the transepts projecting off the main axis forming the other part of the cross, and so forth. What is worthy of note here is that the exemplars, unique as they are, are also all essentially alike for practical purposes: they are all cathedrals with shared perceptible properties and social purposes.

Some of the exemplars of the cathedral are more closely related to one another than they are to others; for example, Chartres and Amiens cathedrals are very much alike because the latter adopted the style (known as "High Gothic") of the former. But this variability is also true in the case of sound shapes. Some pronunciations of words are more similar among themselves than they are with others. Stylistic differences are apparent in sound shape just as they are in architectural form; for example, the American English [mam] has a more open and lower vowel than the British English [mʌm].

There is a further similarity between the cathedral and the sound shape as regards the motion of culture. Not only do the specific objects—a particular cathedral or a specific utterance of a word—represent exemplars of general types; additionally, the replicator (B in fig. 10.1) can extract some (even if not all) of the culture that went into the production of the object by observation of the object. By listening to exemplars of the sound shape [mam], one could learn to reproduce the sound shape and hence, effect the motion of culture between individuals. Similarly, one could (in theory, at least) learn how to produce a cathedral by careful study of the object. I will qualify this

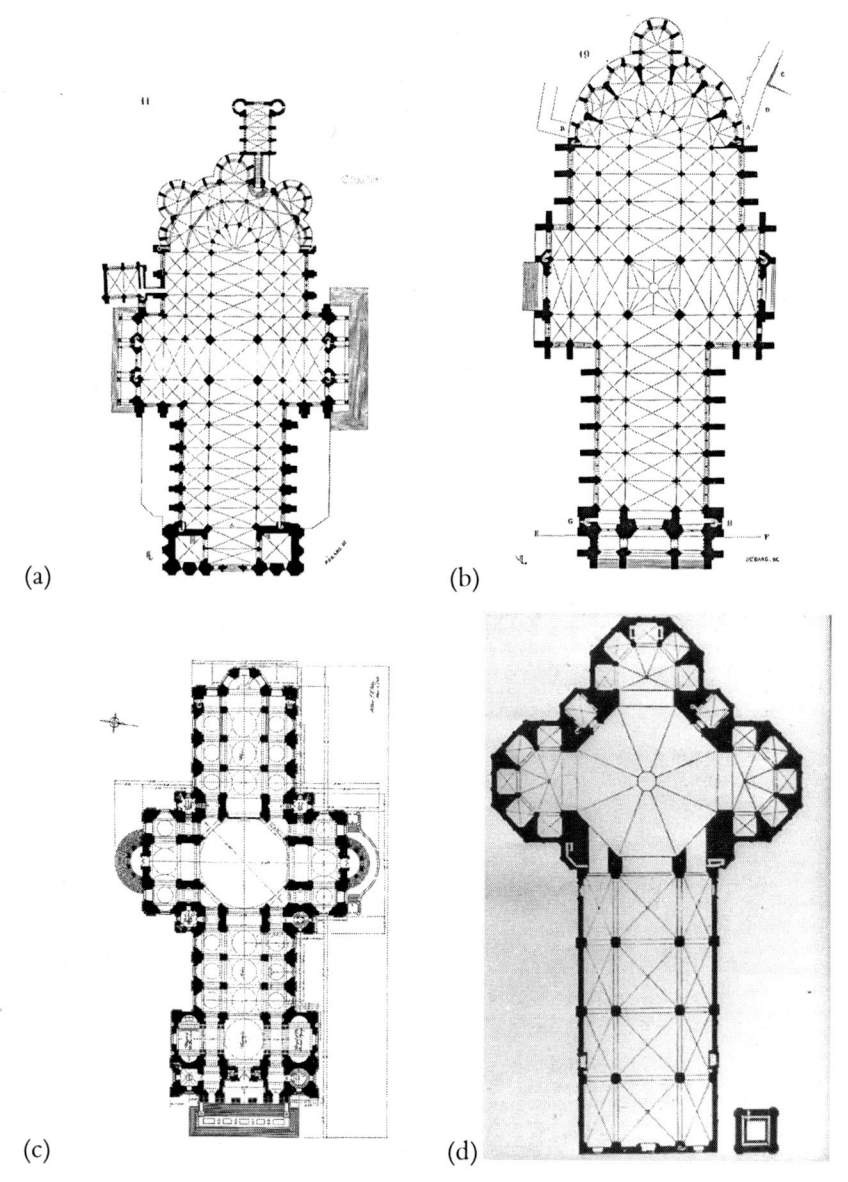

Objects, Social Relations, and Cultural Motion ◉ 211

Figure 10.2 Floor plans of cathedrals: distinct objects linked to a single cultural element. (a) Chartres Cathedral, Chartres, France (1194–1224) (b) Amiens Cathedral, Amiens, France (1220–1247); (c) St. Paul's, London, England (1675–1710); (d) Santa Maria del Fiore, Florence, Italy (1420–1436). Credits: (a) and (b) are from Eugène Viollet-le-Duc, *Dictionnaire raisonné de l'architecture française du XIe au XVIe siècle* (1856); (c) is from Arthur F. E. Poley, *St. Paul's Cathedral, London* (1927); (d) is adapted from Joseph Gwilt, *An Encyclopaedia of Architecture, Historical, Theoretical, and Practical* (1859).

claim subsequently, but some measure of the culture that goes into an object can be extracted from the object by close scrutiny. The object is, in this sense, essential to the motion of culture.

The mechanism of motion depicted in figure 10.1 has its analog in the concept of "reverse engineering" or "back engineering" used in industry. A company such as a pharmaceutical firm researches, develops, produces, and markets a new drug. This company would be the social actor A in figure 10.1. Let's suppose that the new drug is manufactured in pill form. The pills are the objects 1 through n in figure 10.1. Another company (social actor B in figure 10.1) then tries to copy these pills, producing exemplars that have the same chemical composition and pharmacological properties. To do this, researchers in company B analyze the materials and then attempt resynthesis in an effort to produce a drug that is for all practical purposes identical to the one produced by company A. Some if not all of the culture that went into the production of the original drug thereby moves through the world from company A to company B. One can imagine the basic process of cultural motion—whether of a sound shape, a ceramic type, or an architectural form—as a form of reverse engineering.

Cathedral scholars engage in a sort of virtual reverse engineering. They endeavor to extract the culture that went into the making of the cathedral by a careful study of it. However, the goal of the virtual back engineering carried out by scholars is not the production of new objects that are for all practical purposes the same as the ones under investigation. It is rather to convert the culture that went into the cathedral into knowledge encodable in language and other representations. So, for example, Anne Prache (1993:58) and other scholars have concluded, from the masonry of Chartres Cathedral, that the nave was "built at one go," and George Henderson (1968:82) and others conclude from "a small anomaly" that the "western-crossing piers had reached the height of the springing of the vault before those on the east side." Careful observation of the object, in this case, reveals aspects of its original making. However, the reverse engineering results not in the replication of a similar object but rather in representations (such as books and articles) about the object.

Reverse engineering is fundamental to the movement of culture between social actors, but the matter is more complex than I have been letting on. Even in the case of sound objects, like exemplars of the sound shape [mam], the replicator may have perceptual access not just to the sound objects, but also to other aspects of the behaviors that go into their production—for example, the shape of the mouth, its relative openness or closeness, its movement from one position or shape to the next, and so forth. Access to such knowledge is all the more likely in the case of thurmatic objects like cathedrals, where masons may acquire knowledge and skills from observing and working with other masons, carpenters from observing and working with other carpenters, and so forth. Observation of the finished tangible object—the cathedral—is only part of the process through which replication takes place.

Indeed, in the limiting case, replication of an object could be done in the absence of any direct observation of that object. This occurs when the object is replicated thanks to the transmission of instructions about how it is to be produced, instructions being part of what I have elsewhere (Urban 2001) referred to as "metaculture"—culture that is about culture.

We might think of the behavioral and representational (or metacultural) objects that go into the replication of another object, such as a ceramic pot or a cathedral, as *enabling objects*. What I am proposing here is that the greater the quantity of enabling objects, the more thurmatic the object to be replicated is. The least thurmatic (or the most athurmatic) objects require relatively little in the way of enabling objects. A bodily movement, such as an easy-to-learn dance step, could spread between peoples by replication based on direct observation. More thurmatic objects, such as difficult-to-learn ballet movements, require instruction and enabling behaviors (exercises leading up to the ability to perform a movement), in addition to observation. A medieval cathedral would require an enormous number of enabling objects—all the behaviors of masons, carpenters, even townspeople carrying stones from a quarry, not to mention representations in the form of words or plans. And it would require the use of many different tools, themselves objects requiring replication.

Since each enabling object is an exemplar of a cultural element participating in the processes of social learning and social transmission, to say the more thurmatic the object, the greater the number of enabling objects it requires is also to say the more thurmatic the object, the greater the quantity of culture that goes into it and, correspondingly, the greater the quantity of culture that must be extracted from it in the process of reverse engineering.

It is perhaps obvious, therefore, that the transmission of culture must ultimately rest upon elementary replication processes and upon objects with few or no enabling objects, except for basic biological hard wiring. How otherwise could an infant be capable of acquiring culture in the first place? The elementary forms of cultural motion must rest upon the replication of the patterns carried in maximally athurmatic objects—objects in need of no enabling cultural objects.

A corollary of this proposition is that replication of relatively more thurmatic cultural objects—and, hence, the transmission of the culture contained in them—is easier when more of the enabling culture is already shared between the original producer and the replicator (A and B in figure 10.1).

In the case of the reverse engineering of pharmaceuticals, for example, the process is facilitated by the sharing of culture (in the form of knowledge, skills, and techniques) between the scientists and engineers who originally produced the objects (the pharmaceuticals) and the scientists and engineers who are producing the copies. I stress this point because of its relevance to broad, epochal changes in society, such as when civilization began to shift its locus from the eastern Mediterranean area to the west with the rise of Greece and then Rome. Rather than viewing that shift as a parallel and autochthonous development, the view of cultural motion grounded in replication of objects suggests that it begins with the "trinkets," the *athurmata*, that are brought by the traders. With the *athurmata* comes some of the enabling culture of the great centers of civilization. As relatively more thurmatic objects are reverse engineered, with all of the change that process entails, more of the enabling culture necessary to produce thurmatic objects is transported to the receiving population, although in the course of that transportation, change takes place, something new is created, and a new civilization is born.

Exchange and Social Relationships

I want to turn now to the creation and maintenance of social relationships through the movement of culture and, in particular, through the passage of cultural elements via objects from individual to individual, group to group. There is a mutually enabling relationship between cultural motion (understood as the passage of cultural elements via objects) and social relations. The passage of culture via objects necessitates the existence of social relationships. Conversely, relationships are the pathways along which culture flows. Created by the past motion of culture, social relationships are also themselves facilitators of future motion.

From this perspective, exchange relationships are particularly important. I have been talking more generally about the passage of culture via objects, but I now want to focus on the specificity of exchange, as I think it is crucial for the development of a theory of cultural motion, as well as of social relationships. Exchange is not the prototype for the motion of culture. The prototype is probably something more like learning to speak a language growing up in a household. Children learn a language through the sounds and gestures of those around them. They pick it up simply because it is there.

What they do, in particular, is replicate speech or gestural patterns, for example, pronouncing the word [mama], a bilabial nasal stop followed by open oral vowel and then that sequence repeated. Here the sounds and observable articulations are the objects that appear at the interface between parent and child. As I have argued, such objects must be at first maximally athurmatic, requiring no enabling cultural objects. They are exemplars of classes of objects. But what is important for this kind of inertial motion of culture is that the child is able to replicate the objects produced by the parent, to articulate a sound that reminds the adults of the word they have produced, [mama]. This kind of cultural motion is all about replication of objects and with it, the movement of elements, which I have diagrammed in the upper part of figure 10.3, adjacent to the heading "replication."

In the lower part of figure 10.3, adjacent to the heading "dissemination," I have endeavored to represent a somewhat different type of motion that can be called "secondary replication." Both replication (or "primary" replication) and secondary replication involve a dissemination phase. B has perceptual access to objects produced by A that are exemplars of a cultural element. A in this way has disseminated the element through the objects. In primary replication—such as the parent-child bonds through which language is passed—the dissemination by A (the parent) results in the replication of the cultural element by B as manifested in B's production of new objects that are, for all practical purposes, identical to those produced by A. However, in secondary replication, B does not endeavor to reproduce the disseminated objects but merely to extract some of the culture contained in them.

If the social actor A is, for example, a corporation—say, a manufacturer of SUVs—and B is an individual, A has disseminated the culture that goes into making the SUV by producing specific objects, that is, specific SUVs. When the SUV is passed to B, B does not, except in the case of reverse engineering, set out to make another object that is for all practical purposes identical to the SUV. Instead, B extracts some of the culture that went into the making of the object through patterns of use of that object. Processes of secondary replication tend to be associated with social relationships that can be characterized as exchange relations.

The key difference is that in exchange as a form of social relationship, the individuals (or groups) who receive the object do not, in general, intend to replicate that object. Instead, they want to replicate only part of the culture contained in the object, patterns of usage of the object or aspects of the object. But they also want to take the object up in their own local processes of cultural transmission. This is true, for example, of the endeavors by the Brazilian government Indian agency (FUNAI)

Replication

Cultural Element 1   Cultural Element 1'

A → B → C

Dissemination phase of replication process.

Dissemination

Cultural Element 1

A → B

↓ Secondary replication

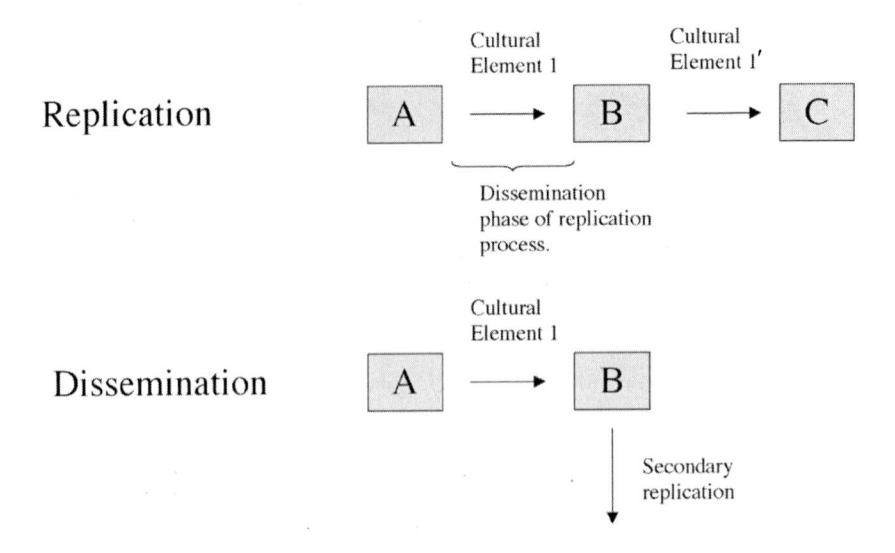

Figure 10.3 Prototypical cultural motion (*top*) versus motion facilitated by exchange (*bottom*). The traditional idea of cultural motion is based on replication. The individual or group B has access to objects that are exemplars of a cultural element produced by A. B then produces replicas that can allow the passage of that element (perhaps slightly modified) to C. An example would be learning words in a language. In the case of exchange, however, B receives the object produced by A, but this does not in general result in B's replicating the whole object. Instead, B extracts only some of the culture that has gone into making the object, such as a pattern of use. An example would be acquiring an automobile in order to use it, not to make another one like it. Courtesy of the author.

to attract and "pacify" isolated Indian populations in the interior, such as the Uru-eu-wau-wau of the far western state of Rondônia during the early 1980s. The attraction was done by means of objects such as metal pots and knives. The government was in the position of disseminator A in figure 10.3 (although it is an intermediate disseminator, with the corporations that manufacture the pots and knives being the original producers). The Uru-eu-wau-wau were actors B in the dissemination process. The Uru-eu-wau-wau took up the metal pots and knives to use them in their ongoing local processes of cultural transmission, substituting them for existing containers and cutting implements. They did not reverse engineer the pots and knives, making new ones. They did not, of course, in part because they did not already possess all of the enabling culture that would make the reverse engineering of these relatively thurmatic objects possible.

This suggests the necessity of differentiating between an *absolute* scale of thurmaticity, and *relative* thurmaticity—that is, the difference between the quantity of culture embodied in an object and the quantity of culture already present in the individual or group that seeks to replicate the object, whether primarily or secondarily.

Secondary replication can take many forms. I have mentioned the use patterns built into such tangible and relatively thurmatic objects as SUVs and metal pots and knives. The viewer of a cinematic film might extract some of the culture deposited in the film by secondarily replicating lines from the film, hair styles, body postures, gestures, ways of talking, plot outlines, clothing patterns, and the like. But secondary replication can range from such overt replications to relatively more subtle ones, such as the aesthetic sensibility that goes into the making of film. This is true of thurmatic objects like ballet performances, in which an audience B may be interested primarily in the aesthetic sensibility contained in the performance,[2] although the desire to replicate movements may be present in aspiring dancers who are part of the audience.

My contention is that exchange typically involves such processes of dissemination and secondary replication, in which the object passing in one direction is relatively thurmatic and the recipient of the object may not want to replicate all of the culture contained in the object, and, indeed, may not be able to do so for want of the necessary enabling culture. In exchange as imagined by Adam Smith in *The Wealth of Nations* (2000 [1776]), the exchange parties would be those who produce objects that are equally thurmatic but who do not share the enabling culture. This is, of course, the idea of the division of labor. However, it may be more typical of exchanges that they are asymmetrical, with A giving relatively thurmatic objects to B (SUVs, metal pots, ballet performances, films), B giving back to A relatively athurmatic objects—labor or skills deposited into money.

What is exciting about exchange is that it typically involves more than the inertial motion of culture. In the acquisition of language or comportment within the family, culture moves via inertia. The objects (such as sounds or gestures) and elements are reproduced because they are there to be reproduced. Exchange, however, necessarily involves a force of interest in objects that goes beyond inertia. The objects are vehicles for what can be termed accelerative culture. The Uru-eu-wau-wau came to want the metal pots and knives. Their interest in these objects kindled a social relationship with the giver, even if it was not at first fully an exchange relationship.

The purchaser of the SUV is attracted to it, desires the culture contained in it, which may not be only the patterns of mundane usage but also the aesthetic or expressive sensibility embodied in it as an exemplar of a cultural element. Even parishioners or pilgrims visiting a medieval cathedral are attracted to the object for some, albeit not all, of the culture that went into its making. And the parishioners or pilgrims give back something in the form of offering to those in charge of the cathedral.

More generally, exchange of objects is about the attractive force exercised by the different and at least partially inaccessible culture that produced the objects being received. The participants in the exchange want some (although typically not all) of the culture contained in the objects they receive. The objects are the vehicles that bring some of that culture to them. Asymmetrical exchange occurs where the object moving in one direction is considerably more thurmatic than the objects moving the other direction. Symmetrical exchange, with equally thurmatic objects moving in opposite directions, as imagined in the division of labor as cooperation, may be a limiting case rather than the norm. More typical may be asymmetrical exchange, with different degrees of thurmaticity involved, although the amount of difference may itself vary.

I have said that the more thurmatic the object, the more the culture that has gone into the object. One aspect of the culture that goes into the production of highly thurmatic objects has to do with the social relations necessary for the object's production. This is obvious in the case of the medieval cathedral, in whose construction masons and carpenters as well as ordinary laborers and townspeople must cooperate.

It is intriguing, indeed, that even the seemingly athurmatic enabling behavior of hauling stone from a quarry to the construction site may have considerable culture behind it. Henderson (1968:36–37) mentions the "cult of the carts," which began at Chartres Cathedral in 1145, before the fire of 1194 and the subsequent rebuilding. He quotes Robert of Torigni, Abbot of Mont-Saint-Michel, to the effect that in the year 1145 "men at Chartres began to drag carts, harnessed to their own shoulders, laden with stones and wood, corn and other provisions, needed for the new church" (1968:36–37). The practice of townspeople hauling stones for the cathedral thus had antecedents at Chartres and was part of local cultural practices. Cart hauling may have been part of "village outings, organized by local priests" (1968:79).

In any case, the key point here is that the production of highly thurmatic objects, such as cathedrals, or SUVs for that matter, may require complex social relations. Pilgrims from other areas might come to a cathedral for religious purposes, that is, to extract some of the culture contained in it in the form of secondary replication. If, however, they wish to extract all of the culture contained in it and to build another cathedral back in their home village or town that was for all practical purposes identical to the one they visited, they would have to have already established the kinds of social relations that are necessary for such replication effort or they would have to bring those relations into existence. Exchange relationships (if they can be called that) of the highly asymmetrical sort involved in a pilgrimage can result over time and after numerous instances of secondary replication in the gradual transportation to a new site of the local culture deposited in a highly thurmatic object. This is also the way in which civilizations might begin to shift their locus, as the culture underpinning the civilization comes to be reproduced, albeit in modified form, in a new location.

A last point is that the construction of extraordinarily thurmatic objects, such as cathedrals or, indeed, whole cities—if they are immovable and only transportable by means of replication—results not only in asymmetrical exchange but also in centralization. The thurmatic object attracts relatively less thurmatic cultural objects to itself. The thurmatic continuum in this way appears to be relevant to understanding not only asymmetrical and symmetrical exchange of objects but also the processes of centralization that are fundamental to the rise of civilizations.

Thurmaticity, Acceleration, and Emergence

Exchange, as a momentary act, produces a social relationship, however transitory. That relationship consists in a pattern of interactions. If the pattern is replicated, the relationship becomes something more than a momentary encounter. It becomes a part of culture that gets transmitted over time.

I have been arguing that the momentary encounters that form the basis for a new social relationship come into existence because of the attractive force of objects, into which culture has been deposited. Referring back to figure 10.1, the attractive force of an object produced by A (an individual or group) is the attractive force of the culture deposited in that object. The attraction stems from the desire of B to extract the culture from the object in the form of secondary replication. B is the recipient of some of the culture deposited in the object, and by means of B's interaction with the object, some of that culture flows through the world, moves between individuals and groups.

However, if the relationship between A and B is emergent, just coming into being, and the directionality of cultural flow is from A to B, does anything come back to A? In an exchange-as-division-of-labor model, A gets from B an equivalent object or objects. Making use of the present terminology, that means an object or objects of the same thurmaticity. A desires the objects given by B, just as B desires the objects given by A, in order to extract from the objects the culture contained in them through processes of secondary replication.

But what are we to make of highly asymmetrical exchanges, such as donations to a cathedral made by parishioners or pilgrims or even tourists? Further, what if the visitor gives nothing back to the cathedral? The question can be extended to the gift more generally. The answer, given by Marcel Mauss (1967) in his celebrated essay *The Gift*, is that what is returned to the giver is the (possibly new) social relationship between giver and receiver, between the Brazilian government's "attraction" team and the Uru-eu-wau-wau in the early 1980s.

The concept of thurmaticity proposed here suggests a modification of the Maussian account. The social relationship created by the gift is not given back to the giver. Rather, the social relationship—as an emergent cultural phenomenon consisting in a set of interactional patterns—becomes part of the enabling culture for the objects transmitted. I have referred to the enabling culture as what makes the production of the object possible in the first place—the skills and knowledge of the masons and carpenters, for example, in the case of the medieval cathedral. The pilgrims and parishioners' donations contribute to the original construction of the cathedral and the ongoing upkeep and operations of the cathedral—the cathedral not just as stones, mortar, and wood, but also as cultural object, as physical thing into which otherwise abstract and inaccessible patterns or forms have been deposited. The practice of being a donor to a cathedral is part of the enabling culture that makes the cathedral as cultural object possible, that enables it continue into the future as culture. And it is the cathedral as an object in the world through which culture passes that is the source of attraction for the pilgrim or parishioner or tourist, for that matter, in the first place. Hence, exchange (of this admittedly highly asymmetrical type) is enabling of the culture that is deposited in the object and that will reside in the object (or in another produced from the culture) in the future.

The cathedral is an extreme example because of its temporal properties. We have to imagine the physical object at one time (call it time t_1) as distinct from the physical object at another (t_2). Without additional culture deposited in it, the physical object would run down, be subject to entropic forces. If it remains the same through care and upkeep, that apparent continuity in the physical thing is the result of additional culture that has been added to it. Similarly, if the physical object at t_2 is the result of additions or modifications of the earlier object, that change is the result of additional culture. In such cases, donations are enabling in that they contribute to the physical shape of the thing. The future physical shape is a precipitate of the culture moving forward in time and infusing the thing with its ethereal shape, and the donation is what enables the forward movement.

This process is perhaps more obvious in the case of culture that results in the production of multiple objects—ceramic pots, for instance, or SUVs. Each individual object may participate in a distinct exchange, and each exchange may in turn enable the culture deposited in the object to move forward into the future. I have attempted to diagram this in figure 10.4.

When exchange brings new individuals or groups together, thereby enabling the flow of culture through the relations thus created, the culture itself undergoes "acceleration." Such situations, in which attractive forces are operative, are to be distinguished from those in which culture is acquired willy-nilly, that is, because it is there to be acquired—as when a child learns to speak a mother tongue because that is the language used in the household. The latter form of motion is inertial, with culture moving forward

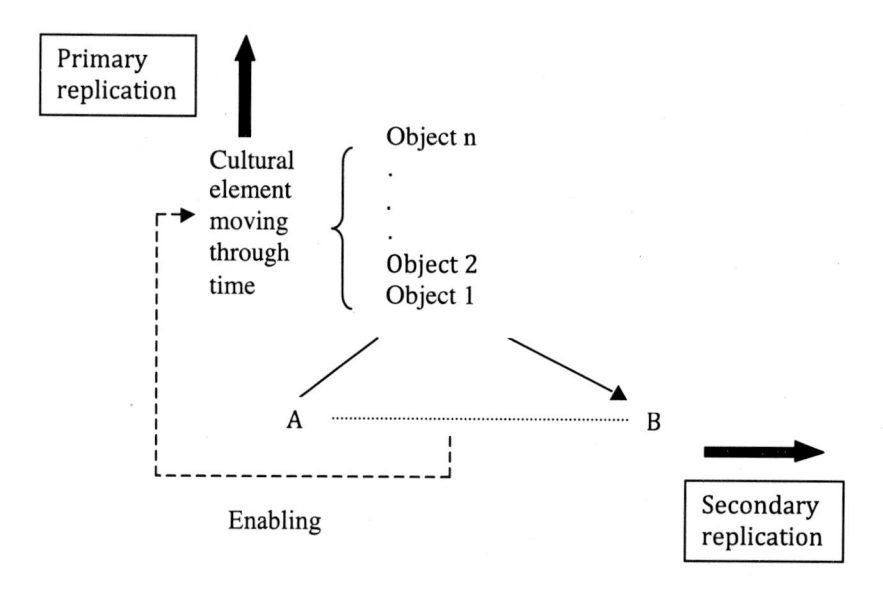

Figure 10.4 Exchange relations enable the movement of culture through time. A gives Object 1 to B. B in return gives something to A (whether a relationship, as in the gift, or another object). That something enables the production of an additional object (Object 2). In this way, the culture deposited in Object 1 moves forward into the future, inhabiting new objects. And, of course, the culture may change in the course of its movement through time. Consequently, the exchange relationship may be said to enable the forward movement of the culture through time. Without the exchange, which is grounded in the interest of B in the object for purposes of extracting some of the culture deposited in it, the culture would cease its motion through time. Courtesy of the author.

through time because it is already in motion, not spreading to new individuals because of positive attraction. Where culture passes because of attraction, as in the case of emergent exchange relationships, culture itself must be undergoing acceleration. What is producing the acceleration is the attractive force of the objects.

There is in turn a connection between the attractive (or accelerative) forces at work in the case of exchange, as I have been arguing, and the relatively thurmatic properties of the objects involved in the exchange. Trade augments the culture that produces relatively thurmatic objects, enabling objects of still greater thurmaticity in the future. The culture, in this sense, does not simply continue forward in time, as if inertial. It also grows, like a living thing. Acceleration renders possible an increase in the thurmaticity of objects produced.

At the same time, however, once a thurmatic object has been produced or reproduced, the culture contained in it moves outward from it into the world. I am not referring only to secondary replication, as when a pilgrim visits a cathedral or an individual drives an SUV. Additionally, what one might think of as the "idea of the object" is let loose into the world. When the pilgrim comes to worship at a cathedral, the pilgrim also acquires the idea of it, the possible thought that the object could be replicated elsewhere, that a new cathedral could be built. From the pilgrim's point of view, the idea of the object—were the thought of replicating it to occur—would also require thinking through how to enable the reproduction of that object. That is, it would require thought about the kinds of social relations that might produce the object. Hence, the relatively thurmatic object, when it participates in new exchange relationships, also enables the transmission of possible ideas about social reorganization.

I am thus arguing for a connection between the acceleration of culture through exchange, the thurmaticity of the objects forming the focus of attraction for the exchange, and the replication (or "reverse-engineering") of the social relations that enable production of the object. Thurmaticity, in other words, is consequential for social relations.

This is most obvious in the case of highly thurmatic objects, like cathedrals or whole cities, in which the objects, because of their immobility, attract people to them. Such objects reorganize social relations in physical space, creating centers of attraction. Centers of attraction in turn create peripheries, where the attractive forces are less potent. The periphery feeds the growth of the center. However, the center also allows the idea of it to move forth into the world, and, hence, it enables the possibility of its replication elsewhere. But, in the course of its replication elsewhere, change occurs. New objects of different attractiveness emerge. The relationship between center and periphery is thus not stable but itself subject to change over time. Moreover, the sum of the thurmaticities of the objects produced—if one can imagine such a sum—is not fixed, but rather capable of growth and expansion.

This argument also suggests that, when objects are of relatively low levels of thurmaticity and relatively easily reproduced, those objects circulate readily among individuals and groups. Their attractive forces propel the culture contained in them through space and over time. The culture itself does not get localized, or rather, centers of attraction are not created within physical space, and the desire for trade is minimal. Any individual or group could replicate the culture of any other individual or group, given access to the objective manifestation of the culture carried by that individual or group.

Trade becomes significant when objects of higher levels of thurmaticity are produced, from which the culture cannot be readily extracted by primary replication. In such cases, new individuals or groups desire the relatively thurmatic objects, but because they cannot immediately replicate them, they are limited to secondary replication. Trade in turn enables an increase in the thurmaticity of objects produced. But that increased thurmaticity is contingent on the social reorganization that enables the production of the objects. Hence, objects are not the passive vehicles for the motion of inertial culture but themselves entities capable of growth whose growth in turn depends on and stimulates transformation in social relations. They are able to do this because the attractive force they exert brings new individuals and groups into contact with the culture that is moving through the world by means of them.

I have spoken of the "idea of the object" that is contained in the cultural object and that, consequently, gets out of the object through trade. But as I have also suggested, it is possible for the idea of the object to move through world in the absence of any direct perceptual contact with the object. This happens when the idea is encoded in metaculture—as in blueprints or sketches or verbal descriptions of the object. An object is capable of stimulating reflection on it, but reflection on it can also be part of culture.

Indeed, if the attractive force exerted by relatively thurmatic objects is a desire to replicate at least some of the culture contained in them, we are led to ponder the processes by which the culture gets into the objects in the first place. That is, how could primary replication result in an increase in thurmaticity? Such increases could occur by chance, as when random errors in replication produce something of greater interest, greater attractive force—for example, when the highly thurmatic objects of a center such as a city are reproduced on the periphery. But they might also occur by design, by reflective processes. If the latter is a real possibility—and I am suggesting that it is—then increases in the force of attraction of objects may be the result of reflective cultural processes, that is, metacultural processes responsible for getting culture into objects in the first place.

From this perspective, the anthropological study of matter (as culturally shaped) and motion is also the study of reflection on matter and of the motion (though metaculture) of that reflection. I have suggested here that the forces responsible for motion also produce the growth of thurmaticity. These are forces that go beyond inertia, beyond the perpetuation of culture that is already in motion. They bring into existence new culture; they reorganize social relations. If I am correct, they have something to do with reflection, and with the role of reflection—in the form of circulating metaculture—in relationship to matter. They are the result of two kinds of motion, one material and one ideal. The contact and interaction between these two kinds of motion is generative, transforming and organizing matter and bringing new culture into being. Consequently, the anthropological inquiry into cultural motion is an inquiry into something fundamental (and fundamentally mysterious) about the universe in which we reside: the energy unleashed in the interaction between matter and reflection on matter, as the two participate in parallel processes of motion.

Notes

1. I will qualify this later, since Object 1 could be a representation or instruction or blueprint, part of metaculture. But I would like to first develop the notion of replication as linked to the copying of perceptible objects.
2. The ghostlike form of an object or objects that can be aesthetically appreciated and replicated resonates with Pierre Bourdieu's (1984 [1975]) idea of taste as a key component of the habitus.

References

Bourdieu, Pierre
1984 [1975] *Distinction: A Social Critique of the Judgment of Taste*. Translated by R. Nice. Harvard University Press, Cambridge, Massachusetts.

Henderson, George
1968 *Chartres*. Penguin Books, Baltimore, Maryland.

Mauss, Marcel
1967 *The Gift: Forms and Functions of Exchange in Archaic Societies*. Translated by I. Cunison. W.W. Norton, New York.

Miller, Malcolm
1991 *Chartres Cathedral*. Riverside Book Company, Hong Kong.

Prache, Anne
1993 *Chartres Cathedral: Image of the Heavenly Jerusalem*. Translated by Janice Abbott. CNRS Editions, Paris.

Smith, Adam
2000 [1776] *An Inquiry into the Nature and Causes of the Wealth of Nations*, edited by Edwin Cannan. Modern Library, New York.

Urban, Greg
2001 *Metaculture: How Culture Moves through the World*. University of Minnesota Press, Minneapolis.

About the Authors

Anna S. Agbe-Davies (PhD, University of Pennsylvania, 2004) is an assistant professor of anthropology at the University of North Carolina, Chapel Hill. Her research interests include the African diaspora in the plantation societies of the southeastern United States and the Caribbean, as well as the cities and towns of the nineteenth- and twentieth-century Midwest. Ongoing field projects include excavation and community collaboration at the sites of New Philadelphia, Illinois, and the Phyllis Wheatley Home for Girls on the south side of Chicago, as described in in-press contributions to the journal *Historical Archaeology* and the edited volume *Archaeology of the Recent African American Past*.

Alexander A. Bauer (PhD, University of Pennsylvania, 2006) is an assistant professor of anthropology at Queens College, City University of New York. His research interests include Old World prehistory, ancient trade, archaeological semiotics, and cultural heritage policy. He is the assistant director of the Sinop Region Archaeological Project, an integrated regional project aimed at exploring the dynamics of interaction and culture change in the Black Sea region from the Neolithic to the present day. Since 2005 he has served as editor of the *International Journal of Cultural Property*, an interdisciplinary journal on cultural heritage law and policy issues published by Cambridge University Press.

Eleanor Casella (PhD, University of California, Berkeley, 1999) is a senior lecturer in archaeology at the University of Manchester. She is the author of *The Archaeology of Institutional Confinement* (University of Florida Press, 2007), and co-editor of *The Archaeology of Plural and Changing Identities* (Springer, 2005) and *Industrial Archaeology: Future Directions* (Springer, 2005). She does work on gender and sexuality, household archaeology, places of confinement, and British colonialism.

About the Authors

Owen Doonan (PhD, Brown University, 1993) is associate professor of art history at California State University, Northridge, and director of the Sinop Regional Archaeological Project. His primary interests include the economic and cultural impact of Greek colonization on local and Greek communities in the first millennium bc and the long-term implications of Greek and subsequent trade diaspora communities in the Black Sea region. He has authored more than forty publications, including *Sinop Landscapes: Exploring Connection in the Hinterland of a Black Sea Port* (University of Pennsylvania Museum Monographs, 2004).

Paul Farnsworth (PhD, University of California, Los Angeles, 1987) is a research affiliate of the Archaeological Research Facility at the University of California, Berkeley, and a project director with William Self Associates in Orinda, California. His research interests include the African diaspora in the plantation societies of the southern United States and the Caribbean. His work focuses primarily on the Bahamas and Louisiana in the late eighteenth- through the mid-twentieth centuries. His other research interests include the western United States from the Spanish colonial period through the twentieth century, and he has recently participated in projects in Arizona, California, Nevada, Texas, and Utah.

Kenneth G. Kelly (PhD, University of California, Los Angeles, 1995) is associate professor of anthropology at the University of South Carolina, where he teaches historical archaeology and African archaeology. His long-standing research focus has been on developing a transatlantic perspective on the archaeology of the African diaspora and exploring the diaspora's impact in both West Africa and the Caribbean. He has conducted long-term archaeological research in Bénin, Jamaica, Guadeloupe, and Martinique. His research has been supported by grants from the Fulbright Program, the Wenner-Gren Foundation for Anthropological Research, and the French Ministry of Culture. He has published the results of his work in a variety of edited volumes and journals, including *American Anthropologist, World Archaeology, Journal of Archaeological Method and Theory, Archéologiques, Journal of Caribbean Archaeology,* and *Ethnohistory*.

Marisa Lazzari (PhD, Columbia University, 2006) is currently a lecturer in the archaeology department of the School of Geography, Archaeology, and Earth Resources (SoGAER) at the University of Exeter, United Kingdom. She specializes in the archaeology of circulation and social interaction in the south-central Andes, particularly focusing on Northwest Argentina. She looks at ancient regional connections and how these shaped landscapes over the long term. Her research combines the technological analysis of stone tools, sourcing studies of raw materials (lithics and clays), and intrasite and regional distributions of material culture within social archaeology frameworks. Other interests include issues of materiality and landscape in connection with the contemporary claims made by Indigenous groups in the field of cultural heritage. Her website may be found at http://sogaer.exeter.ac.uk/archaeology/staff/lazzari.shtml

Susan Sherratt (DPhil, Oxford University, 1982) is currently a research fellow in the department of archaeology, University of Sheffield. Her research interests focus on the Bronze and Early Iron Ages of the Aegean, Cyprus, and the wider Eastern Mediterranean, particularly all aspects of trade and interaction within and beyond these regions. She is also interested in exploring the ways in which the Homeric epics and the archaeological record can most usefully be combined.

Greg Urban (PhD, University of Chicago, 1978) is the Arthur Hobson Quinn Professor in the department of anthropology at the University of Pennsylvania. His principal interest is in the motion of culture through space and time and the forces affecting that motion. He has conducted field research among indigenous populations in Brazil and has more recently begun to study modern business corporations. His publications include *Metaculture: How Culture Moves through the World* (University of Minnesota Press, 2001).

Laurie A. Wilkie (PhD, University of California, Los Angeles) is professor of anthropology and the director of the Archaeological Research Facility at the University of California, Berkeley. Wilkie's research explores issues related to social inequality and social justice. Her recent publications include *The Archaeology of Mothering* (Routledge, 2003) and *The Lost Boys of Zeta Psi* (University of California Press, 2010).

Index

A

Abaucán Valley, 60
Abbot of Mont-Saint-Michel, 218
acceleration, 219, 221–222
accelerative culture, 217
acculturation, 31, 40, 74
Achaeans, 125
Aconquija Mountains, 52; assemblage, 55; clay sourcing, 60; subsistence, 52, 58
Adams, Robert McC., 35, 37, 41
African aesthetic, 152
African American archaeology, 143
Africanisms, 146
Afro-Virginians, 75
Agadja (King of Dahomey), 111
agency, 13, 15, 41, 191–192; and identity, 191
agrarian ideal, 135
Albemarle, 79
Alderson, West Virginia, 178
Allada, 101, 103, 111
Ambato Valley, 60
Amiens, 210, 211
Andean Formative, 22, 52, 55; ceramic fluidity, 59; ceramic motifs, 59; obsidian, 60
Angolan, 150
Angolite, The, 174
Aniakor, Chike, 155
Ankara, 186
Annales School, 38
Annual Customs, 112
Antofagasta de la Sierra, 60
Appadurai, Arjun, 191
Argives, 125
Argos, 130
Armenians, 196
Arvad, 122
Athenaeus of Naukratis, 192
Athens, 192
athurmata, 126, 207, 209, 214, 224. *See also* thurmata/thurmaticity
Atlantic slave trade, 100, 143, 147
Attica, 130
Auschwitz concentration camp, 172

B

Babylonia, 132–133
Bacon's Rebellion, 78, 79
Bahamas, 143–144, 146–151, 153; Loyalist migration, 144; Loyalist Period, 143; plantation population, 144
BaKongo, 158
barter, 15, 52–53, 54, 58, 172, 174, 183
Beka'a Valley, 133
Bell Beaker Culture, 29
Bellér-Hann, Ildikó, 195
"belly bowls," 82
Bender, Barbara, 18
Bénin, 101. *See also* Bight of Benin
Bennett Farm, 91
Berchéres, 208
Berkeley, William, 77–79
"big men," 174
Bight of Benin, 100–101, 105, 151, 153
Bight of Biafra, 147
Binford, Lewis, 13, 75
Black Sea, 185, 188, 191, 198; Early Bronze Age, 198; fish, 197–198; metals, 200; pottery manufacture, 200
Bookbinder pipes, 86, 88
Bosman, W., 107
Bourdieu, Pierre, 10, 17, 50, 175, 177
Boztepe, 193
Braudel, Fernand, 38, 189

Brazil, 208, 215, 220
British Home Office, 166
"broken down daddies," 178
Byblos, 122

C

Cajon, 57, 59
Caldwell, Joseph R., 33, 39
Campo del Pucara, 57, 59
Carrier, James, 21
cathedrals, 208–213, 218–220; floor plans, 210; High Gothic, 210
Catling, H. W., 132
Caucasus, 198, 200
centers of attraction, 222–223
centralization, 57, 103, 219
Chalcidice, 123, 130
Charrière, Henri, 170
Chartres Cathedral, 208–212, 218
Chesapeake region, 69–77, 85, 88, 92; demographics, 70; elites, 77
Childe, V. Gordon, 29–31
Circassians, 196
Clifton Plantation, 144–146, 151–160; assemblage, 152–153; ceramic diversity, 156; ceramic overlap, 159; ceramics, 153; diet, 153; driver's house, 159; excavation strategy, 153; social networks, 59; structures, 153, 154
Colalao, 60
Colono pipes, 88
communicative material culture, 7, 13, 19, 111
"community of culture," 24
Congo, 144–147, 150–153
consumption, 7, 20–21; definition, 20; households and, 21
context, 37, 60, 92, 100, 114, 119–120, 138, 159, 186, 190–191; definition, 16; malleability, 190
coping behaviors, 166–167
core-periphery, 38, 119, 186
cosmogram (Bakongo), 158
Cotton, Robert, 77
Cox, C. Jane, 76
Creole, 147, 151
Crete, 122–123, 130
"cult of the carts," 218
cultural element, 23, 188, 209, 213–218
culture areas, 31
Cyclades, 130

Cypriots/Cyprus, 124, 130, 132

D

Dahomey, 101–103, 111–114; expansion, 111; king of, 111; trade strategies, 112
Danaans, 125
Davidson, Thomas E., 77
Dedekoy, 197
Deipnosophists, 192
diaspora, 40, 188; African, 75, 143–145, 158; European, 71
Diodorus, Siculus, 132, 134
dissemination, 215–217
Dolmen, 200
double consciousness, 145, 152, 160
Drummond, William II, 79
Drummond's Field, 78–79, 83
DuBois, W. E. B., 152
Dunn, James, 174, 176
Durağan, 195

E

Earle, Timothy, 22, 36, 37
Early Bronze Age (Black Sea), 198
Early Iron Age (Greece), 120–121, 136
ecological complementarity, 49, 51, 54
economic anthropology, 22, 33–34, 53
Eltis, David, 147
Emerson, Matthew, 75, 89
enabling objects, 213, 222
Erfelek, 183–188, 192
ethnicity, 16, 18–21, 29, 49, 69, 74–76, 92, 143–145, 158, 196
ethnogenesis, 122
Euboea, 126, 135
Eumaios, 124
Eve, Jack and Sue, 158
événement, 101
ex oriente lux, 31
exchange and trade: academic abandonment of, 30; administered, 35; archaeological/ material aspects, 15–17; asymmetrical, 218; as coping behavior, 167; definitions, 15; distance and, 54; emergent relations, 208; as facilitator, 201; interaction without material, 200; landscape and, 18; markets, 15, 17, 20, 34–35, 41, 49–50, 53, 110, 133, 151, 153, 155, 158, 165, 167–169, 174, 175, 177–179, 192, 195, 212; non-linear, 187; physical dimensions, 17; social aspects,

16, 19; sociopolitical complexity, 103; symmetrical, 218; themes, 16; western/non-western, 50. *See also* theoretical approaches to exchange
exploitation, 17–18, 119–120, 170

F

faience, 126, 130–131, 137
Federal Reformatory for Women, 178
Ferguson, Leland, 146
fictive kinship, 167, 170
Finley, Moses, 192
Flannery, Kent, 18
Flynn, Elizabeth, 178
French Guiana, 170
FUNAI (Brazilian agency), 215

G

Gadsby, Dave, 76
"gal-boys," 176, 179
gambling, 172–174
Garman, James, 168
Georgia Sea Islands, 147
Georgians, 196
Gift, The, 220
Gold Coast, 101, 147, 151, 153
Gomez, Michael, 144, 145
Greeks: Early Iron Age, 120–121, 136; deception, 192; identity, 121–122, 124, 125, 136
Green Spring, 77–80, 83–85
"gutta-percha," 173

H

habitus, 79
Hall, Gwendolyn Midlo, 144
Hamilton, 197
Hann, Christopher M., 195
Harrington, J. C., 73
Heffernan, Esther, 171
heirloom, 133, 137
Hellas, 125
Henderson, George, 212, 218
Henry, Susan, 74
Heroon, 132
Herskovitz, Melville, 146
Hesiod, 125, 135
Heyman, Josiah, 21
Higman, Barry, 146

Hodder, Ian, 37
Homer, 121–122, 124–126, 134–136
Honeyman Inscription, 134
Hualfín, 57, 59
Hueda, 101–114; identity, 110–111; landscape manipulation, 104–110; networks, 103; palace, 110; trade strategies, 104
Huelva, 130
hybridity, 145, 152
Hyde Park Barracks, 172
hypothetico-deductive approach, 30

I

Ibn Battutah, 197
"idea of the object," 222–223
identity, 70; group identity, 23, 120; self-identity, 136, 152
Igbo, 145, 150, 151, 155
Iliad, 121, 124, 126, 136
index/indexicality, 18–20, 29, 61, 76, 92, 191; artifacts, 20; index of similarity, 88–91
interaction, 39, 101, 103, 120, 185–190, 219–220; intercultural, 100, 114; interregional, 15, 37, 39–40, 186; peer-polity, 39; sphere of, 33, 39

J

James, Erwin, 168
Jamestown, Virginia, 71, 73, 77–81, 83–86, 88–89, 91; Structure 19: 79; Structure 100: 78–79, 83; Structure 112: 78; Structure 127: 79, 83, 84; Structure 144: 78, 79, 85

K

kaolin, 71
Kastamonu, 195
Kelso, William, 77
Kemp, Richard, 78–79
kilns, 77, 208
King, Julie, 76
"kingpins," 171, 174, 177, 178
Kirch, Patrick, 22
Kiser, Taft, 85, 86
Kohl, Philip, 15
Kossina, Gustav, 29
kula, 17, 34
Kulturkreise school, 30
Kusimba, Chapurukha, 15

L

La Aguada cultural complex, 60
La Candelaria, 59
labor, 7, 38, 54, 70–72, 76–78, 84–86, 92, 217–219
Laguna Blanca, 57, 60, 61
Lambe, Bulfinch, 111
landscape, 18, 22, 51, 54–55, 61
Lattimore, Richmond, 131
Laz, 196
Lecoq, Patrice, 53
Lefkandi, 126
Lemnos, 126
Lerma, 59
Levi, Primo, 172
Lévi-Strauss, Claude, 50
libido, 175–177, 179
Linear B, 122
llama caravans, 53, 55
lo andino, 49, 50
longue durée, 101
Louisiana State Penitentiary, 174
Lower Dniester Valley, 200
Luckenbach, Al, 76, 85, 86, 88
Ludwell, Philip, 78, 79
Ludwell, Thomas, 79

M

Magoon, Dane, 71
Maikop, 200
Malinowski, Bronislaw, 17, 34, 35, 41, 50
maritime trade, 119–122, 124–125, 130, 135–136, 138, 188, 191
Matron Mamma Morton, 165, 175
Mauss, Marcel, 34, 41, 50, 61, 165, 167, 172, 220
Meeker, Michael, 196
Melanesia, 22, 174
merchant, 49, 77, 126, 132, 187, 189, 195, 201
metaculture, 24, 213, 223–224
metallurgy, 31, 58
Middle Plantation, 77
migration, 17, 22, 29, 31, 144, 198
Miletus, 193
Miller, Daniel, 20
Miller, Henry, 74
Miller, Malcolm, 208
Mintz, Sidney, 146
"mode of integration," 195
Monroe, J. Cameron, 88, 89
Montpelier, Jamaica, 146
Mount Pangaion, 130
Mullin, Michael, 144
multi-sited frameworks, 188–189
multivalency, 76, 111
Munn, Nancy, 51
Murra, John, 52–53
Mycenaean chamber tombs, 121

N

Nassau, 144
nation-states, 38, 41
Neiman, Fraser, 76
New Orleans, 151
New Providence, 144, 146
Nielsen, Axel, 53
Novosvobodnaya, 200

O

obsidian: Aconquija assemblage, 57; ambiguity, 60; frequencies, 57; properties, 57; social significance, 58
Occoquan, Virginia, 171, 176
Odyssey, 121, 122, 124, 125, 126, 131, 134, 136, 138
Oka, Rahul, 15
Old Baton Rouge Penitentiary, 173
Ona-Las Cuevas, 57
Opium Wars, 136
Ottoman period, 195, 197
Ouidah, 102, 104, 112, 113
Out (Family) Islands, 150

P

Page, John, 77, 79
Pasbehaye, 79
penal institutions: gendered roles, 176–179; same-sex relationships, 175–176; social networks, 167; value commodities, 168; violence, 174–175
Phaiakians, 135
Phoenicians, 121; cargos, 126, 134; curse, 134; as hustlers, 126, 132, 136, 138
phoinikios, 122
phoinix, 122
Peirce, Charles Sanders, 19
Pliny, 135
Polanyi, Karl, 35, 53, 192, 195
Pope's Fort, 74

Port Anne, 73, 78, 83
Prache, Anne, 212
production, 7, 16, 21, 24, 39, 69, 76, 77–80, 89, 173, 193, 210, 212, 218, 221
puna, 57, 60

Q

"queens," 179

R

reciprocity, 49, 50, 52, 166, 169, 175, 189; anticipation and, 177; balanced, 169, 171, 172, 179; gift exchange, 13, 15, 34, 41, 50, 53–54, 137, 165, 167, 172, 175–180, 186, 190, 220; infinite, 54; negative, 169, 174; positive, 169–170
regionality, 51, 61
Renfrew, Colin A., 15, 19, 35, 39, 201
replication, 177, 207–208, 212–222
reverse engineering, 212
Rhode Island State Prison, 168
Rhodes, 130
Rice, Prudence, 89
Rich Neck Plantation, 78, 79, 83
Richardson, David, 147
Rideau, Wilbert, 174, 176, 177, 179
Robert of Torigni, 218
Ross Female Factory, 169

S

Sahlins, Marshall, 166, 169, 170, 171, 174
Santa María, 57, 59
Savi, 104–113
scale, 167, 188–190
Schneider, Jane, 37, 38
secondary replication, 215, 217–220, 223
Senegambia, 147, 150, 151
Sidon, 122, 124–126
Sierra Leone, 147, 151
Sikes, Katherine, 76
Sinop, 183, 187–188, 192–202; burial tumuli, 193; ceramics, 200; communication networks, 197; economy, 183; ethnic distribution, 196; trade network expansion, 195. *See also* Sinope
Sinop Regional Archaeological Project, 193
Sinope, 193, 194. *See also* Sinop
Siphnos, 130
Slave Coast, 100, 101, 104
"slaves" (in penal institutions), 174

slavery, 20, 23, 100–104, 110, 122, 143–161; in households, 146; regional selection, 147; resale, 151; self-sufficiency, 151
Smith, Adam, 217
Snelgrave, William, 111
social exchange theory, 37
social fields, 16
social "habits," 198
Solitary Cellblock, 169
sound form, 209
Star Maker pipes, 86
Stein, Gil, 15, 39, 40
stereotypes, 126, 135–137
Steward, Julian, 31
Straube, Beverly, 77
"studs," 178, 179

T

Tafí, 57, 59
Tebenquiche, 57, 60
technomic, 13, 75
Terrell, John Edwards, 16, 24
theoretical approaches to exchange: adaptationalist, 34, 166; cultural diffusion, 30–31, 33–34; cultural evolution, 22, 31, 33–34, 38; culture-history, 7, 20, 73; formalist, 7, 34–37, 41; modernist, 192; postprocessual, 7, 9, 14–16, 20, 30, 39–41, 75, 187–188, 190; primitivist, 192; processual, 7, 9, 15–16, 20, 23, 30, 40–41, 74, 80, 92, 187; substantivist, 35, 192; systemic approach, 74
Thomas, David Hurst, 81
Thorikos, 130
thurmata/thurmaticity, 207, 209, 217. *See also* athurmata
tobacco pipes, 69; adjunct style, 84; decoration, 70, 72, 75, 76; distribution, 71, 84; economics, 77, 78; interpretations, 74, 75, 76; isochrestic styles, 80; local or imported, 71; production, 69, 77; sourcing, 80; technical *vs.* decorative traits, 80–81
tomb robbing, 133–134
"total social phenomenon," 61
trade. *See* exchange and trade
trafficking, 166; artifact assemblage, 169; general functions, 175; material signatures, 168; people as commodities, 175; status hierarchy, 178
Trobriand Islands, 34
Turks and Caicos Islands, 150

types, 85, 86
Tyre, 122, 125, 130

U

Ukraine, 198, 200
Uru-eu-wau-wau, 216–217
Uruk, 40
Usatovo, 200

V

Van Diemen's Land, 169
vertical archipelago/verticality, 52
Virginia Company, 77
Viru Valley, 33

W

Wallerstein, Immanuel, 38, 39

Walnut Street Prison, 173
Wealth of Nations, The, 217
Weiner, Annette, 50
West Africa, 100
"white devils," 136
Willey, Gordon, 33
Williamsburg, 77
Windward Coast, 147
Wobst, Martin, 201
world-systems theory, 14, 33
Wylie, Alison, 41
Wyllys, William, 144, 151, 153, 159, 161

Y

"yellow peril," 136
Yoruba, 144
Yovogan, 112
yungas, 60